HIKING NEBRASKA

A GUIDE TO THE STATE'S GREATEST HIKING ADVENTURES

Seth Brooks

FALCONGUIDES

ESSEX, CONNECTICUT

To Mom and Dad, for always encouraging me to explore.

FALCONGUIDES®

An imprint of Globe Pequot, the trade division of
The Rowman & Littlefield Publishing Group, Inc.
4501 Forbes Blvd., Ste. 200
Lanham, MD 20706
www.rowman.com

Falcon and FalconGuides are registered trademarks and Make Adventure Your Story is a
trademark of The Rowman & Littlefield Publishing Group, Inc.

Distributed by NATIONAL BOOK NETWORK

Photos by Seth Brooks unless otherwise noted
Maps by Melissa Baker and The Rowman & Littlefield Publishing Group, Inc.

British Library Cataloguing in Publication Information available

Library of Congress Cataloging-in-Publication Data available

Names: Brooks, Seth (Conservationist), author.
Title: Hiking Nebraska : a guide to the state's greatest hiking adventures / Seth Brooks.
Description: Essex, Connecticut : Falcon Guides, [2023] | Includes bibliographical references. |
   Summary: "Hiking Nebraska features detailed hike descriptions, miles and directions, trailhead
   GPS coordinates, and informative maps for 45 of the greatest hikes in the cornhusker state.
   From the wooded bluffs near the Missouri River to the badlands of the western half of the
   state, discover the plethora of hiking trails that might just be Nebraska's best kept secret"
   —Provided by publisher.
Identifiers: LCCN 2022050471 (print) | LCCN 2022050472 (ebook) | ISBN 9781493069163
   (paperback) | ISBN 9781493069170 (epub)
Subjects: LCSH: Hiking—Nebraska—Guidebooks. | Nebraska—Guidebooks. | LCGFT: Guidebooks.
Classification: LCC GV199.42.N22 B76 2023 (print) | LCC GV199.42.N22 (ebook) | DDC
   796.5109782—dc23/eng/20221229
LC record available at https://lccn.loc.gov/2022050471
LC ebook record available at https://lccn.loc.gov/2022050472

CONTENTS

OVERVIEW MAP   vii

ACKNOWLEDGMENTS   viii

MEET YOUR GUIDE   ix

INTRODUCTION   1

BEFORE YOU HIT THE TRAIL   8

TRAIL FINDER   16

MAP LEGEND   17

THE HIKES

High Plains   *19*

1. Toadstool Trail, Bison Trail, and Great Plains Trail, *Oglala National Grasslands* (Crawford)   20
2. Fossil Hills Trail and Bone Cabin, *Agate Fossil Beds National Monument* (Harrison)   25
3. Saddle Rock Trail, *Scotts Bluff National Monument* (Gering and Scottsbluff)   29
4. Turkey Run Trail to Monument View, *Wildcat Hills State Recreation Area* (Gering and Scottsbluff)   33
5. Chimney Rock Trail, *Chimney Rock National Historic Site* (Bridgeport)   38
6. Oregon Trail to Medicine Wheel, *Ash Hollow State Historical Park* (Lewellen)   42

Honorable Mention

A. Bead Mountain, *Bead Mountain Ranch* (Gering and Scottsbluff)   46

Pine Ridge   *49*

7. Trooper Trail and Boots and Saddle Trail, *Soldier Creek Wilderness* (Crawford)   50
8. Turtle Rock Trail, *Fort Robinson State Park* (Crawford)   55

9. Mexican Canyon, *Fort Robinson State Park* (Crawford) 59
10. Lovers Leap and Red Cloud Buttes, *Fort Robinson State Park* (Crawford) 63
11. Roberts Loop, *Nebraska National Forest Pine Ridge Ranger District* (Chadron) 68
12. Black Hills Overlook Trail, *Nebraska National Forest Pine Ridge Ranger District* (Chadron) 72
13. Steamboat Butte Trail, *Chadron State Park* (Chadron) 76
14. Spotted Tail Loop, *Nebraska National Forest Pine Ridge Ranger District* (Chadron) 80
15. The Cliffs, *Nebraska National Forest Pine Ridge Ranger District* (Chadron) 84

Honorable Mentions

B. Pine Ridge Trail, *Nebraska National Forest Pine Ridge Ranger District* (Crawford and Chadron) 88
C. Coffee Mill Butte, *Nebraska National Forest Pine Ridge Ranger District* (Chadron) 90
D. Strong Canyon, *Nebraska National Forest Pine Ridge Ranger District* (Chadron) 92

Sandhills 95

16. Sandhills Nature Trail, *Crescent Lake National Wildlife Refuge* (Oshkosh) 96
17. Blue Jay Trail, *Samuel R. McKelvie National Forest* (Cody) 100
18. CCC Fire Tower Trail, *Valentine National Wildlife Refuge* (Valentine) 104
19. Scott Lookout National Recreation Trail, *Nebraska National Forest Bessey Ranger District* (Halsey) 108
20. Olson Nature Preserve, *Prairie Plains Resource Institute* (Petersburg) 112

Honorable Mentions

E. Island Lake Loop, *Crescent Lake National Wildlife Refuge* (Oshkosh) 116
F. East End Access Trail, *Valentine National Wildlife Refuge* (Valentine) 118

Niobrara Valley **121**

  21. Government Canyon, *Valentine State Fish Hatchery* (Valentine) 122
  22. Fort Falls Trail, *Fort Niobrara National Wildlife Refuge* (Valentine) 126
  23. Smith Falls Trail and Jim MacAllister Nature Trail, *Smith Falls State Park* (Valentine) 130
  24. Niobrara Valley Preserve, *The Nature Conservancy* (Johnstown) 135
  25. Long Pine Creek and Dale Mundorf Memorial Nature Trail, *Long Pine State Recreation Area* (Long Pine) 139

Honorable Mention

  G. Cowboy Trail, *Nebraska Game and Parks Commission* (Valentine) 143

Platte Valley **145**

  26. North Platte River Trail, *Buffalo Bill State Recreation Area* (North Platte) 146
  27. Derr House Prairie, *The Nature Conservancy* (Wood River) 150
  28. Crane Trust Prairie Trail, *Crane Trust* (Alda) 154
  29. Gjerloff Prairie, *Prairie Plains Resource Institute* (Marquette) 158
  30. Hackberry Trail and Red Cedar Trail, *Schramm Park State Recreation Area* (Gretna) 162
  31. Stone Creek Falls, *Platte River State Park* (Louisville) 166

Honorable Mentions

  H. Rowe Sanctuary, *Iain Nicolson Audubon Center at Rowe Sanctuary* (Kearney) 172
  I. Dark Island Trail, *Platte PEER Group* (Central City) 174

Southern Nebraska **177**

  32. New Camp Loop, *Potter's Pasture* (Brady) 178
  33. Rock Creek Prairie Loop, *Rock Creek Station State Historical Park* (Fairbury) 182

34. Upland Prairie Loop, *Homestead National Historical Park* (Beatrice) 186

35. Spring Creek Prairie, *Spring Creek Prairie Audubon Center* (Denton) 190

36. Martin Prairie and Wetlands Loop, *Pioneers Park* (Lincoln) 194

37. Nine-Mile Prairie, *University of Nebraska* (Lincoln) 199

38. Frank Shoemaker Marsh, *City of Lincoln Parks and Recreation* (Lincoln) 203

Honorable Mentions

J. Willa Cather Memorial Prairie, *Willa Cather Foundation* (Red Cloud) 208

K. Oak Creek Trail, *Lower Platte South Natural Resources District* (Valparaiso) 210

L. Wilderness Park, *City of Lincoln Parks and Recreation* (Lincoln) 212

Missouri Valley *215*

39. South Shore Trail, *Lewis and Clark State Recreation Area* (South Yankton) 216

40. Old Oak Trail and Bloodroot Trail, *Ponca State Park* (Ponca) 220

41. Cottonwood and Grassland Nature Trails, *DeSoto National Wildlife Refuge* (Blair) 224

42. North Island Trail and Oriole Trail, *Boyer Chute National Wildlife Refuge* (Fort Calhoun) 228

43. Neale Woods, *Fontenelle Forest* (Omaha) 234

44. Upland North and Floodplain, *Fontenelle Forest* (Omaha) 239

45. Indian Cave via East Ridge Trail, *Indian Cave State Park* (Shubert) 244

Honorable Mentions

M. Deer Creek Trail, *Niobrara State Park* (Niobrara) 248

N. Steamboat Trace Trail, *Nemaha Natural Resources District* (Brownville and Peru) 250

HIKE INDEX 252

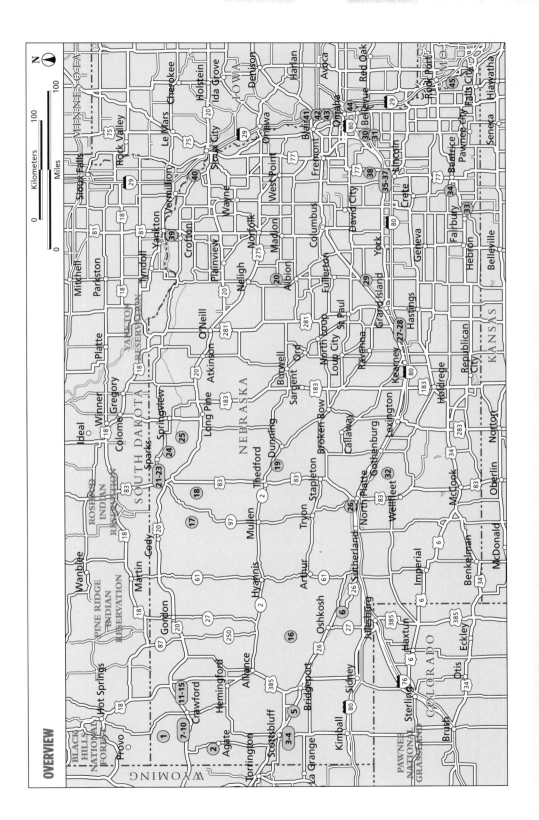

OVERVIEW

ACKNOWLEDGMENTS

There are numerous people to thank who helped bring this book to publication. Thank you to all the hikers, outdoor recreationists, and travelers who were curious about my project and shared my passion for the state of Nebraska. I hope this book introduces more like-minded people to the natural beauty and cultural wealth that the Cornhusker State offers.

First, I must thank everyone at Globe Pequot and FalconGuides. Mason Gadd, thank you for offering guidance, answering my questions, and encouraging me during this project. I am honored that you entrusted me with such a special project to write the first ever hiking guidebook about Nebraska.

I also must thank the staff at the Iain Nicolson Audubon Center's Rowe Sanctuary: Amanda, Anne, Beka, Bill, Catherine, Cody, and Soncey. What an exciting time to be a part of Rowe Sanctuary!

A hearty thank-you to the following park managers, rangers, biologists, naturalists, administrators, and inspirations who shared their knowledge to improve the accuracy of this guidebook or helped spark a curiosity: Eric Grunwald; Timothy Buskirk and the Pine Ridge Ranger District staff; Kevin Poague and the Spring Creek Prairie Audubon Center staff; Shae Caldwell; Hannah Clark; Dana Meyer and the Fontenelle Forest staff; Tony Korth; Lance Foster; Ashley Rippe; Neal Bryan and Andrea Fass; Hunter Baillie and Tom Krolikowski; Candy Downer; Julie Bain and Amber Pearson; Brian DeVries; Juancarlos Giese; Amy Kucera; Sara McClure; Tamara Cooper; Deb Kennedy; Matt Sprenger; Susan Rodenburg; Mindy Sheets and Peter Rea; Wendy Bailey; Amy Jones; Jan Alexander; Adam Johns; Michaela Clemens; Parker Robinson; Terry Lee; the late Paul Johnsgard; and Ron Cisar.

Finally, and most importantly, I must thank my parents, Lloyd and Betty, for always encouraging me to explore. Thank you for all your support during this journey. Without your help, this book would not have been possible. I could not have done this without you. I love you.

MEET YOUR GUIDE

Seth Brooks has been interested in travel and the natural world since an early age. Family trips were common growing up, including trips to Fort Robinson State Park in western Nebraska, a road trip to California, and visits to Wrigley Field in Chicago to root on the Cubs, among many other adventures. Seth frequently accompanied his father on business trips to Alaska, where the two braved the high seas to fish halibut and the giant mosquitoes on wild Alaskan rivers while fishing for king salmon.

While traveling the state and writing this guidebook, Seth worked as a conservation technician at the Iain Nicolson Audubon Center's Rowe Sanctuary near Kearney. His work assisting the conservation team cultivated Seth's knowledge of the natural ecosystems of Nebraska and the importance of conservation work. With extensive hiking and backcountry experience, Seth explored Nebraska searching for the best trails to include in this guidebook.

Seth called the rainy, mystical region of Galicia in northwestern Spain home for seven years, where he spent holidays hiking the Camino de Santiago and exploring Europe. He has worked in environmental education and conservation since returning to the United States in late 2020. Seth currently resides in his home state of Nebraska and works in rural western Iowa, where he enjoys spending time with his partner Chelle in the Loess Hills and exploring with his dog Jasper.

To follow Seth's photography and writing, you can find him on Instagram @sethfromsomewhere and his website, www.sethfromsomewhere.com.

The braided north channel of the Platte River.

HELP US KEEP THIS GUIDE UP TO DATE

Every effort has been made by the author and editors to make this guide as accurate and useful as possible. However, many things can change after a guide is published—trails are rerouted, regulations change, techniques evolve, facilities come under new management, etc.

We appreciate hearing from you concerning your experiences with this guide and how you feel it could be improved and kept up to date. While we may not be able to respond to all comments and suggestions, we'll take them to heart and we'll also make certain to share them with the author. Please send your comments and suggestions to the following e-mail address: falconeditorial@rowman.com

Thanks for your input, and happy trails!

INTRODUCTION

Hiking in Nebraska faces two obstacles: perception and land. The state moniker, the Cornhusker State, does nothing to dispel the stereotypical Nebraska landscape consisting of crop fields and pastures, center pivots, grain silos, and barns and farmhouses. Venture away from I–80, however, and the traveler will encounter a state with a diversity of eco-systems rivaling any other.

The High Plains in the panhandle have been home to incredibly diverse megafauna, most recently bison, grizzly bears, wolves, elk, pronghorn, and bighorn sheep before Europeans arrived and hunted them to complete or near extirpation. The "American Serengeti" described by Dan Flores in the book of the same name was wiped out in

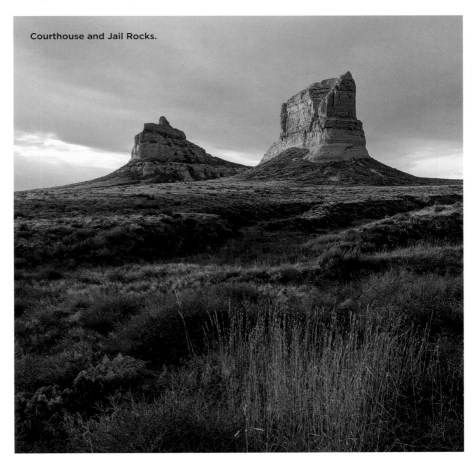

Courthouse and Jail Rocks.

the nineteenth century by market hunting, but the mixed-grass prairie of the Oglala National Grasslands and the sandstone buttes of the Wildcat Hills remain for hikers to explore.

The Pine Ridge escarpment is the eroded remnant of a high tableland between the White and Niobrara rivers in the northwestern corner of the state. The ponderosa savanna, sandstone buttes, and rugged canyons were the scene of many confrontations during the tragic conflict between American westward expansion and Native American resistance. Fire was an essential part of the Pine Ridge ecology before European settlers arrived. However, with their arrival and the suppression of fire, ponderosa forests became too dense, and the result has been devastating wildfires that have threatened not only the health of the ponderosa savanna but also towns like Chadron.

The Sandhills is the largest dune complex in the western hemisphere. The rolling, treeless landscape is wilderness par excellence in the state, with wild, wide-open spaces stretching as far as the eye can see. Much of the Sandhills are privately owned by ranchers. However, there are a handful of federally protected lands that allow hikers to explore this pristine ecosystem, namely Crescent Lake National Wildlife Refuge and the Nebraska National Forest near Halsey and the Samuel R. McKelvie National Forest near Valentine.

The Niobrara River, especially the Middle Niobrara beginning in Valentine and heading east, is a major transition zone for plant and animal species, some of which can only be found in the river valley and its cool spring-branch canyons. Waterfalls and forests, with locally uncommon trees like paper birch and aspens, shatter the stereotype of Nebraska. The river is popular with paddlers and floaters, but there are numerous protected areas open to hiking along the Niobrara National Scenic River.

Every spring, the Central Platte Valley hosts one of the greatest migrations on the planet, as hundreds of thousands of sandhill cranes use the shallow river and adjacent wet meadows and mixed-grass prairies to rest and refuel for their journey to northern breeding grounds. The river is an unimposing one, shallow and a mile wide, but gives Nebraska its name and is the site of outstanding conservation work done by multiple organizations. The important sandhill and whooping crane migrations have spurred noble conservation work by different organizations, notably The Nature Conservancy and the National Audubon Society. They have protected and restored habitat along the Platte River that will allow future generations to witness the annual spring migration.

Southern Nebraska is largely cropland, but the sandsage prairies in the southwest, combined with the Loess Canyons, Rainwater Basin, and tallgrass prairies and eastern deciduous forest in the southeast provide a diversity of natural areas to explore. Waterfowl and other birds congregate in the hundreds of thousands in the Rainwater Basin every spring during their annual migration. There are several public areas where hikers and birders can witness this spectacle. Most of the tallgrass prairie in Nebraska fell to the plough, but some remnant prairies have been protected, many of them by the University of Nebraska in the southeastern corner of the state.

Finally, the Missouri River Valley is where the eastern hardwood forest reaches its westernmost range. It too is an important migratory route for many bird species, such as snow geese, which often congregate in the thousands in spring at places like DeSoto National Wildlife Refuge. The warbler migration is another sight to see, especially at Fontenelle Forest and Indian Cave State Park.

Once you realize Nebraska offers a wealth of natural areas for the hiker to explore, the second obstacle makes itself abundantly clear. Nebraska is in the bottom three of all states

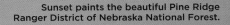

Sunset paints the beautiful Pine Ridge Ranger District of Nebraska National Forest.

with regards to publicly accessible land. Western states typically have a high percentage of publicly owned land; however, Nebraska is a Great Plains state in a transitory zone between east and west. The extreme contrast between its public lands and those to the west is confusing considering their proximity. What all this means is that for the curious hiker, one must drive long distances to experience the natural beauty of Nebraska. Most of the population lives near I-80, but the state's numerous scenic byways give access to areas of the state that challenge the stereotype that is formed when you only stick to the freeway. This guidebook encourages adventures to all corners of Nebraska in order to experience its natural and cultural heritage.

WEATHER AND SEASONS

Every season in Nebraska presents challenges to hikers, but every season also rewards hikers with great experiences. Spring in Nebraska is unpredictable. A snowstorm in May is not uncommon, to be followed by a heat wave reaching into the 90s. What can be counted on, however, is that Nebraska begins to thaw by April and wildflowers like Dutchman's breeches in the Missouri Valley signal that summer is ahead. Spring in Nebraska is highlighted by the awesome spectacle of the annual crane migration along the Central Platte Valley. Hundreds of thousands of sandhill cranes, as well as the rare whooping crane, rest and refuel along this stretch of the river before continuing their ancient and epic migration north to Canada, Alaska, and Siberia.

Summers in Nebraska are hot and humid. Ticks are abundant, and thunderstorms are frequent. These factors complicate hiking excursions from June through August, but the lure of wildflowers should be enough to entice hikers to explore the prairies of the state throughout the summer. Temperatures reach into the triple digits in summer, however,

Storm passing over the Nebraska National Forest near Chadron (Spotted Tail Loop).

and the lack of shade and water on many trails in Nebraska presents challenges for the hiker. The arrival of fall brings milder temperatures and brilliant colors, from the reds, yellows, and browns of the Missouri Valley's hardwood forest to the copper big bluestem towering 6 feet and taller on the tallgrass prairie. Autumn also means the beginning of hunting season, and hikers would be wise to wear blaze orange when they hit the trails. Winters are bitter and long in the Cornhusker State, but often cold days are accompanied by blue skies, so if you are willing to bundle up and brave the cold, you will find quiet trails and prime bird-watching, especially along rivers as bald eagles have spectacularly recovered in the state.

FLORA AND FAUNA

Nebraska lies at the crossroads of the Great Plains, and as such is home to a wide array of plant and animal species. As you move across the state from east to west, you will transition through the three major prairie ecosystems in North America. Eastern Nebraska is home to tallgrass prairie, or what little of it remains. Much of the tallgrass prairie was plowed under after the arrival of European settlers, however places like Homestead National Historical Park and Spring Creek Prairie Audubon Center have both restored and remnant prairies to explore. The eastern deciduous forest reaches its westernmost range along the Missouri Valley on the eastern edge of the state. Oak and hickory forests drape the river bluffs that provide habitat for migrating warblers in the spring. Tallgrass prairie gives way to mixed-grass prairie as you travel west through Nebraska, with short-grass prairie found in the Panhandle. The boundaries between the three are not fixed but change depending on the amount of precipitation. The rain shadow created by the Rocky Mountains is the main influence, as the farther you travel east through Nebraska, the average annual rainfall increases.

Other ecosystems can be found in Nebraska, like islands of biodiversity in the sea of cropland that covers much of Nebraska. Rocky and rugged escarpments, with deep pine-studded canyons that provide habitat for mule deer, mountain lions, bighorn sheep, elk,

Dickcissel at Rowe Sanctuary.

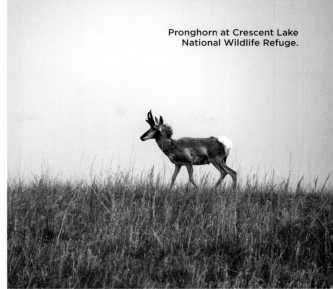
Pronghorn at Crescent Lake National Wildlife Refuge.

and bobcats, rise out of the prairie to give the state topographical diversity. The Wildcat Hills and Pine Ridge are the best examples that provide numerous hiking opportunities. The Sandhills are essentially sand dunes stabilized by grasses, the largest dune complex in the western hemisphere and one of the largest intact grassland areas in the world. Besides the barbed wire fence and grazing cattle, this is true wilderness. Much of the land is privately owned, however, so hiking opportunities are few and far between.

Rivers take up a sizable section of Nebraska's natural landscape. The state has more miles of river than any other in the country. The major rivers covered in this guidebook—Missouri, Niobrara, and Platte—are all major migratory corridors. The Platte is famous for the crane migration every spring, while the Missouri Valley is another important flyway for waterfowl and woodland birds alike. The warbler migrations are a sight to see in the hardwood forests along the Missouri River. The Niobrara Valley has such a unique natural history that an entire book was written about the river.

Paul Johnsgard wrote *The Niobrara: A River Running Through Time* along with more than one hundred books, many of them about the flora and fauna of Nebraska. His work is the place to start when studying Nebraska's natural history. The renowned biologist and emeritus professor at the University of Nebraska passed away in 2021, but his legacy lives on in his books about sandhill cranes, snow geese, prairie dogs, the Niobrara, and many others. Another book to study is *Field Guide to Wildflowers of Nebraska and the Great Plains* by Jon Farrar.

WILDERNESS RESTRICTIONS/REGULATIONS
Native Lands

Native American tribes have occupied Nebraska for thousands of years. Tribes have come and gone over the centuries, following game or pushed out by other tribes. The federal government recognizes several tribes in Nebraska: the Iowa Tribe of Kansas and Nebraska, the Omaha Tribe of Nebraska, the Ponca Tribe of Nebraska, the Sac & Fox Nation of Missouri in Kansas and Nebraska, the Santee Sioux Tribe of the Santee

IOWAY TRIBAL NATIONAL PARK

Ioway Tribal National Park (ITNP) is in the far southeastern tip of Nebraska. These oak-hickory woodlands, loess bluffs, and tallgrass prairie remnants are adjacent to the Missouri River and continue into Kansas. This unique park is entirely owned and administered by the Iowa Tribe of Kansas and Nebraska as a tribal natural and cultural heritage area. The tribe plans to open the park officially in 2025 and will implement a permit system for limited visitation by nonmembers of the tribe at that time. The Rulo Bluffs Preserve was transferred to the tribe by The Nature Conservancy. It is classified as a Biologically Unique Landscape by the state of Nebraska. It is habitat for many unique species such as cerulean warbler and southern flying squirrel. It is managed as a primitive area with only one trail about a mile along one ridge. Trails are planned for the Dupuis Hollow Unit, adding a couple of miles, and connecting it to the 1854 Kansas-Nebraska Act historical boundary marker. Also part of ITNP is an ancestral archaeological site, Leary Site National Historic Landmark, and near Highland about 19 miles to the southeast is the Iowa and Sac & Fox Mission Museum which will have information about the tribes and a short interpretive trail about a half mile long. For more information, contact Lance Foster, director of Ioway Tribal National Park, at 785-595-3258; https://iowaytribalnationalpark.org/.

Reservation of Nebraska, and the Winnebago Tribe of Nebraska. These tribes, and their ancestors, are the original stewards of these lands. Many of the historical tribes associated with Nebraska, like the Pawnee and Lakota Sioux, sold their land to the federal government or exchanged it in treaties only to have seen the treaties broken by the United States soon after.

State Parks

The Nebraska Game and Parks Commission manages state parks, state historical parks, and state recreation areas. These parks are some of the most popular recreation spots in Nebraska, with camping, fishing, hunting, horseback riding, boating, and archery the most popular activities. A valid park entry permit is required for all three categories of parks. A permit can be purchased at the parks themselves but also at statewide Game and Parks offices and permit vendors or online at outdoornebraska.gov.

Most of the parks managed by the Nebraska Game and Parks Commission have hiking trails. However, some parks have well-maintained trails with signage that aids hikers navigating the trail system. Other parks, however, lack information at the trailhead and on the trails themselves with little to no waymarking or navigational directions at major junctions. Park maps, available at park headquarters or online, provide guidance for hikers but sometimes have inaccurate trail information.

Hunting is allowed at most state recreation areas and some state parks. Check hunting season dates if you are hiking in the fall and winter. Always wear blaze orange when you hike during these months; two items of clothing with blaze orange is recommended and do not forget to dress your dog appropriately.

County, Municipal, and Natural Resources District Parks

Rules and regulations for parks owned and managed by counties, municipalities, and natural resource districts vary. Check with the land manager before visiting to inquire about the state of trails. Many county and municipal parks have well-maintained trails, many of them ADA accessible on paved paths.

National Parks Service, National Forest Service, and National Wildlife Refuges

National Park, National Forest Service, and National Wildlife Refuge areas are the most protected and therefore have the most rules and regulations. They also typically have the best-maintained trails with excellent waymarking and information at the trailhead for most hikes. Pets are mostly allowed on federal land but check beforehand before bringing your four-legged friends. Always stay on designated trails, pack out what you pack in, and be respectful of wildlife.

Private Land and Nature Preserves

There are several nonprofit organizations that allow public access to their land. Notable organizations include The Nature Conservancy, the National Audubon Society, and the Prairie Plains Resource Institute, which manage multiple reserves. Like county and municipal parks, rules and regulations vary at each reserve. Dogs may be allowed at one place but are not permitted at another.

BEFORE YOU HIT THE TRAIL

Hiking Nebraska focuses on some of the most scenic day hikes in Nebraska. This guide-book is not comprehensive, however, as it does not include every scenic trail in the state. *Hiking Nebraska* aims to provide a survey of the best trails in the state while balancing geography, difficulty, and ecology. Effort was made to not saturate one area of the state at the expense of others while including hikes in different ecosystems, from the High Plains in the Panhandle and the singular Sandhills to the mighty Missouri River. The hikes are organized into seven sections based on geography and ecology to guide you through the various adventures that await you as you explore the Cornhusker State. The fifty-nine hikes covered in this book vary in difficulty to engage novice as well as experienced hikers. Use the Overview Map to locate the hikes nearest you. Detailed information is provided for each of the trails, with chapter sections explained below.

START
This indicates the starting location for the hike.

ELEVATION GAIN
Elevation is generally the most important factor in determining a hike's difficulty. The two numbers listed are the highest and lowest points reached on the hike. Often, but not always, the trailhead lies at the low point and the end lies at the highest point. With canyon hikes, the numbers are sometimes reversed. Hikes along the Missouri River Valley may not have great elevation changes like the Rocky Mountains, but the trails along loess bluffs can have steep ups and downs that can become incredibly slippery when wet or muddy. The butte and canyon country in the Nebraska Panhandle have the most rugged trails and will challenge most hikers; good physical condition is required for these hikes as they have more total elevation gain because they generally cover longer distances. Prairie hikes have very minimal elevation changes.

Absolute elevation also affects difficulty. At high elevations, lower atmospheric pressure creates "thin air" that requires higher breathing rates and more effort to pull enough oxygen into the lungs. Since most of Nebraska lies at low elevations, hikers will encounter thinner air on only a few of the hikes in this guide. As you cross Nebraska from east to west, you gradually gain elevation—from an average of 1,000 feet along the Missouri River Valley to nearly 5,500 feet in extreme western Nebraska. The moderately higher elevations encountered on hikes in the Nebraska Panhandle (Pine Ridge and the High Plains) will require only a little additional effort.

DISTANCE

The distance specified in each description is listed as a round-trip distance from the trailhead to the end of the route and back. Hike lengths have been determined by using the author's GPS unit. Some variability is to be expected between this measurement and those by the land manager or your own GPS device, however any discrepancies should be minimal.

DIFFICULTY

Assessing a hike's difficulty also is very subjective. Elevation, elevation change, and distance all play a role, as do trail conditions, weather, and the hiker's physical condition. However, even my subjective ratings will give some idea of difficulty. To me, elevation gain was the most significant variable in establishing levels of difficulty. Most of the hikes in Nebraska have only small elevation gains and are rated easy or moderate. The majority of the difficult hikes are located in the Nebraska Panhandle, with a handful of hikes in the rest of the state also rated as difficult. Poor trails, excessive heat, high elevations with thin air, off-trail travel, and other factors may result in a more difficult designation than would otherwise seem to be the case from simply the elevation change and hike distance. Carrying a heavy backpack can make even an "easy" day hike fairly strenuous. Each hiker's difficulty rating may be different from my own. A hike rated difficult in Nebraska may be moderate to someone accustomed to hikes in the Rocky Mountains. Difficulty is subjective and unique to each hiker and each hike itself; the best effort was made to provide a rating that takes into consideration the factors listed in this paragraph. The best advice is to consider your own fitness level, hiking experience, and the unique characteristics of the hike (elevation, elevation gain, distance, etc.) and adjust your expectations accordingly.

APPROXIMATE HIKING TIME

The approximate hiking time is a rough estimate of the time within which the average hiker will be able to complete the hike. Very fit, fast-moving hikers will be able to complete it in less time. Slow-moving hikers or those preoccupied with activities such as photography or field identification may take longer. To come up with this information, I estimated that most people hike at 2.5 miles per hour and always rounded total hike time up to the next half hour or hour to consider water breaks, photography, and other activities that add time to a hike. I also tried to consider other factors such as a rough trail or particularly big elevation changes. Carrying a backpack for overnight trips will add significantly to the time required.

SEASONS/SCHEDULE

This section lists when the trails are open to the public. Most trails in Nebraska are open year-round from sunset to sunrise. Some trails close on holidays or at specific times; always contact the land manager or visit their website to verify the status of the trails, not only for opening hours but also current conditions. Some trails close during deer rifle season or important migration periods, such as the annual crane migration during spring along the Central Platte River Valley. Additionally, some agencies use prescribed burns

Fall colors at Fort Robinson State Park (Lovers Leap and Red Cloud Buttes).

to manage their land. Most prescribed fires occur in the spring (late April to early May) but they can occur throughout the year. Contact the land manager or check their website for updates and trail closures.

The season specified for a hike is the optimum or ideal season. This advice is subjective but based on factors such as bird migrations, blooming wildflowers, and other events that will enhance your hike. Hiking a prairie in winter or early spring does not compare to the summer when wildflowers are blooming and native grasses grow nearly 10 feet. There even is great variety throughout the summer as different wildflowers bloom at different times. However, summer is not always the best time to hike in Nebraska. Extreme temperatures and an abundance of ticks can make summer hiking unpleasant. Spring is a good time to hike but snow and cold temperatures can linger into the spring. Fall is an excellent time to hike, perhaps the best season in Nebraska. Temperatures are cooler, insects are largely gone, and leaves begin to change. Winter is often overlooked as a hiking season, especially in Nebraska with the popularity of hunting. However, there are great benefits to hiking in winter, as bird-watching is easier due to lack of foliage. The complete absence of insects is another benefit of hiking in winter. It is imperative, however, that you are aware of hunting seasons and that you wear appropriate clothing for yourself and any pets that hike with you. Ideally, two items of blaze orange clothing (a hat and vest, for example) are appropriate during hunting season.

FEES AND PERMITS

Valid park entry permits are required for state parks, state historical parks, and state recreation areas managed by the Nebraska Game and Parks Commission. These can be obtained at the park entrance, at kiosks located in each respective park, or at licensed vendors near the park. Permits can also be obtained online. Check outdoornebraska.gov for regulations, prices, and places to obtain permits. An annual park entry permit is also available, allowing yearlong entrance to all parks in the Nebraska Game and Parks Commission system. Some of the areas managed by the US Forest Service and National Parks

Service require passes while others are free to the public. In general, organizations like The Nature Conservancy, the National Audubon Society, and other nonprofits do not require an entrance fee.

TRAIL CONTACT

The trail contacts category lists the name, address, phone number, and website of the managing agency for the lands through which the trail passes. Call, write, or check the website for current information about the hike. Sometimes the address listed is not the physical address of the park or area where the hike and trailhead are located, rather it is the office or mailing address of the land manager.

DOG-FRIENDLY

This section describes whether dogs are allowed on the trail. Generally, dogs need to be leashed when they are allowed. Please be courteous and pick up after your dog.

Dogs are allowed, on leashes no longer than 6 feet, on many trails in Nebraska.

TRAIL SURFACE

Trail surface describes the material that makes up the trail. Most commonly it is simply a dirt path consisting of the native materials that were there when the trail was built. On occasion gravel is added or the trail may be paved. In a few instances the hike follows a paved road, dirt road, or a primitive two-track road.

LAND STATUS

The land status simply tells which agency, usually federal or state, manages the land in which the trail lies. In this book the Nebraska Game and Parks Commission, USDA Forest Service, US Fish and Wildlife Service, and the National Park Service are the most common land managers.

NEAREST TOWN

The nearest town is the closest city or town to the hike's trailhead that has at least minimal visitor services. The listed town will usually have gas, food, and limited lodging available. In small towns and villages, the hours these services are available may be limited.

MAPS

The maps in this guide are as accurate and current as possible. When used in conjunction with the hike description and the additional maps listed for each hike, you should have little trouble following the route.

Generally, two types of maps are listed. Most of the state parks have park and trail maps available free at the entrance station, headquarters, or online. Some of the park maps have a rudimentary map of trails, while other parks have more detailed maps. State recreation areas also have maps but some may only contain information about camping, fishing, and other recreation but not include hiking trails. The US Forest Service has two different types of maps available. The motor vehicle use map lists the different types of roads within the national forests. They do not list, however, hiking trails and are not topographical maps. There are printable versions of these maps available on the Forest Service's website as well as digital maps available for download on the Avenza Maps app. The Forest Service website also has color, foldable brochures available for purchase These are excellent maps that list forest roads as well as hiking trails. They are not topographical, however.

USGS topographic quadrangles are generally the most detailed and accurate maps available of natural features. With some practice they allow you to visualize peaks, canyons, cliffs, rivers, roads, and many other features. With a little experience, a topographic map, and a compass, you should never become lost. All the USGS maps noted in this guide are 7.5-minute quads. USGS quads are particularly useful for little-used trails and off-trail travel. Unfortunately, some of the quadrangles, particularly for less-populated parts of the state, are out of date and do not show many newer man-made features such as roads and trails. However, they are still useful for their topographic information. Most of the more developed hikes in this guide do not require a topo map. The state park maps, Forest Service maps, or maps made available by other land managers will suffice on most trails.

GPS (Global Positioning System) units, particularly those with installed maps, can be very useful for route finding when used in conjunction with paper maps. However, anyone that enters the backcountry should have at least basic knowledge in using a paper map and compass. Batteries die and GPS units get dropped. It's best not to be completely dependent on them in case of failure. A GPS unit with maps installed can be particularly helpful on off-trail hikes.

USGS quads can usually be purchased at outdoor shops or ordered directly from USGS at http://store.usgs.gov or from online companies such as www.mytopo.com or www.topozone.com. To order from USGS, know the state, the number desired of each map, the exact map name as listed in the hike heading, and the scale. You can also download USGS quads at https://apps.nationalmap.gov/downloader/#/ and print them yourself.

OTHER TRAIL USERS

This describes the other users that you might encounter on the hike. Mountain bikers, equestrians, and hunters are the most common. On multiuse trails, bikers and hikers must yield to equestrians, while bikers must also yield to hikers.

SPECIAL CONSIDERATIONS

Here is where unique elements of this trail that require extra preparation will be listed. This might include water availability, drastic temperature changes, sun exposure, or extreme crowding.

Cattle grazing is a land management technique used by many agencies.

AMENITIES AVAILABLE

This spec will address necessities like restroom availability, running water, shelter, first aid, vending machines, ramps, etc.

MAXIMUM GRADE

This spec is a good indication of how hard the hardest part of the hike gets. This will tell you how steep the trail gets, and how long the steepest sections last.

CELL SERVICE

It's important to know if you can, or definitely cannot, count on cell services before you head into the woods. If you are traveling with anyone with mobility or disability considerations, make sure all are aware of the communication channels available. If there is no cell service available, make extra sure to read the directions carefully and don't assume you'll be able to follow your GPS.

FINDING THE TRAILHEAD

This section provides detailed directions to the trailhead. With a basic current state highway map or GPS unit, you can easily locate the starting point from the directions. In general, the nearest town or interstate exit is used as the starting point. Federal highways use the abbreviation US in this guide, while Nebraska state highways are listed as NE. County roads are sometimes paved but often are gravel country roads.

Distances were measured using Google Maps. Be sure to keep an eye open for the specific signs, junctions, and landmarks mentioned in the directions, not just the mileages. The map services available on cell phone GPS systems are often inaccurate or nonexistent in remote areas, so use them with care. In addition, many require decent cell service to work, further lessening their value. A current map is your best option for finding the trailhead.

Dotted gayfeather (*Liatris punctata*).

Most of this guide's hikes have trail-heads that can be reached by any type of vehicle. A few, as noted, require a high-clearance or four-wheel-drive vehicle. Rain or snow can temporarily make some roads impassable. The forest roads in the Pine Ridge and the sandy tracks in the Sandhills are notoriously difficult to manage after precipitation. Before venturing into the country, you should check with park or forest headquarters. On less-traveled back roads, particularly in the Sandhills, you should carry basic emergency equipment such as a shovel, chains, water, a spare tire, a jack, blankets, and some extra food and clothing. Make sure that your vehicle is in good operating condition with a full tank of gas.

Try not to leave valuables in your car at all; if you must, lock them out of sight in the trunk. If I have enough room, I usually put everything in the trunk to give the car an overall empty appearance. In my many years of parking and hiking at remote trailheads, my vehicle has never been disturbed.

TRAIL CONDITIONS

All hikes are not created equal. Some hikes are well maintained and well-marked with trail signs, markers, and more that make navigation incredibly simple. Other hikes have nonexistent trail infrastructure that can frustrate even the most experienced hiker and make your hike unexpectedly long, or worse, you get lost. This section addresses trail infrastructure such as waymarking, trail signage, and other helpful navigational assistance created by land managers and volunteers. While there are exceptions, in general trails on land managed by the US Forest Service and National Parks Service are superbly maintained while the trails at parks managed by the Nebraska Game and Parks Commission vary greatly from park to park. This section also lists potential hazards that may be encountered on your hike. Sun exposure, ticks, and tree snags are the most common hazards you will encounter hiking in Nebraska. Finally, an estimate of the foot traffic the hike receives is given to give you an idea of how popular the trails are in the area where the hike is located.

THE HIKE

All of the hikes selected for this guide can be done easily by people in good physical condition. Scrambling may be necessary for very few of the hikes, while none require any rock-climbing skills. A few of the hikes, as noted in their descriptions, travel on very faint trails. You should have an experienced hiker, along with a compass, USGS quad, and a GPS unit, with your group before attempting those hikes.

The waymarking on trails depends on the agency that manages the land where the hike is located. The US Forest Service does an excellent job maintaining and marking their trails, using brown posts painted white at the top as well as a few other types of trail markers. There is no uniform trail waymarking used by the Nebraska Game and Parks Commission; each state park or state recreation area uses different types of trail markers and signage. Some parks, like Fort Robinson, Indian Cave, and Ponca, have trail systems that are well marked and maintained, while state recreation areas and some state parks, like Niobrara and Platte River, have little to no trail signage. Most of the time the paths are very obvious and easy to follow, but the marks help when the trails are little-used and faint or when there are numerous intersecting trails throughout the park. Fresh snow can obscure footpaths, so always know the type of trail markers used where you are hiking and bring a map, compass, and GPS unit with fresh batteries. Be sure not to add your own trail waymarkings—it can confuse the route. Leave such markings to the official trail workers.

Steamboat Butte Trailhead at Chadron State Park.

Possible backcountry campsites are often suggested in the descriptions. Many others are usually available. In the national forests, there are usually few restrictions in selecting a campsite, provided that it is well away from the trail or any water source; always check Forest Service regulations before camping. The state parks and recreation areas do not allow backcountry camping but some do have hike-in campsites that require registration. The state parks charge a small fee for camping at hike-in sites as well as developed and primitive campgrounds.

After reading the descriptions, pick the hike that most appeals to you. Go only as far as ability and desire allow. There is no obligation to complete any hike. Remember, you are out hiking to enjoy yourself, not to prove anything.

MILES AND DIRECTIONS

To help you stay on course, a detailed route finder sets forth mileages between significant landmarks along the trail.

TRAIL FINDER

BEST HIKES FOR FAMILIES
31. Stone Creek Falls
23. Smith Falls Trail and Jim MacAllister Nature Trail
13. Steamboat Butte Trail

BEST HIKES FOR EPIC VIEWS
10. Lovers Leap and Red Cloud Buttes
3. Saddle Rock Trail
1. Toadstool Trail, Bison Trail, and Great Plains Trail

BEST HIKES FOR WILDLIFE
16. Sandhills Nature Trail
H. Rowe Sanctuary
9. Mexican Canyon

BEST HIKES FOR WILDFLOWERS
37. Nine-Mile Prairie
43. Neale Woods
35. Spring Creek Prairie

BEST FOREST HIKES
40. Old Oak Trail and Bloodroot Trail
17. Blue Jay Trail
44. Upland North and Floodplain

BEST HIKES FOR HISTORY
2. Fossil Hills Trail and Bone Cabin
6. Oregon Trail to Medicine Wheel
34. Upland Prairie Loop

BEST HIKES FOR BACKPACKING
B. Pine Ridge Trail
7. Trooper Trail and Boots and Saddle Trail
45. Indian Cave via East Ridge Trail

MAP LEGEND

Municipal

🛣 80 Freeway/Interstate Highway

🛣 26 US Highway

🛣 71 State Road

902 County/Paved/Improved Road

⊢—⊢— Railroad

Trails

------ Featured Trail

- - - - - Trail or Fire Road

Water Features

Body of Water

Marsh/Swamp

River/Creek

Intermittent Stream

⌒ Spring

⫽ Rapids

≋ Waterfall

Land Management

National Park/Forest

State/County Park

Reservation

National Monument/
Wilderness Area

Symbols

⤛ Boat Ramp

⏝ Bridge

▪ Building/Point of Interest

⛺ Campground

⌒ Cave

✝ Cemetery

× Elevation

⌶ Gate

⬛ Inn/Lodging

▲ Mountain/Peak

🅿 Parking

🎍 Picnic Area

🚻 Restroom

◈ Scenic View/Overlook

|||||||| Steps/Boardwalk

🗼 Tower

17 Trailhead

⊢——⊣ Tunnel

❓ Visitor/Information Center

🚰 Water

Sunset at Oglala National Grasslands
(Toadstool Trail, Bison Trail, and
Great Plains Trail).

HIGH PLAINS

Panorama Point, the highest natural point in Nebraska, is a nondescript low rise in southwestern Nebraska near the border with Colorado and Wyoming. The shortgrass and sandsage prairies of the High Plains are not all rolling grasslands, however, as it is interspersed with breaks and buttes that have left a mark on all who have passed through the region. Nebraska's two most iconic landmarks, Chimney Rock and Scotts Bluff, marked the beginning of the West as pioneers traversed the California, Mormon, and Oregon Trails. This is the driest and starkest landscape in Nebraska, the place where the sublime simplicity of the prairie reaches its apex.

Bone Cabin, restored to its 1910 condition, at Agate Fossil Beds National Monument.

1 TOADSTOOL TRAIL, BISON TRAIL, AND GREAT PLAINS TRAIL

Each of the three hikes comprising this loop is a journey through time. Toadstool Trail is a short loop through stark badlands, a landscape unlike any other in Nebraska. Bone fragments and fossils, including 30-million-year-old fossil tracks, continue to draw paleontologists to the area. Bison Trail meanders through a canyon carved by Big Cottonwood Creek, then over mixed-grass prairie to the Hudson-Meng Education and Research Center containing the bones of nearly 600 bison that roamed these grasslands 10,000 years ago. Great Plains Trail leaves recent history to the imagination, however, as the bison, grizzly bears, wolves, pronghorn, wild horses, and other megafauna that once roamed the "American Serengeti" of the Great Plains were largely gone by the end of the nineteenth century.

Start: Toadstool Campground
Elevation gain: 3,791 to 4,180 feet
Distance: 7.92-mile loop (Toadstool Trail is a 1-mile loop; Bison Trail is 3 miles one-way to Hudson-Meng)
Difficulty: Difficult, due to length and sun exposure
Hiking time: 3–4 hours
Seasons/schedule: Trails open year-round; best during the fall for cooler temperatures
Fees and permits: Day-use fee required year-round (interagency passes are valid); self-register and pay at the campground
Trail contact: Nebraska National Forest Pine Ridge Ranger District, 125 N Main St., Chadron 69337; (308) 432-0300; fs.usda.gov/recarea/nebraska/recarea/?recid=30328
Dog-friendly: Yes, on leash
Trail surface: Grass and dirt
Land status: Oglala National Grasslands
Nearest town: Crawford 19 miles to the southeast
Maps: USGS Roundtop, NE 2021; available at fs.usda.gov/main/nebraska/maps-pubs

Other trail users: Foot traffic only in Toadstool Geologic Park; equestrians and cyclists are allowed outside the geologic park
Special considerations: Fossil collecting is prohibited in Toadstool Geologic Park. There is no water at Toadstool Campground and none along the trail; please plan accordingly, as the Forest Service has had to rescue numerous hikers in recent years due to poor planning. Check road conditions with the Pine Ridge Ranger District after inclement weather; the roads to Toadstool Geologic Park are rough but manageable in most vehicles.
Amenities available: At Toadstool Campground, there are vault toilets, parking, 6 primitive campsites, and picnic tables. There are restrooms at Hudson-Meng; check with the Pine Ridge Ranger District for opening hours.
Maximum grade: 17%
Cell service: Full coverage at the campground, reliable coverage on open grasslands, and limited to no coverage in Big Cottonwood Creek.

FINDING THE TRAILHEAD

From Crawford proceed to the intersection of US 20 and NE 2. Take NE 2 north for 4.2 miles to Toadstool Road. Follow Toadstool Road for 11.4 miles to FR 902 and continue on FR 902 for 1.4 miles to Toadstool Campground. **GPS:** N42° 51.466' W103° 35.073

The contrast between stark badlands and golden grasslands is sublime on Great Plains Trail.

Trail Conditions: The Forest Service does an excellent job maintaining the trail, waymarking it with brown posts painted white at the top. Grazing cattle may knock over the posts, so keep an eye on the next post in the distance or around a bend. The canyon bottoms and badlands can get muddy after rain and snow. Flash floods are a danger in Big Cottonwood Creek after storms. Heat and sun exposure are serious hazards during the summer. There is no water at Toadstool Campground or on the trail; please plan accordingly. Toadstool Trail receives heavy traffic, while Bison Trail and Great Plains Trail receive light foot traffic.

THE HIKE

Oglala National Grasslands is geographically closer to the Pine Ridge region but is ecologically closer to the High Plains, which is why it has been included in this section. The hike uses three trails to create a loop, beginning in Toadstool Geologic Park before traversing the national grassland via Bison and Great Plains Trails.

Toadstool Trail is a 1-mile self-guided loop taking you past eroded sandstone slabs resembling toadstools, giving the park its name. There is a box at the gated entrance with brochures providing information for the numbered stops along the loop. Feel free to follow the loop in numerical order if you wish, however, this hike begins in the opposite direction by keeping left after the gate and immediately ascending a steep path. Pass self-guided stop #8 (0.15 mile) and maneuver around a large sandstone pillar before reaching an area with steep cliffs (0.27 mile). Follow the trail posts down into Big Cottonwood Creek, where you turn left (southwest) to follow Bison Trail at 0.42 mile for 1.5 miles out of the canyon.

Bison Trail snakes along the dry creek bed, although be cautious during May to July, as a sudden thunderstorm could lead to flash flooding in the canyon. The landscape here is completely alien to stereotypical Nebraska farmland—you'd be forgiven

Mushroom-like sandstone formations give Toadstool Geologic Park its name.

for thinking you were in the American Southwest. Pay attention to the trail posts so you don't end up off the trail in a slot canyon. Reach a sign at 0.51 mile reading, "Leaving Toadstool Park, Trail to Hudson-Meng 2.7 miles" and continue in a southerly direction along the canyon bottom. Pass through a gate at 1.61 miles and immediately turn right indicated by a trail post to climb out of the canyon.

The junction with FR 918, at 1.9 miles, is on the canyon's southern rim. Continue south on Bison Trail toward Hudson-Meng, 1.3 miles away according to a trail sign. From here to Hudson-Meng, Bison Trail crosses the mixed-grass prairie of Oglala National Grasslands. Cattle may be present on the pastures; if so, treat them with caution and respect and close all gates behind you. As you hike south, look for Roundtop and Pine Butte on the horizon rising behind Hudson-Meng.

The trail to the bison bonebed is not flat prairie the entire way, as you find out reaching the canyon rim of Whitehead Creek after 2.2 miles. After climbing out of the canyon, Bison Trail enters Pasture 33B at 2.62 miles and then reaches the rim of a smaller canyon at 3.0 miles. Head south to reach Hudson-Meng after climbing out of the canyon. The center has been closed since early 2020 but the ranger district plans to open May to September; check ahead of your hike for current operating hours. Even if it is closed, Hudson-Meng makes a nice resting stop with shade and benches outside the building. The bison found at the site are ancestors to today's modern bison. There is no consensus on how they came to rest at this spot, but one leading theory suggests the area was used as seasonal hunting grounds for thousands of years by nomadic indigenous peoples.

After visiting Hudson-Meng, return to FR 918 via Bison Trail, traversing the two canyons and shortgrass prairie. When you reach the forest road, turn left (north) to follow FR 918 for 1.5 miles. Before they were hunted to near extinction, bison and pronghorn freely roamed the grasslands that stretch out before you. While a few pronghorn still graze the sagebrush, sadly the only bison are the bones of their distant relatives at Hudson-Meng.

Reach the junction with Great Plains Trail and turn right (east). Great Plains Trail crosses a broad desertlike area covered in many places with agate. Enter the badlands again as we near Toadstool Geologic Park. The views of the badlands here are splendid. At the junction with Toadstool Trail, turn left (east) to return to the trailhead. If you wish to explore Toadstool some more, turn right to follow the self-guided loop through the park and back to the campground.

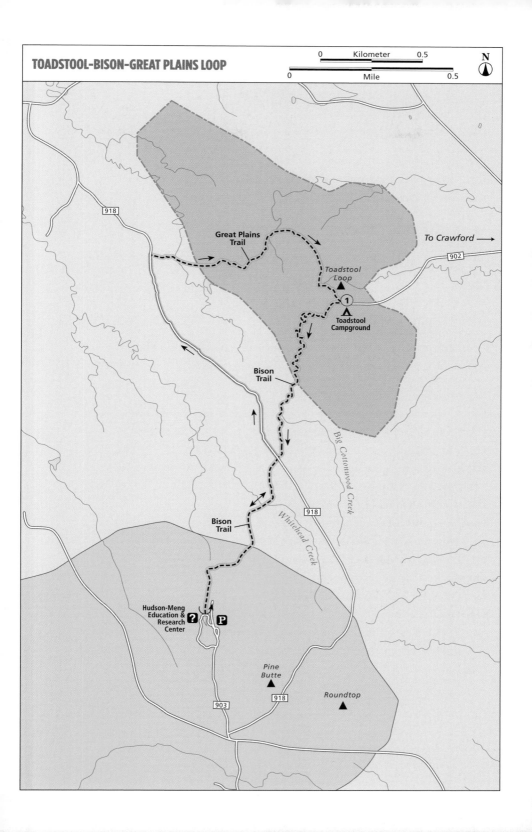

TOADSTOOL–BISON–GREAT PLAINS LOOP

Kilometer
0   0.5
Mile
0   0.5

N

918

Great Plains
Trail

To Crawford →

902

Toadstool
Loop

1

Toadstool
Campground

Bison
Trail

Big Cottonwood Creek

918

Whitehead Creek

Bison
Trail

Hudson-Meng
Education &
Research
Center

?   P

Pine
Butte

Roundtop

903   918

MILES AND DIRECTIONS

0.00 Begin at Toadstool Campground; pass through a gate and keep left (west) at the fork marked by a small "Self-guided trail" sign.

0.10 Scramble over a rocky section.

0.15 Continue straight (south) past a side trail on your left leading to self-guided spot #8.

0.27 Reach an area with steep cliffs.

0.38 Follow the posts as the trail descends into Big Cottonwood Creek.

0.42 Turn left (southwest) onto Bison Trail; follow the posts as the trail winds along the creek bed.

0.51 Reach a sign, "Leaving Toadstool Park, Trail to Hudson-Meng 2.7 miles." Continue south.

1.61 Pass through a gate, then immediately turn right (southwest) indicated with a trail post.

1.90 Climb out of the canyon to reach FR 918; cross FR 918 to continue south on Bison Trail through shortgrass prairie toward Hudson-Meng.

2.20 Reach the rim of a canyon with Whitehead Creek at its bottom; descend following the trail posts.

2.32 Reach the canyon bottom; continue south to climb out of the canyon.

2.50 Bison Trail runs south parallel to a barbed wire fence; Roundtop and Pine Butte are on the horizon ahead to the south.

2.62 Cross through the fence into Pasture 33B; continue west.

2.90 Reach the east rim of a ravine; cross the wooded creek bottom heading west.

3.00 Climb out of the ravine and turn left (south) toward Hudson-Meng.

3.07 Pass through a gate to enter the Hudson-Meng property.

3.29 Hudson-Meng Education & Research Center; return to FR 918 via Bison Trail.

3.49 Reach the gate; head north.

3.56 Descend into the ravine heading east.

3.66 Reach the east rim of the ravine and continue east.

3.93 Cross through the fence into Pasture 33C; continue north.

4.13 Descend into Big Cottonwood Creek.

4.47 Turn left (north) onto FR 918.

4.91 Enter Unit 33D; continue north on FR 918.

6.14 Reach a junction; turn right (east) onto Great Plains Trail.

7.15 Pass through a gate and continue east through badlands.

7.71 Reach a junction; turn left (east) onto Toadstool Trail to return to the trailhead.

7.92 Arrive back at Toadstool Campground.

2 FOSSIL HILLS TRAIL AND BONE CABIN

Agate Fossil Beds National Monument's isolation lends to its appeal: Unbroken vistas of mixed-grass prairie and dramatic Nebraska sunsets give way to a night sky free of light pollution. The hike to University and Carnegie Hills is a great way to learn about the Miocene mammals that roamed western Nebraska more than 16 million years ago. The trail also leads to Bone Cabin, restored to its 1910 appearance, that was used during fossil excavations. Make sure you stop in the visitor center to see life-sized displays of the extinct animals and James H. Cook's collection of gifts he received from Chief Red Cloud.

Start: Fossil Hills Trailhead next to a picnic shelter east of the visitor center
Elevation gain: 4,395 to 4,566 feet
Distance: 3.60-mile loop
Difficulty: Easy
Hiking time: 1.5–2 hours
Seasons/schedule: Trail open year-round, sunrise to sunset; best in fall for milder temperatures
Fees and permits: None
Trail contact: Agate Fossil Beds National Monument, 301 River Rd., Harrison 69346; (308) 665-4113; nps .gov/agfo
Dog-friendly: Yes, on leash
Trail surface: Asphalt and mowed grass
Land status: Agate Fossil Beds National Monument

Nearest town: Harrison 25 miles to the north, Mitchell 37 miles to the south
Maps: USGS Agate, NE 2021; paper trail guide available at visitor center or on the National Park Service app
Other trail users: None
Special considerations: There are no services near the national monument, so plan accordingly.
Amenities available: Restrooms, water, and information at the visitor center
Maximum grade: 7%
Cell service: Cell reception is spotty or not available for most carriers. Free public Wi-Fi is available inside the visitor center.

FINDING THE TRAILHEAD

From Harrison, head south 22 miles on NE 29, then 3 miles east on River Road. From Mitchell, head 34 miles north on NE 29, then 3 miles east on River Road. The trailhead can also be accessed via NE 71 by driving 25 miles west on the unpaved portion of River Road. **GPS:** N42° 25.523' W103° 44.008

Trail Conditions: Well maintained with covered benches and interpretive panels along the trail. The trail to Bone Cabin is a mowed path through the mixed-grass prairie. Prairie rattlesnakes may be present. The only shade is provided at the interpretive panels on Fossil Hills Trail. Summer hazards also include extreme heat and sudden thunderstorms; hike early in the morning to avoid both.

THE HIKE

Before the discovery of fossils, Agate Fossil Beds National Monument was known as Agate Springs Ranch. James and Kate Cook purchased the ranch from Kate's parents and soon discovered fossil remains on their range. Seventeen years later, Olaf Peterson of the

University Hill (left) and Carnegie Hill (right).

Sunset over the frozen Niobrara River.

Carnegie Museum in Pittsburgh excavated the "Fossil Hills," one of which is now known as Carnegie Hill (the other is University Hill). James also became friends with Red Cloud; the famous Lakota chief made a 150-mile journey from the Pine Ridge Reservation in South Dakota to visit James at his Agate Springs Ranch, during which Red Cloud and other Lakota Sioux and Northern Cheyenne gave James numerous gifts. The James H. Cook Collection in the visitor center houses these gifts, including Red Cloud's shirt and Crazy Horse's whetstone. The visitor center also has interpretive information about the fossils found in the area and life-sized displays of some of the Miocene mammals, such as the bison-sized piglike Dinohyus (not related to modern pigs, however).

Fossil Hills Trail begins just east of the visitor center next to a picnic shelter on the south side of the parking lot. The trail first passes through lush wetlands created by the Niobrara River, which is miniscule here compared to the deep valley it carves down river near Valentine. A boardwalk at 0.2 mile takes you over the narrow river and into restored mixed-grass prairie. Although it is unlikely you will see one, be mindful of prairie rattlesnakes sunning themselves along the side of the trail. While there are no trees in sight, the covered benches next to interpretive panels offer a shaded place to sit and contemplate the sublime simplicity of the prairie.

The trail climbs around University Hill to approach it from the south and finally reaches the hill itself at 1.2 miles. There are several interpretive displays at the excellent viewpoint with the Niobrara River below and beyond the visitor center. Continue on the paved trail as it wraps around the north side of Carnegie Hill to reach more interpretive panels on the west side of the hill. After learning about the Miocene animals that roamed the area 23 million years ago, take the mowed path at 1.42 miles. Fossil Hills Trail

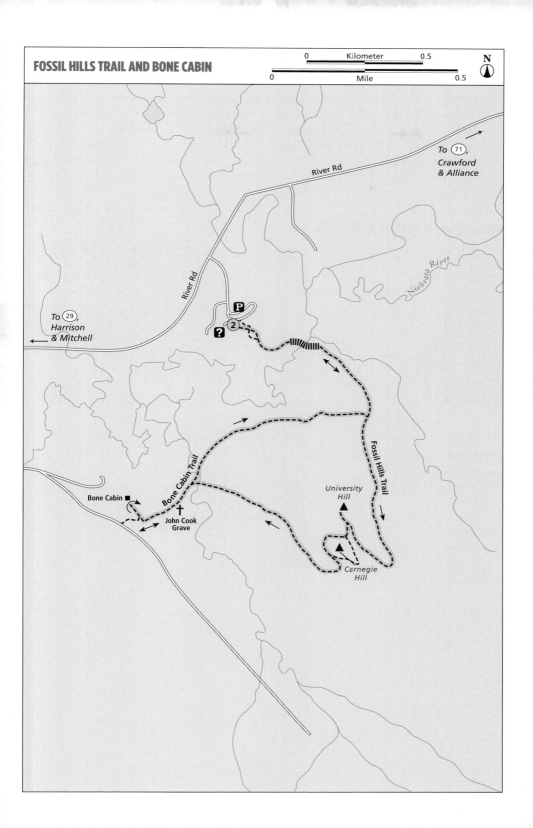

FOSSIL HILLS TRAIL AND BONE CABIN

0   Kilometer   0.5

0   Mile   0.5

N

River Rd

To 71, Crawford & Alliance

Niobrara River

River Rd

To 29, Harrison & Mitchell

P

?

2

Fossil Hills Trail

Bone Cabin Trail

Bone Cabin

John Cook Grave

University Hill

Carnegie Hill

was explicitly built to meet accessibility standards, so if you have mobility difficulties, return to the trailhead via the paved Fossil Hills Trail.

The unofficial Bone Cabin Trail first heads south then north as the trail bends on itself to head toward Bone Cabin. Head west at the junction at 1.97 miles, pass John Cook's gravesite at 2.02 miles, and then turn north at 2.15 miles to reach Bone Cabin. Restored to its 1910 condition when Harold and Eleanor Cook lived there, the cabin was used after 1914 by scientists during fossil excavations. After visiting the cabin, head east on Bone Cabin Trail through mixed-grass prairie with views south of Carnegie and University Hills. Once back on Fossil Hills Trail, the hike back to the trailhead is roughly one-half mile.

MILES AND DIRECTIONS

0.00 Begin at the trailhead next to the picnic shelter; head east on a paved trail.

0.20 Boardwalk.

0.47 Covered bench and interpretive panel.

0.50 Continue straight (south) on Fossil Hills Trail at junction with Bone Cabin Trail.

0.92 Covered bench and interpretive panel.

1.15 Continue straight (north).

1.20 University Hill.

1.25 Keep right (south) at the next two forks.

1.29 Turn right (west).

1.39 Carnegie Hill.

1.42 Keep right, leaving the paved trail to follow the mowed path to Bone Cabin.

1.46 Path bends to head north.

1.97 Keep left (west).

2.02 Gravesite of John Cook.

2.15 Turn right (north).

2.22 Bone Cabin; turn around.

2.47 Keep left (northeast).

3.05 Turn left (north) onto Fossil Hills Trail.

3.60 Arrive back at the trailhead.

3 SADDLE ROCK TRAIL

Scotts Bluff has stood as a landmark on the "Great American Desert" for 10 million years. To emigrants on the Oregon Trail, it marked the beginning of the West. To Plains Indians, it is Me-a-pa-te, or "hill that is hard to go around." Rather than go around, Saddle Rock Trail goes up Scotts Bluff: The climb is strenuous yet rewarding with expansive views of the Wildcat Hills, North Platte River Valley, Chimney Rock, and on a clear day, the Laramie Mountains in Wyoming.

Start: Behind the visitor center on the northeast corner
Elevation gain: 4,205 to 4,767 feet
Distance: 3.96 miles out and back
Difficulty: Moderate due to climb up Saddle Rock
Hiking time: 2–3 hours
Seasons/schedule: Trails open year-round, sunrise to sunset; best in spring and fall due to lack of shade
Fees and permits: None
Trail contact: Scotts Bluff National Monument, 190276 Old Oregon Trail, Gering 69341; (308) 436-9700; nps.gov/scbl/index.htm
Dog-friendly: Dogs allowed on leash; please pick up all waste
Trail surface: Asphalt
Land status: Scotts Bluff National Monument
Nearest town: Gering to the east, Scottsbluff to north

Maps: USGS Scottsbluff South, NE 2021; park map available online and at visitor center; a topographic map is also available at the visitor center
Other trail users: None
Special considerations: Check forecast for thunderstorms as trails are exposed. Be aware of prairie rattlesnakes in the area. No climbing is allowed on named rocks and where otherwise posted. Off-trail hiking is permitted on South Bluff (directly south of the visitor center across the highway); consult with a park ranger before venturing up South Bluff.
Amenities available: At the visitor center, an information desk is staffed by park rangers, restrooms, water, picnic tables, and trash bins.
Maximum grade: 21%
Cell service: Full coverage on all parts of the trail

FINDING THE TRAILHEAD
From Gering, head west on Old Oregon Trail (M Street in Gering). After stopping at the four-way stop intersection with Five Rocks Road, continue west on Old Oregon Trail for 2 miles, passing the Legacy of the Plains Museum. Turn right (north) into the Scotts Bluff National Monument Visitor Center parking area (no permits needed). The trailhead is located behind the visitor center near its northeast corner. **GPS:** N41° 49.718' W103° 42.427

Trail Conditions: There are some uneven spots from frost heave and erosion but there are no hazards or obstacles along the trail apart from some mild exposure on Saddle Rock. The trail is not marked but is easy to follow with moderate foot traffic.

THE HIKE
Saddle Rock Trail leads to the top of Scotts Bluff National Monument, first traversing a restored prairie, then climbing up Saddle Rock and literally walking through it via a pedestrian tunnel. Atop Scotts Bluff, ponderosa pines weather the constant winds of the High Plains, the views of which are spectacular from the north and south overlooks.

Sentinel Rock (left) and Eagle Rock rise above Mitchell Pass.

The trail begins behind the National Park Service visitor center at its northeast corner, following an asphalt path all the way to the summit of Scotts Bluff. There are no trail markers until you reach the top, however, there are markers along the trail for a cell phone audio tour to follow as you hike.

The first half mile crosses an undulating prairie of needle-and-thread grass, little bluestem, and yucca with Scotts Bluff rising on your left. As you head north, you will pass two ravines choked with eastern redcedar, providing both forage and shelter to herds of mule deer. The second ravine, Scotts Spring, is named after fur trader Hirman Scott, who died in the area and gave his name to the national monument.

After Scotts Spring, your first look of Saddle Rock comes into view. Take in the view at a bench (0.57 mile) dedicated to Albert Mathers, the custodian of Scotts Bluff National Monument from 1925 to 1934. From the bench you can view the weathered sandstone formations atop Saddle Rock, the tunnel which pierces the butte, and two thin layers of white volcanic ash that were deposited by western volcanoes millions of years ago.

The trail begins to climb steeply after leaving the bench, reaching a switchback at 0.81 mile to climb the south face of Saddle Rock with a steep drop on your right. The path enters the tunnel at 0.94 mile through Saddle Rock to reach its north-facing slope with views of Gering and Scottsbluff. The foot tunnel was built as a test prior to the construction of the vehicle tunnels in 1933—lucky for us it has stood the test of time!

The trail continues to climb, passing the original but now closed Zig-Zag Trail on the steep slope on your right, until it reaches several switchbacks to eventually reach a gap in Saddle Rock at 1.18 miles to return to the south face of the butte. The trail runs west along the cliff face with steep exposure on your left but the asphalt path is wide and safe. Shortly before reaching a staircase at 1.28 miles you can touch one of the volcanic ash layers that is about 6 feet above the trail on your right.

The trail reaches the summit of Scotts Bluff at 1.53 miles. Keep right (west) at the various forks, passing a metal survey post that proves Scotts Bluff is still eroding beneath your feet, as well as a memorial to the monument's namesake. The trail ends at the North Overlook with views of the Wildcat Hills, North Platte River, and on a clear day, Wyoming's Laramie Mountains on the western horizon.

Turn around and keep right (southwest) at each fork until you reach the parking area. Continue southwest along the sidewalk to reach the South Overlook at 1.98 miles.

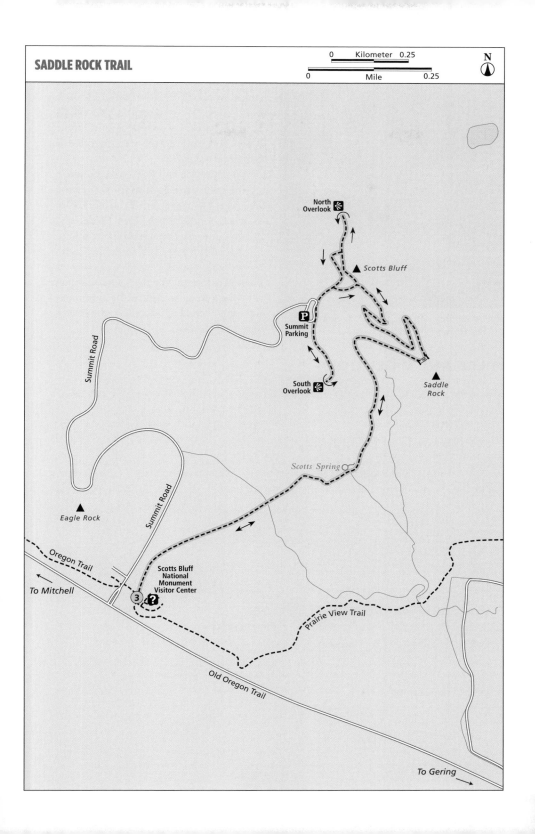

SADDLE ROCK TRAIL

0 Kilometer 0.25

0 Mile 0.25

N

North Overlook

Scotts Bluff

P Summit Parking

South Overlook

Saddle Rock

Summit Road

Summit Road

Scotts Spring

Eagle Rock

Oregon Trail

To Mitchell

Scotts Bluff National Monument Visitor Center

3 ?

Prairie View Trail

Old Oregon Trail

To Gering

Mule deer forage in the juniper ravines surrounding Scotts Bluff.

The trail cuts through a redcedar grove and shortly reaches the overlook. Looking directly south, try to locate the other named rocks of Scotts Bluff and South Bluff: (from west to east) Eagle Rock, Sentinel Rock, Crown Rock, and Dome Rock. You can also see Chimney Rock farther to the east.

This is an out-and-back trail, so return via the same path. Return to the parking area, keeping right (north) at each fork to reach Saddle Rock Trail to descend via the same paved path. Once you have descended the butte and are hiking south toward the visitor center, look west at Eagle Rock to see the first of two tunnels allowing vehicle access to the summit—the only vehicle tunnels in the entire state of Nebraska!

MILES AND DIRECTIONS

0.00 Begin behind the visitor center at its northeast corner near an accessible restroom.

0.81 The trail switches back across the ravine and climbs up Saddle Rock heading northeast.

0.94 Reach the tunnel through Saddle Rock.

1.18 Reach a gap in Saddle Rock as the trail curves right (west) to traverse the south-facing slope of Saddle Rock. Take caution here with the steep drop-off on your left.

1.53 Reach the top of Scotts Bluff. Keep right (west) until you reach the North Overlook.

1.70 North Overlook. Turn around and keep right, heading southeast, until you reach the parking area.

1.93 At the parking area, continue along the sidewalk toward the South Overlook trailhead.

1.98 Reach the South Overlook trailhead and follow the path heading southeast.

2.12 South Overlook. Turn around and return to the parking area.

2.27 Reach the parking area and continue north.

2.33 North Overlook trailhead. Keep right until you reach the Saddle Rock trailhead.

2.42 Turn right (east) onto Saddle Rock Trail.

2.74 The trail passes through the gap in Saddle Rock and curves left (west) heading toward the switchbacks down the north-facing slope of Saddle Rock.

2.95 Continue through the tunnel.

3.96 Arrive back at the visitor center.

4 TURKEY RUN TRAIL TO MONUMENT VIEW

Evergreen canyons and sandstone buttes define the rugged terrain of the Wildcat Hills, unique in Nebraska with its mix of prairie and mountain plant species. Turkey Run Trail meanders through Rocky Mountain juniper, mountain mahogany, eastern redcedar, and ponderosa pine before reaching the ridgetop Monument View Trail with views of Scotts Bluff National Monument. If you're lucky you might spot a bobcat, the park's elusive namesake, but you're more likely to see birds such as mountain bluebird, red crossbill, and wild turkey.

Start: Turkey Run Trailhead at the first primitive campsite upon entering the park

Elevation gain: 4,487 to 4,656 feet

Distance: 4.18 miles out and back

Difficulty: Difficult due to rugged terrain

Hiking time: 2–3 hours

Seasons/schedule: Trails open year-round, sunrise to sunset; best in spring for wildflowers

Fees and permits: A park entry permit is required and may be purchased at the park, statewide Game and Parks offices and permit vendors, or online at outdoornebraska.gov.

Trail contact: Wildcat Hills State Recreation Area, 210615 NE 71, Gering 69341; (308) 436-3777

Dog-friendly: Yes, on a 6-foot leash

Trail surface: Dirt and rocky terrain

Land status: Wildcat Hills State Recreation Area

Nearest town: Gering and Scottsbluff to the north

Maps: USGS Wildcat Mountain; park map available at visitor center, some trailheads in the park, and outdoornebraska.gov/maps

Other trail users: Equestrians and mountain bikers

Special considerations: Prairie rattlesnakes are common in the area. Take precautions if you encounter one. The alternative trailhead for Turkey Run Trail is 0.5 mile farther on the park road.

Amenities available: Vault toilets at the primitive campsites and hand water pumps in-season; 2 picnic shelters along the trails

Maximum grade: 16%

Cell service: Coverage on park roads and open ridges; none in canyons or under tree cover

FINDING THE TRAILHEAD

From Gering, head south on NE 71 / John McLellan Jr. Expressway for 8 miles. Turn left at the entrance to Wildcat Hills State Recreation Area. Continue on the park road, passing a shooting complex on your right and the visitor center on the left. After 0.3 mile, arrive at a primitive campsite. Turkey Run Trailhead is at the west end of the campsite. Before going past the kiosk or Nature Center, visitors must obtain a park entry permit. **GPS:** N41° 42.423' W103° 40.446

Trail Conditions: Trails are mostly marked but there are some unmarked junctions and forks. There is a tricky footbridge crossing because the handrails are too far away to hold while crossing the footbridge.

THE HIKE

This hike follows four trails in the Wildcat Hills State Recreation Area: Turkey Run, Pine Top, Muley, and Monument View. The Turkey Run, Pine Top, and Muley trails travel mostly underneath forest canopy while Monument View traverses a ridge with expansive views of the rocky escarpment of Wildcat Hills and Scotts Bluff National Monument.

There are two trailheads for Turkey Run, and we begin at the trailhead located at the first primitive campsite you encounter after entering the park. Heading west, the trail passes under ponderosa pines before reaching a small clearing at 0.1 mile. On your right (north) you will see a No Camping sign and farther a sign for Turkey Run Trail: Do not follow that sign but continue straight (west). At 0.23 mile you will reach a junction with White Tail Trail. Continue north on Turkey Run as it bends around a large eastern redcedar.

Turkey Run Trail winds through the forested canyon, interspersed with clearings on sunnier, drier canyonsides. The south and west-facing slopes receive more sun, creating conditions that favor prairie grasses, while the moist and cool north- and east-facing slopes are ideal for pine, redcedar, and juniper.

Shortly after Turkey Run bends sharply to the southeast, you will reach an unmarked junction with Cedar Ridge Trail. Unless you want to hike up the ridge to the Depression-era Civilian Conservation Corp shelter, keep left (southeast) to continue on Turkey Run Trail. Farther ahead, at 0.83 mile, pass a short spur trail on your right that leads to another shelter on the hillside. On this next stretch of trail you can see evidence of the cooler, moister west-facing slope and canyon bottom: The ponderosa pine and, to a lesser extent, eastern redcedar, are covered in lichen along this stretch of the trail.

Cross a footbridge at 1.09 miles and at 1.27 miles reach an unmarked fork. Keep left onto Pine Top Trail, which immediately bends sharply to the left to reach another unmarked fork at 1.3 miles. Look up to see two wooden walkways clinging to the hillside. Keep right at the fork to cross both as the trail climbs up the hill. Turn right (east) to climb the stairs leading to another CCC shelter. Note: This spur trail with the two wooden walkways is not marked on the park map but is safe to hike.

The picnic shelter is a great place to have a snack and rest. Continuing past the shelter and through the small parking area, follow the road until you reach a sign indicating restrooms. Turn left (north) onto Muley Trail toward the restrooms, passing them and a small stone memorial at 1.45 miles, before reaching a junction. Turn left (northwest), then keep right near a picnic table, to reach the fenced grilling area of the group campsite. Here, head uphill toward the parking area for the Monument View Trailhead at 1.61 miles.

Snap a picture at the selfie station, then walk northwest along the ridgetop Monument View Trail. At 1.68 miles, continue straight (northwest) at the junction with Pine Top Trail. The trail opens up with excellent views of the surrounding Wildcat Hills. As you near the viewpoint, the ridge narrows considerably on both sides but the walking is easy until you reach the end of the trail. Enjoy the views of Scotts Bluff National Monument in the distance to the north, then turn around to return via Monument View.

At 2.38 miles, turn right (west) onto Pine Top Trail to descend into the canyon. The trail is rutted out, especially in the middle, so take caution in wet conditions. Turn left (southeast) at 2.5 miles to continue on Pine Top Trail. You can turn right (north) at this junction to follow Pine Top Trail to the northern boundary of the park, however you will have to return to this junction as it's an out-and-back route.

Monument View.

Continuing due south on Pine Top Trail, you will reach a footbridge at 2.59 miles. The crossing is tricky, as the handrails are too wide to hold while you cross, however the drop is only 5 feet and the bridge is short. The trail heads west briefly then bends south again to continue up the canyon until you reach the junction with Turkey Run Trail at 2.96 miles. Turn right (northwest) at the unmarked junction onto Turkey Run, staying on the trail as you pass the spur trail for Cedar Ridge at 3.61 miles and the junction with White Tail Trail at 3.97 miles until returning to the trailhead. Make sure to stop by the visitor center before or after your hike, as it has an interesting exhibit on the natural and cultural history of the Wildcat Hills plus gifts and information.

MILES AND DIRECTIONS

0.00   Begin at Turkey Run Trailhead heading northwest.

0.10   Arrive at a clearing and continue straight (northwest), passing an overgrown spur trail on your right.

0.23   Continue north on Turkey Run Trail at the junction with White Tail Trail.

0.60   Keep left to stay on Turkey Run Trail at an unmarked junction with Cedar Ridge Trail.

   Side trip: Turn right (south) onto Cedar Ridge Trail to climb the rocky trail to the CCC shelter, then return to this junction.

0.83   Continue east on Turkey Run Trail, passing a spur trail on the right leading to a shelter on the hillside.

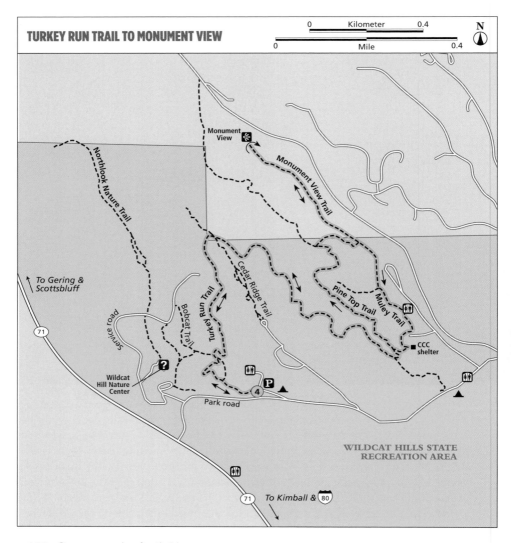

Monument View

Monument View Trail

Northlook Nature Trail

To Gering & Scottsbluff

71

Service road

Bobcat Trail

Turkey Run Trail

Cedar Ridge Trail

Pine Top Trail

Muley Trail

CCC shelter

Wildcat Hill Nature Center

Park road

4

P

WILDCAT HILLS STATE RECREATION AREA

71   To Kimball & 80

1.09   Cross a wooden footbridge.

1.27   At an unmarked fork, bear left onto Pine Top Trail, which immediately curves sharply left.

1.30   Reach another unmarked fork. Keep right to follow a windy path up a rugged hillside, crossing two wooden footbridges.

1.35   Turn right (north) at the trail marker and climb the steps to the CCC shelter.

1.37   Reach the CCC shelter and a small parking area. Continue north on the gravel road and turn left (northwest) onto Muley Trail and follow the sign to the restrooms.

1.45   Reach the restrooms on your right. Continue north and turn left (northwest) at the next junction, heading toward the group campsite.

1.54   Next to the grilling area for the group campsite, take the wide grass path uphill (north) to reach a parking area.

Shelter built by Civilian Conservation Corps during the Great Depression.

1.61 Reach the parking area, which is Monument View Trailhead. Follow Monument View Trail north along the ridge.

1.68 Continue straight (northwest) at the junction with Pine Top Trail on the left.

2.02 Reach Monument View. Turn around and return to the junction with Pine Top Trail.

2.38 Turn right (west) onto Pine Top Trail.

2.50 Turn left (southeast) to continue on Pine Top Trail.

Option: Turn right (northwest) to follow Pine Top Trail to the park's northern boundary.

2.59 Reach a tricky footbridge crossing.

2.94 Continue straight on Pine Top Trail, passing the hillside footbridges on the left.

2.96 Turn right (northwest) onto Turkey Run Trail.

Option: Turn left to follow Turkey Run Trail to its alternative trailhead, then return to the original trailhead following the park road.

3.12 Cross a wooden footbridge.

3.38 Continue straight at the spur trail on the left leading uphill to a shelter.

3.61 Keep right at the unmarked junction with Cedar Ridge Trail.

3.97 Continue east on Turkey Run Trail at the junction with White Tail Trail.

4.09 Continue straight on Turkey Run Trail.

4.18 Arrive back at Turkey Run Trailhead.

Turkey Run Trailhead.

5 CHIMNEY ROCK TRAIL

By far the most mentioned landmark in their journals, the sight of Chimney Rock made emigrants "glad to see we are going in the right direction." It's difficult to go the wrong way on this 1-mile out-and-back trail, but beware of prairie rattlesnakes and prickly yucca along the narrow footpath to the base of Chimney Rock. The pioneer cemetery adjacent to the trailhead offers a quiet place to reflect on the history of Nebraska's most famous landmark.

Start: Chimney Rock Pioneer Cemetery
Elevation gain: 3,986 to 4,043 feet
Distance: 0.92 mile out and back
Difficulty: Easy
Hiking time: 1 hour
Seasons/schedule: Trail open year-round; best in spring and fall due to sun exposure
Fees and permits: None
Trail contact: Chimney Rock Museum, 9822 CR 75, Bayard 69334; (308) 586-2581; history.nebraska .gov/rock
Dog-friendly: Yes, on leash
Trail surface: Narrow dirt footpath
Land status: Chimney Rock National Historic Site

Nearest town: Bayard 5 miles to the north, Gering and Scottsbluff 21 miles to the northwest
Maps: USGS South Bayard, NE 2021
Other trail users: None
Special considerations: Prairie rattlesnakes are present in the area. Also, long pants are recommended as the trail is narrow with yucca and other rough or sharp plants. Check museum opening hours during the off-season (late Sept to late Apr). There are no services or amenities near the trailhead.
Amenities available: None
Maximum grade: 9%
Cell service: Reliable reception throughout the trail and next to Chimney Rock

FINDING THE TRAILHEAD

From Gering, head east on NE 92 for 17 miles. Turn right (south) onto Nebraska 62F. After 1.3 miles, turn left (west) onto CR 98. Continue for 0.5 mile until you reach a dead end at Chimney Rock Cemetery. The trail head is opposite (west) of the entrance to the cemetery. **GPS:** N41° 41.951' W103° 20.494'

Trail Conditions: This is not a maintained trail; please hike with caution. Prairie rattlesnakes may be present. The trail is a single-track footpath leading from the parking area at the cemetery to the landmark at the base of Chimney Rock. The trail receives light traffic. Climbing Chimney Rock is not permitted.

THE HIKE

Chimney Rock is never out of view on this short and easy hike. The sandstone spire was substantially higher during the heyday of the Oregon Trail in the mid–1800s: Wind, erosion, and lightning have reduced Chimney Rock's height by 30 feet over the last century and a half. Today, the landmark rises 470 feet above the North Platte River Valley, and this hike leads you to its base. Thousands of emigrants and others carved their names into the base of the spire, but do not follow their example. To prevent further erosion and preserve this natural monument, please do not climb Chimney Rock.

Chimney Rock, one of the most famous landmarks on the Oregon Trail.

Beginning in front of the Chimney Rock Pioneer Cemetery, find the narrow footpath heading west toward Chimney Rock. The trail immediately descends into a shallow draw. The narrow single-track path climbs out of the draw and heads west, running parallel with a barbed wire fence on your right (north) and a large bluff to the south. Watch for mule deer bounding away in the short-grass prairie. The narrow footpath weaves through sagebrush and yucca, so it's best to wear long pants during this hike.

After 0.2 mile, the trail continues west as it leaves the barbed wire fence, which turns northwest. There are prairie rattlesnakes in the area, so keep your eyes on the trail ahead and your ears open for their telltale warning signal. After 0.3 mile, the trail climbs in and out of two more shallow draws, the second choked with a dense thicket on its bottom. The footpath continues through the short-grass prairie until it reaches the base of Chimney Rock, marked with a commemorative plaque at 0.5 mile.

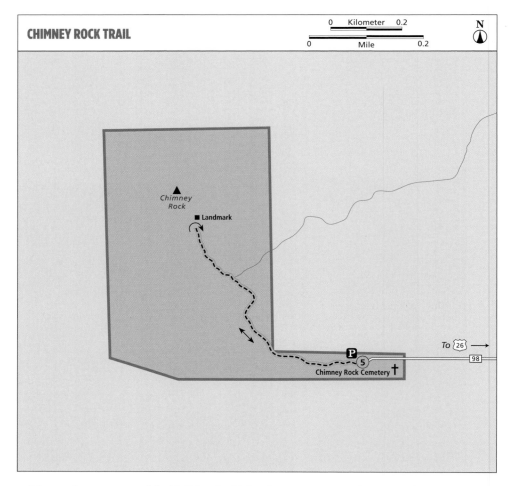

The marker was erected in 1940 by the Nebraska State Historical Society after Roszel Frank Durnal donated the 80-acre property to the public. The site became a National Historic Site in 1956, and the image of Chimney Rock was chosen in 2006 to feature on Nebraska's state quarter.

There are several faint footpaths that continue past the marker. The path around the south side of Chimney Rock is more defined and can be followed all the way to the

COURTHOUSE AND JAIL ROCKS

Even if they have never visited them, most Nebraskans are familiar with Chimney Rock and two other famous buttes, Courthouse and Jail Rocks. All three served as milestones on the Oregon Trail, as pioneers saw them as the beginning of the West and the end of the sun-drenched and treeless prairie. While not on the Oregon Trail, pioneers would make an excursion just to see the famous rocks. Current visitors can follow signs and country roads to reach the two, which tower next to each other above the surrounding prairie. A short 0.3-mile loop trail takes hikers to the foot of the buttes.

Left: The trailhead is adjacent to Chimney Rock Cemetery.
Right: Erosion has exposed layers of sediments and volcanic ash deposited over millions of years. Chimney Rock is shaped by wind, water, and lightning.

opposite eastern side of the landmark, where the trail disappears. The hike described here follows the half-mile trail to the marker and then turns around to return to the cemetery. If you decide to explore around the base of Chimney Rock, please be responsible and respect this national historic landmark. Under no circumstances is climbing Chimney Rock allowed.

After returning to the parking turnaround, explore the Chimney Rock Pioneer Cemetery. The cemetery is a peaceful place to remember those who lost their lives in search of a better one.

MILES AND DIRECTIONS

0.00 Begin opposite the cemetery entrance and take the narrow footpath that descends into a draw.

0.31 The trail descends into the first of two shallow draws.

0.50 Reach the marker at the base of Chimney Rock. Turn around and return via the same path.

0.92 Arrive back at the trailhead at the cemetery.

6 OREGON TRAIL TO MEDICINE WHEEL

The trails at Ash Hollow State Historical Park span human history dating back 6,000 years. The hike begins at Ash Hollow Cave, a National Historic Landmark, occupied by a succession of indigenous cultures. The creek below, its course diverted by the modern highway, was an idyllic oasis of water, food, and timber for natives and emigrants alike, as it was an important staging point on the Oregon Trail. The hike continues to a medicine wheel replica overlooking the North Platte River Valley, a nod to the Lakota Sioux people who inhabited the area before European settlers, commercial fur merchants, and sport hunters arrived.

Start: Ash Hollow State Historical Park visitor center
Elevation gain: 3,395 to 3,585 feet
Distance: 4.09-mile loop
Difficulty: Moderate due to sun exposure
Hiking time: 2–3 hours
Seasons/schedule: Trails open year-round, sunrise to sunset; best in fall for ash leaves turning color and spring and summer for wildflowers
Fees and permits: A park entry permit is required and may be purchased at the park, statewide Game and Parks offices and permit vendors, or online at outdoornebraska.gov.
Trail contact: Ash Hollow State Historical Park, 4265 NE 26, Lewellen 69147; (308) 778-5651; outdoornebraska.gov/ashhollow/
Dog-friendly: Yes, on leash
Trail surface: Asphalt, gravel road, dirt footpath, and mowed grass path
Land status: Ash Hollow State Historical Park

Nearest town: Lewellen 3 miles to the north, Ogallala 28 miles to the southeast
Maps: USGS Ruthton, NE 2021; park map available at outdoornebraska .gov/maps and at the visitor center
Other trail users: None
Special considerations: More than half of the hike has no protection from the sun; plan and pack accordingly with plenty of water and personal sun protection. Part of the hike follows the park road. Traffic is light but be aware of potential vehicles. The visitor center rents binoculars, scopes, and bird books.
Amenities available: Restrooms and water at the visitor center; vault toilets and water at the picnic area near Ash Hollow Spring
Maximum grade: 9%
Cell service: Coverage available in most of the park, with the exception of limited coverage in Ash Hollow Creek

FINDING THE TRAILHEAD

From I-80 exit 126, head north on NE 26 for 0.6 mile toward Ogallala. At the first intersection in Ogallala, turn left (west) onto US 26 / US 30 / E 1st Street. After 2 miles, turn right (north) and follow US 26 for 3.1 miles. Turn left (west) to continue on US 26 for 24 miles. After passing Windlass Hill, turn right (east) to enter Ash Hollow State Historical Park. Continue east on the park road for 0.4 mile, then turn left (north) to reach the visitor center. The trail begins near the southwest corner of the visitor center. **GPS:** N41° 18.088′ W102° 7.258′

Trail Conditions: There is considerable sun exposure on this hike. Prairie rattlesnakes are common in the area.

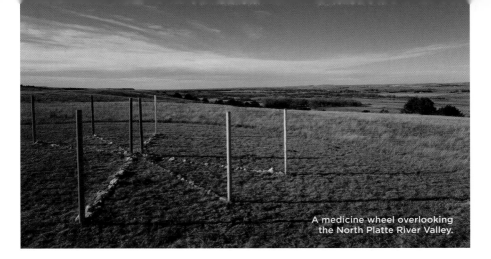
A medicine wheel overlooking the North Platte River Valley.

THE HIKE

Timber, shelter, wild game, and sweet spring water have drawn humans to Ash Hollow for more than 6,000 years. The cave above the springs was used as a camp for much of that time, most recently by the Dismal River People, ancient ancestors of the Apache. Less than a century after they left, pioneers arrived and gave Ash Hollow its name for the parklike grove of green ash lining the creek bottom. The channel of Ash Hollow Creek has since been diverted because of the highway, but you can still hike the very same section of the Oregon Trail that westward wagons took across the High Plains.

Beginning on the west side of the visitor center, head north on the asphalt path to Ash Hollow Cave after 0.08 mile. After visiting the cave, turn east onto Spring Trail and descend a steep asphalt path into a ravine with limestone outcroppings on both sides. A bench at 0.19 mile near Spring Pond offers the choice of continuing south on the asphalt path or skirting the pond along its west bank under tree cover; both options meet on the south end of the pond next to a sign about Ash Hollow Spring at 0.37 mile. "A number of springs of cold and crystal water gushed forth from under the high barren cliff" is how emigrant Madison Moorman described Ash Hollow in 1850. The shady creek bottom with fresh water was an oasis to emigrants who had trudged across the treeless prairie after crossing the Missouri River.

From the sign, continue south underneath power lines across a grassy field with swells from emigrant wagons tearing up the sandy soil. Cross the park entry road at 0.73 mile and continue south on a wide mowed path, passing a trailhead sign and information about native songbirds. For nearly the next mile the trail follows a sandy path alongside chalky outcroppings and underneath the shade of ash trees—if it were the mid-1800s, you'd be passing wagons loaded with emigrants and supplies. The trees give way to open prairie just before 1.6 miles and the Rock School, which was in use from 1903 until 1919.

WINDLASS HILL

Windlass Hill is located 2.5 miles south of Ash Hollow State Historical Park on NE 26. There is a short but steep paved path leading up a hill to a marker commemorating the Oregon Trail. Visible ruts can still be seen on the hillside that were cut by thousands of wagons as they descended the steep hill heading to the water, timber, and shade that Ash Hollow provided.

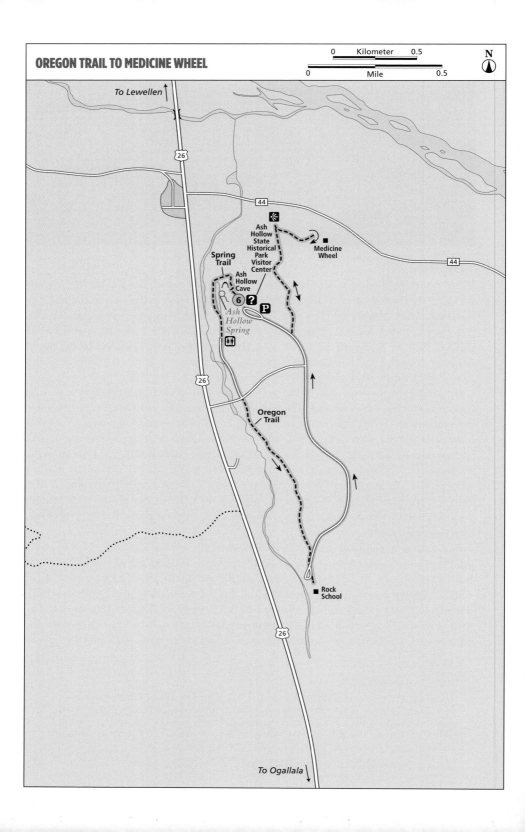

OREGON TRAIL TO MEDICINE WHEEL

0   Kilometer   0.5

0   Mile   0.5

N

To Lewellen ↑

26

44

Ash
Hollow
State
Historical
Park
Visitor
Center

Medicine
Wheel

**Spring
Trail**

Ash
Hollow
Cave

6

?

P

*Ash
Hollow
Spring*

44

26

**Oregon
Trail**

Rock
School

26

To Ogallala ↓

Head north on the park road as it climbs out of the hollow to shortgrass prairie upland. There are great views of the surrounding High Plains from the road. Continue south at the intersection with the park entry road at 2.65 miles until you reach the trailhead at 2.8 miles for Medicine Wheel, a 1.5-mile out-and-back trail to a replica of a Lakota Sioux medicine wheel marking the solstices and equinoxes. Veer left onto the mowed grass trail as the North Platte River Valley lays to the north. A viewpoint with a picnic table at 3.25 miles provides a rest stop and photo opportunity. Continue east to reach the medicine wheel at 3.45 miles. Head back via the same trail to reach the park road and the visitor center. Be sure to find the aromatic pine bottle-brush in front of the visitor center!

The Oregon Trail as it passes through Ash Hollow.

MILES AND DIRECTIONS

0.00 Begin near the southwest corner of the visitor center on the asphalt path toward the cave.

0.08 Reach the cave entrance. Turn right (east) to follow Spring Trail.

0.10 Turn left (north) onto Spring Trail and descend down a steep path.

0.37 Reach the south end of the pond. Continue south toward the vault toilets.

0.50 Arrive at the vault toilets and follow the gravel road south.

0.73 Cross the park road and catch the trail between two large eastern redcedars heading south.

1.00 Continue south at the picnic area and a spur trail on the right.

1.09 Reach a fork. Bear left onto the trail marked with a "Pedestrian Traffic Only" sign.

1.40 Reach a fork and bear left, keeping the rock outcropping on your left.

1.50 Reach a trailhead sign and mailbox. Continue south on the park road toward Rock School.

1.60 Rock School. Turn around and walk north on the park road.

2.65 Continue straight at the junction with the park entry road.

2.80 Bear right (north) off the park road to follow Medicine Wheel Trail at the trailhead sign.

3.25 Reach a viewpoint with a picnic table. Turn right (east) toward Medicine Wheel.

3.45 Medicine Wheel. Turn around and return to the trailhead junction at the park road.

3.90 Turn right (northwest) onto the park road.

4.09 Arrive back at the visitor center and parking area.

A **BEAD MOUNTAIN**

Named for the beads that pioneer schoolchildren found on an ancient Native American burial site, Bead Mountain offers the rare opportunity to bag a peak in Nebraska. Bead Mountain Ranch and the adjacent surrounding areas (Buffalo Creek WMA, Wildcat Hills SRA, and Murphy Ranch) offer more than 10,000 acres of contiguous publicly accessible land to hike. However, there are no maintained trails at Bead Mountain, so the best approach is to climb to the saddle and then scramble up each summit, both offering sweeping views of the Wildcat Hills.

Start: Bead Mountain PRBE parking area
Elevation gain: 4,205 to 4,628 feet
Distance: 2.00 miles out and back (off-trail)
Difficulty: Difficult due to steep ascent and descent of Bead Mountain
Hiking time: 1–2 hours
Seasons/schedule: Open year-round, dawn to dusk; best outside of hunting season
Fees and permits: None
Trail contact: Nebraska Game and Parks Commission; (402) 471-0641; outdoornebraska.gov/
Dog-friendly: Yes, on 6-foot leash
Trail surface: Dirt and grass

Land status: Bead Mountain Ranch, Platte River Basin Environments
Nearest town: Gering 8 miles to the north
Maps: USGS Wright Gap, NE 2021
Other trail users: Bikers, equestrians, hunters
Special considerations: Hunting is allowed during the season; thunderstorms are a significant hazard during the summer, especially in the afternoon.
Amenities available: None
Maximum grade: 29%
Cell service: Yes, coverage on the approach and at the summit of Bead Mountain

FINDING THE TRAILHEAD

From Gering, drive south on NE 71. After 6 miles, turn left (east) onto CR W. Continue for 2.8 miles until reaching the Bead Mountain parking area. **GPS:** N41° 44.485' W103° 37.227'

Trail Conditions: There is no trail to the summit, as all hiking is off-trail. Any trails are footpaths worn over time or game paths. Rattlesnakes, thunderstorms, and steep slopes with loose and dry dirt are potential hazards. Light trail traffic.

The hike to the summit of Bead Mountain is off-trail and steep.

Saddle Rock at Fort Robinson State Park
(Lovers Leap and Red Cloud Buttes).

PINE RIDGE

Pine Ridge is a steep escarpment that separates the western High Plains from the northwestern Great Plains and the Missouri Plateau. The landscape shatters the stereotype of flat Nebraskan farmland: Parklike ponderosa pine savanna, pine-studded canyons, and rugged sandstone buttes evoke the American West. Indeed, the region is steeped in Native American history, especially from the tragic conflict in the late nineteenth century that culminated in the Wounded Knee Massacre in South Dakota. Stretching 100 miles through Sioux, Dawes, and Sheridan Counties in northwestern Nebraska, Pine Ridge provides habitat for some of the state's most elusive wildlife, including bighorn sheep, bobcats, elk, and mountain lions.

An eroded butte in Soldier Creek Wilderness.

7 TROOPER TRAIL AND BOOTS AND SADDLE TRAIL

Trooper Trail and Boots and Saddle Trail combine to form this loop that traverses most of 7,794-acre Soldier Creek Wilderness, the largest of two wilderness areas in Nebraska. Much of the area was burned in the 1989 Fort Robinson Fire and again in 2007 during the Soldier Creek Complex Fires, leaving barren, sandy hills strewn with snags and dead timber. Some stands of ponderosa survived while regrowth is slow but encouraging in other areas. The South, Middle, and North Forks of Soldier Creek, however, turn beautiful colors in fall and offer trout fishing and wonderful backcountry camping opportunities.

Start: South Fork Trailhead
Elevation gain: 4,115 to 4,743 feet
Distance: 14.48-mile loop
Difficulty: Difficult due to distance, rugged terrain, and multiple creek crossings
Hiking time: At least 5 hours
Seasons/schedule: Trails open year-round; good any time of year except during the heat of summer
Fees and permits: None
Trail contact: Nebraska National Forest Pine Ridge Ranger District, 125 N Main St., Chadron 69337; (308) 432-0300
Dog-friendly: Yes, on leash
Trail surface: Dirt and grass footpaths
Land status: Soldier Creek Wilderness, Nebraska National Forest Pine Ridge Ranger District
Nearest town: Crawford 10 miles to the east
Maps: USGS Smiley Canyon, NE 2021 and USGS Andrews, NE 2021; brochure with map available in visitor register box at trailhead;

Forest Service maps available at fs.usda.gov/main/nebraska/maps-pubs
Other trail users: Equestrians and mountain bikers on trails within the national forest
Special considerations: There is no shade along most of the trail, so plan accordingly and avoid hiking during hot days. Be aware of thunderstorms; also be cautious of tree snags during windy conditions. Check hunting season dates and wear appropriate clothing. Cattle graze in the wilderness and national forest areas; be respectful and do not approach cattle. This is a remote wilderness area; pack the Ten Essentials and practice Leave No Trace principles.
Amenities available: At trailhead: vault toilets, hand water pump, parking, primitive campsites; water available at South and Middle Forks of Soldier Creek (filter or purify)
Maximum grade: 21%
Cell service: Clear at South Fork Trailhead and on ridges and clearings; unreliable near creek forks

FINDING THE TRAILHEAD

From Crawford take US 20 west for 2.5 miles to Fort Robinson State Park. Turn north on Soldier Creek Road for 6 miles. After crossing a high-water clearance and entering the recreation area, keep left at the fork to park at the South Fork Trailhead past the horse corral. **GPS:** N42° 41.708' W103° 34.141

Trail Conditions: The trail is waymarked with wooden posts, some painted white at the top. Cows can and do knock over the posts, especially near stock tanks where they congregate, so always be looking for the next trail marker post. At times the footpath is faint or disappears, so focus on the next trail marker post ahead.

THE HIKE

Soldier Creek Wilderness was created when the US Congress passed the Nebraska Wilderness Act in 1986. It gets its name from its use as a timber reserve, horse pasture, and recreation area by military personnel when Fort Robinson was in operation. Shortly after its dedication in 1989, 90 percent of the pines in the wilderness area were burned during the Fort Robinson Fire. Another fire in 2007 burned one-third of the wilderness area, however, it was similar to the low intensity natural fires that indigenous people used to maintain open savanna ponderosa forest, resulting in a less catastrophic fire. The 1989 fire was similar to the devastating fires that have ravaged the western United States for the past decade.

Besides pockets of ponderosa that survived the fires and new growth, the three forks of Soldier Creek—South, Middle, North—are also forested. Cottonwood, box elder, and ash line the creek beds while prairie sandreed, needle-and-thread, and little bluestem grow on the treeless sandy-slope prairie. Lupine, sego lily, and shell-leaf penstemon are just three of the kaleidoscope of prairie wildflowers that bloom in spring and summer. Mule deer, elk, bobcats, coyotes, bald eagles, and more wildlife can be spotted in this pristine wilderness. Besides two functioning windmills, their accompanying stock tanks, and barbed wire fence, the only sign of human activity are the Forest Service trail posts marking the two trails and old double-track paths that comprise historic military routes. Logging, mining, and any other activity is prohibited in the wilderness area.

Begin the loop at the South Fork Trailhead, which has a large horse corral and a hand pump to collect potable water year-round. Trooper Trail heads southwest for almost two and a half miles following the level and wooded creek bed of Soldier Creek's south fork. Some of the surrounding hillsides have eroded into sheer cliff faces. The trail crosses the creek several times and passes two excellent sites to camp at 1.94 miles and 2.05 miles. Trooper Trail leaves the creek to head northwest into rugged, treeless hills.

Damage from wildfires in 1989 and 2007 is most extensive on Boots and Saddle Trail.

The trail follows the spine of a ridge, climbing more than 400 feet in 1.5 miles. After crossing a ravine at 4.81 miles, Trooper Trail doubles back at 5.35 miles to head east toward a functioning windmill and stock tanks. The trail continues southeast for nearly 2 miles along a wide, flat ridge.

The junction with Boots and Saddle Trail after 7.33 miles marks the midpoint of the loop. The trail heads north descending over 300 hundred feet through ponderosa savanna until it reaches Middle Fork Soldier Creek after 8.54 miles with several nice spots near the creek to camp.

The trail from the creek bed climbs over 300 hundred feet north into rugged canyon country to leave the wilderness area at 9.98 miles and enter the Nebraska National Forest. The trail turns southeast to descend 350 feet to reach the North Fork of Soldier Creek at 10.78 miles. Once again the trail climbs out of the creek into rugged canyon country before turning south at the boundary with Fort Robinson State Park at 12.5 miles. Continue south as the trail descends via a ridge to reach open prairie and the North Fork once again at 13.52 miles. There are multiple creek crossings before you reach Soldier Creek Campground at 14.16 miles and North Fork Trailhead. Follow the forest road back to the South Fork Trailhead.

MILES AND DIRECTIONS

0.00 Begin at South Fork Trailhead; head south through two gates following brown and white posts.

0.11 Cross the South Fork of Soldier Creek.

0.38 Cross a fence to enter Unit 53SE.

0.53 Creek crossing.

1.00 Veer left (south) at a trail marker to descend toward the creek.

1.05 Turn right (northwest) at a Trooper Trail sign.

1.61 Keep left (southwest) at a trail post.

1.72 Creek crossing.

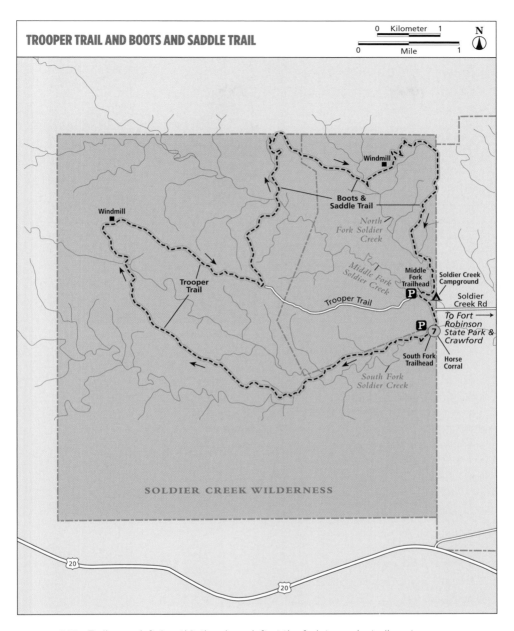

TROOPER TRAIL AND BOOTS AND SADDLE TRAIL

Windmill

Boots &
Saddle Trail

North
Fork Soldier
Creek

Windmill

Middle
Fork Soldier Creek

Trooper
Trail

Middle
Fork
Trailhead

Soldier Creek
Campground

Trooper Trail

Soldier
Creek Rd

To Fort
Robinson
State Park &
Crawford

7

South Fork
Trailhead

Horse
Corral

South Fork
Soldier Creek

SOLDIER CREEK WILDERNESS

20

20

1.89   Trail veers left (south), then keep left at the fork toward a trail post.

2.04   Creek crossing.

2.15   Enter Unit 53SW

2.23   Turn right (northwest) at the Trooper Trail sign

2.29   Veer right (north) at a trail post and climb the hillside.

2.39   Fence.

2.56 Veer left (northwest) at a trail post to enter a treeless area.

2.76 Turn right (northwest) at a trail post.

3.66 Veer right (north) at a trail post.

4.42 Enter Unit 53NW and continue north.

4.81 Ravine bottom.

4.90 Veer left (west) toward two posts climbing the crest of a hill.

5.35 Trail bends right to head northeast toward stock tanks.

5.50 Stock tanks.

5.59 Broken trail sign: "South Fork 3 miles, trailhead 5.5 miles."

7.20 Switchbacks.

7.33 Reach the junction of Trooper Trail and Boots and Saddle Trail; turn left (north) onto Boots and Saddle Trail.

> **Option:** Continue southeast on Trooper Trail to reach the Middle/Nork Fork Trailhead.

Ponderosa pine savanna.

8.31 Turn left (northeast) at a trail post to head downhill (no defined trail, follow posts).

8.42 Fence.

8.54 Cross the Middle Fork of Soldier Creek; head north toward the trail post and past the Boots and Saddle Trail sign.

8.60 Trail heads north with a deep canyon on the left.

9.41 Head east uphill near a large tree snag; few trail posts in this section and numerous snags make route finding difficult.

9.60 Reach a barbed wire fence; the trail bends east.

9.98 Boundary of Soldier Creek Wilderness and Nebraska National Forest.

10.66 Reach a creek and follow it southeast.

10.78 Reach a trail sign; cross the creek to head northeast toward Soldier Creek Campground.

11.07 Pass stock tanks to the left.

11.20 Enter canyon country; trail winds along canyonsides.

12.02 Leave the canyon country.

12.90 Cross a ravine.

13.35 Continue south at a trail post.

13.52 Cross the North Fork of Soldier Creek; six more creek crossings over the next half mile.

14.04 Reach a fork; keep right (northwest).

14.16 North Fork Trailhead; turn left (south) onto FR 803.

14.35 Keep right at the fork.

14.48 Arrive back at the South Fork Trailhead.

8 TURTLE ROCK TRAIL

Turtle Rock Trail packs a mighty punch in just over 2 miles. The trail climbs nearly 400 feet in the first mile to reach Cheyenne Buttes, named after the tragic Cheyenne Breakout that took place at Fort Robinson in January 1879. Despite the steep climb, the short distance and easy navigation makes this hike appropriate for children with experience hiking. The effort will be rewarded with breathtaking views of the White River Valley, Pine Ridge, and Fort Robinson State Park.

Start: Turtle Rock Trailhead
Elevation gain: 4,045 to 4,403 feet
Distance: 2.31-mile loop
Difficulty: Moderate due to sun exposure and steep climb at the beginning of the hike
Hiking time: 1–2 hours
Seasons/schedule: Trail open year-round, sunrise to sunset; best in spring and fall to avoid heat and sun exposure
Fees and permits: A park entry permit is required and may be purchased at the park, statewide Game and Parks offices and permit vendors, or online at outdoornebraska.gov.
Trail contact: Fort Robinson State Park, 3200 US 20, Crawford 69339; (308) 665-2900; outdoornebraska .gov/fortrobinson/
Dog-friendly: Yes, on leash
Trail surface: Dirt two-track

Land status: Fort Robinson State Park
Nearest town: Crawford 4 miles to the east
Maps: USGS Smiley Canyon, NE 2021; park map available online; detailed trails map available at main park office
Other trail users: Mountain bikers and equestrians; guided jeep tours during the summer season
Special considerations: Turtle Rock Trail can be extended with Southwest Boundary Trail or Smiley Canyon Trail to explore the western section of Fort Robinson State Park. The state park offers guided jeep tours on this trail during the summer season. Hunting is allowed in the state park.
Amenities available: None
Maximum grade: 19%
Cell service: Moderate to good reception on the entirety of the trail

FINDING THE TRAILHEAD

From Fort Robinson State Park, head west on US 20. After one-half mile, turn right (north) onto Old Smiley Scenic Drive. Continue for 2.5 miles until reaching Turtle Rock Trailhead. **GPS:** N42° 40.000' W103° 30.923'

Trail Conditions: The trail is in excellent condition and easy to follow with trail signage at important junctions. There is no shade along the trail, so heat and sun exposure are serious concerns during the summer. Ticks are a nuisance during the summer. The state park offers guided jeep tours during the summer season, so be aware of vehicles while hiking. The trail receives light to moderate traffic.

THE HIKE

In September 1879, a group of Northern Cheyenne, led by Dull Knife, left abysmal conditions on an Oklahoma reservation and headed north to return to their homeland on the Northern Plains. After months of evading US soldiers across Oklahoma, Kansas,

Turtle Rock Trail climbs nearly 400 feet in 1 mile to reach Cheyenne Butte.

and Nebraska, 149 of the tribe members were captured and sent to Fort Robinson. Dull Knife hoped to relocate his people to their former homeland or to the Pine Ridge Reservation, where Red Cloud's band had settled, instead of returning to Oklahoma.

However, on January 3, 1879, they were ordered to return to Oklahoma. After Dull Knife refused, soldiers confined the Cheyenne to their barracks and withheld food and fuel. After six days enduring hunger and bitter cold, Dull Knife and his band broke out of their barracks and followed the banks of the White River before climbing the steep buttes known today as Cheyenne Buttes. They were pursued across the rugged Pine Ridge area for twelve days until they were captured northwest of Fort Robinson. All told, sixty-four Northern Cheyenne died in the escape. Dull Knife and his family survived and found refuge with Red Cloud on the Pine Ridge Reservation in South Dakota.

Turtle Rock Trail begins on the northern side of Cheyenne Buttes; the view from the top of the buttes offers a stark and sobering view of the climb that Dull Knife and the Northern Cheyenne undertook as they escaped the oppressive conditions they endured

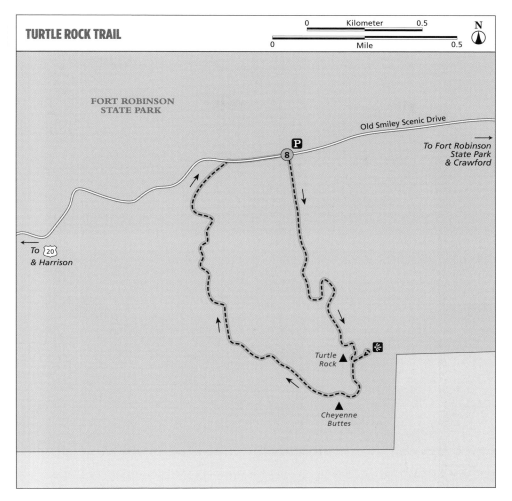

FORT ROBINSON
STATE PARK

Old Smiley Scenic Drive

To Fort Robinson
State Park
& Crawford

To 20
& Harrison

Turtle
Rock

Cheyenne
Buttes

at Fort Robinson. The trail follows a two-track loop that is used by guided jeep tours offered by the state park during the summer season. The track is sandy at times, making the nearly 400-foot climb over 1 mile strenuous. After reaching the top at 0.79 mile, turn left onto a short loop track that leads to incredible views of the White River Valley and Pine Ridge. The viewpoint at 0.86 mile is fenced to provide added security due to the precipitous drop atop the buttes.

Return to the previous junction and head west along the two-track. Paying attention for any oncoming jeeps, be sure to locate the band of white volcanic ash that was uniformly deposited millions of years ago by a volcano in the Great Basin area of Nevada and Utah. Also imagine the desperation of the Northern Cheyenne as they climbed up the steep buttes pursued by cavalry and gunfire.

As you continue along the second half of the loop, look east at Turtle Rock. It is not hard to see how the butte got its name: The shell, long neck, and head, complete with an eroded hole for an eye, bear a striking resemblance to a turtle. Continue on the trail at 1.48 miles, passing the junction with the Southwest Boundary Trail. If you wish to

Turtle Rock seen from the western half of the loop.

Dull Knife led his band of Northern Cheyenne up the steep cliffs after escaping from Fort Robinson.

extend your hike, you can take this trail and then connect with Smiley Canyon Trail before returning to Turtle Rock Trailhead. If not, continue on Turtle Rock Trail until reaching Old Smiley Scenic Drive at 2.15 miles. Turn right (east) and follow the road briefly until returning to the trailhead. After your hike, find the historical marker on US 20 that explains the history of the Cheyenne Outbreak and offers views of the southern face of Cheyenne Buttes.

MILES AND DIRECTIONS

0.00 Begin at the Turtle Rock Trailhead and head south.

0.79 Turn left (east) toward the viewpoint loop.

0.86 Viewpoint.

0.94 Turn left (south).

1.48 Keep right to continue on Turtle Rock Trail.

2.15 Turn right (east) onto Old Smiley Scenic Drive.

2.31 Arrive back at the trailhead.

9 MEXICAN CANYON

The trails in the Mexican Canyon area of Fort Robinson State Park take hikers along razor ridges with exceptional views of towering sandstone buttes and near-vertical cliffs. The hike into and out of the canyon is very steep, but your effort is rewarded with up-close views of the dramatic rock formations. A herd of Rocky Mountain bighorn sheep, introduced in 1981, are frequently seen grazing the rugged terrain around Mexican Canyon.

Start: Mexican Canyon Trailhead
Elevation gain: 3,962 to 4,269 feet
Distance: 2.41-mile loop
Difficulty: Difficult due to steep descent and ascent out of Mexican Canyon
Hiking time: 1–2 hours
Seasons/schedule: Trails open year-round, sunrise to sunset
Fees and permits: A park entry permit is required and may be purchased at the park, statewide Game and Parks offices and permit vendors, or online at outdoornebraska.gov.
Trail contact: Fort Robinson State Park, 3200 US 20, Crawford 69339; (308) 665-2900; outdoornebraska.gov/fortrobinson/
Dog-friendly: Yes, on leash
Trail surface: Grass and dirt

Land status: Fort Robinson State Park
Nearest town: Crawford 4 miles to the east
Maps: USGS Smiley Canyon, NE 2021 and USGS Crawford, NE 2021; park map available online; detailed trails map available at main park office
Other trail users: Bikers and equestrians
Special considerations: Hunting is allowed, so check hunting season dates and dress accordingly.
Amenities available: None at the trailhead or on the trail
Maximum grade: 29%
Cell service: Adequate coverage from most carriers on the trail with the exception at the bottom of Mexican Canyon

FINDING THE TRAILHEAD

From Fort Robinson State Park, take Soldier Creek Road northwest for 1.6 miles. Turn right (north) following the sign for Mexican Canyon. There are several interpretive panels inside a fence at the parking area. The trailhead is located next to the interpretive display. **GPS:** N42° 41.046' W103° 29.326'

Trail Conditions: Signage along the trail indicates trail names and directional guidance. The trail into and out of Mexican Canyon is steep in either direction and could be impassable in wet and muddy conditions. Ticks are abundant during the summer. The trail receives light to moderate traffic.

THE HIKE

Mexican Canyon is one of the most scenic canyons in not only Fort Robinson State Park, but the entire Pine Ridge area as well. The canyon, buttes, and cliffs are ideal habitat for numerous animals, including Rocky Mountain bighorn sheep. In 1981, the Wildlife Division of the Nebraska Game and Parks Commission relocated six sheep from Custer State Park in South Dakota to this rugged section of the state park. Bighorn sheep are native to the Nebraska Panhandle but were extirpated in the early twentieth century due to disease, habitat loss, and unregulated hunting. Additional herds were reintroduced in

The trail into Mexican Canyon is steep and rugged.

the Wildcat Hills south of Scottsbluff. The herds have faced challenges, especially disease, but hikers still have a chance of spotting these rare animals, including at Mexican Canyon.

The hike through Mexican Canyon can be completed in either a clockwise or counterclockwise direction. The benefit of the former is the steep climb up the east side of Mexican Canyon is easier than descending it if you were to hike the loop counterclockwise. The benefit of hiking the loop counterclockwise, however, is the views of the buttes as you head north. The views of Mexican Canyon and the Soldier Creek Valley are wonderful regardless of the direction you hike the trail—the route described here follows the loop clockwise.

From the interpretive display at the trailhead, head north following a two-track path as it climbs up a ridge. The views of Mexican Canyon and the buttes beyond will stay with you as you continue north up the canyon. The trail leaves the two-track after 0.37 mile to follow a footpath along the steep, grassy hillside. The footpath rejoins the two-track after a half mile, then reaches a junction at 0.7 mile. You can continue north for another 0.3 mile to reach a gated fence, which leads into the remote northern section of Fort Robinson State Park. If you have the time and energy, the Spring Creek Loop Trail in this northern section is an excellent way to spend the day hiking the rugged ridges and canyons where you may spot mule deer or even bighorn sheep. Otherwise, turn right (east) toward East Mexican Canyon Trail.

There is a viewpoint atop a rocky outcrop before the trail descends steeply down the narrow ridge, descending from 4,270 feet near the viewpoint to 4,050 feet at the bottom of Mexican Canyon. Many of the trees in the canyon survived the 1989 fire, providing the only shade on this hike. The trail climbs out of the canyon on a steep path with loose rock and dirt; in muddy conditions it might be extremely difficult to hike out of the canyon, so consider avoiding this hike after heavy precipitation.

Soaring buttes and vertical cliff faces are the backdrop as you hike north toward the base of the buttes. After 1.29 miles, turn right (east) onto East Mexican Canyon Trail. The Scenic View Trail to the left is an out-and-back trail leading to the park boundary on the northern side of the buttes in front of you. The herd of bighorn sheep enjoy the

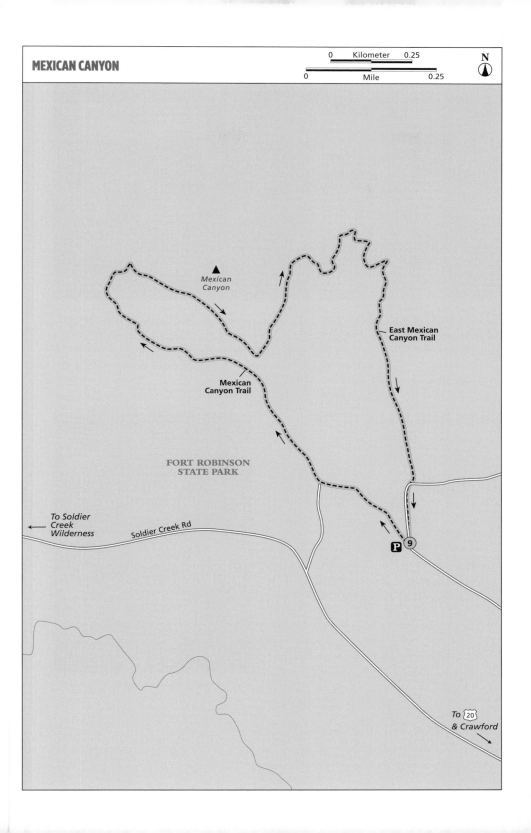

0   Kilometer   0.25

0   Mile   0.25

N

Mexican
Canyon

East Mexican
Canyon Trail

Mexican
Canyon Trail

FORT ROBINSON
STATE PARK

To Soldier
Creek
Wilderness

Soldier Creek Rd

P   9

To 20
& Crawford

The rugged landscape is ideal habitat for bighorn sheep.

rugged terrain of this section of Mexican Canyon and are frequently seen in the area. East Mexican Canyon Trail heads south after 1.6 miles, then begins to descend along a grassy ridge after 1.7 miles. Turn right (northwest) near two white posts at 2.24 miles to follow a footpath that crosses Mexican Canyon one final time before climbing up to the trailhead and parking area.

MILES AND DIRECTIONS

0.00 Begin at Mexican Canyon Trailhead; head north on the two-track path.

0.37 Keep left (west) to leave the two-track and climb the hill following the white trail marker posts.

0.70 Junction of Mexican Canyon Trail and East Mexican Canyon Trail; turn right (east) onto East Canyon Trail.

1.06 Canyon bottom.

1.07 Turn left (northeast) to climb up a steep hill following the white trail marker posts.

1.29 Turn right (east) to continue on East Mexican Canyon Trail.

Option: Left (west) on Scenic View Trail that terminates at the park boundary.

The forested bottom of Mexican Canyon.

1.74 Continue straight (south) on East Mexican Canyon Trail.

2.13 Turn right (west) onto West Mexican Canyon Trail.

2.24 Turn right (northwest).

2.41 Arrive back at the Mexican Canyon Trailhead.

10 LOVERS LEAP AND RED CLOUD BUTTES

Perhaps the best hike in Nebraska, Lovers Leap and Red Cloud Buttes offer challenges that few other hikes in the state can match. The superlatives begin on the approach from the trailhead to McKenzie Pass and continue for the duration of the hike. A short scramble leads to the top of Lovers Leap, named after a local Native American legend. After descending the peak, the trail traverses rugged terrain through ponderosa forest that will make your lungs burn and heart pump. The viewpoint on the rim of Red Cloud Buttes provides exceptional views of Giants Coffins Butte, the White River Valley, and the Pine Ridge escarpment.

Start: McKenzie Pass Trailhead
Elevation gain: 3,793 to 4,364 feet
Distance: 6.27-mile lollipop
Difficulty: Very difficult due to rugged terrain, a short scramble up Lovers Leap, and navigational issues
Hiking time: 3 or more hours
Seasons/schedule: Trails are open year-round, sunrise to sunset; good any time of year, although snow and ice in winter may complicate the hike
Fees and permits: A park entry permit is required and may be purchased at the park, statewide Game and Parks offices and permit vendors, or online at outdoornebraska.gov.
Trail contact: Fort Robinson State Park, 3200 US 20, Crawford 69339; (308) 665-2900; outdoornebraska .gov/fortrobinson/
Dog-friendly: Yes, on leash

Trail surface: Dirt and grass
Land status: Fort Robinson State Park
Nearest town: Crawford 4 miles to the east
Maps: USGS Crawford, NE 2021; park map available online; detailed trails map available at main park office
Other trail users: Equestrians and mountain bikers
Special considerations: Hunting is allowed, so check hunting season dates and dress accordingly.
Amenities available: None at the trailhead or on the trail
Maximum grade: 30%
Cell service: Moderate to good reception is available at the trailhead, in clearings, and along ridges. Weak to no reception under tree cover and in canyons.

FINDING THE TRAILHEAD

From Crawford, head west on US 20 for 2.2 miles. After passing a golf course and a scenic view pull-off, turn right onto a gravel road marked by a Nebraska Game and Parks Commission sign. The trailhead is at the north end of the loop road. **GPS:** N42° 40.697' W103° 26.754'

Trail Conditions: The trail is marked with white posts, and there are trail signs placed at strategic junctions. The myriad of trails can be confusing, so get a detailed trails map from the park office and also follow a GPS track of the hike. Hazards include ticks, tree snags, exposure on cliffs and buttes, and loose rock and soil on several steep sections of the trail. The trail receives light to moderate foot traffic.

THE HIKE

The legend of Lovers Leap, a prominent butte northwest of the town of Crawford, is recounted in the book *Nebraska Folklore* by Louise Pound. According to the legend, a young Sioux chief, Eagle Feather, fell in love with the daughter of a Cheyenne chief. Instead of attacking the camp, Eagle Feather captured the young woman, and with her consent, they fled from the camp. Her father, however, spotted the two lovers escaping and pursued them with his warriors. The couple reached the nearby buttes but were trapped. Realizing escape was futile, the two leaped from the cliff and fell to their death, giving name to Lovers Leap.

There are several trailheads that provide access to this legendary butte. Wagon Wheel Trail begins in Crawford City Park and leads directly to Lovers Leap. Another trailhead located opposite the Mare Barn Complex in Fort Robinson State Park provides access to the western end of Red Cloud Buttes. However, the best trailhead is one located east of the state park along US 20. There is a small parking area and a gate (sometimes locked). The views of Red Cloud Buttes from this trailhead are spectacular, making it a great introduction to this hike. The trailhead connects to Wagon Wheel Trail as it heads across the prairie and climbs up to McKenzie Pass, with Red Cloud Buttes to the west and Saddle Rock to the east. After descending from McKenzie Pass, continue east on Wagon Wheel Trail at a trail sign at 0.69 mile until reaching the trail to Lovers Leap at 0.97 mile. Take in the views of Grant's Thumb and Lovers Leap, as the next mile is an arduous climb to the base of the legendary butte.

Lovers Leap Trail reaches the base of an unnamed rock formation at 1.34 miles. The left fork is the preferred path, however, the right fork is a shortcut that passes by Grant's Thumb and climbs to the ridge leading to Lovers Leap. If you take the easier left fork, you'll have to ascend a short path at 1.41 miles to reach Grant's Thumb and the trail to Lovers Leap. At 1.5 miles you will reach the short scramble path to the top of Lovers Leap. The scramble is not technical, but caution must be taken atop the butte to avoid the same fate as the two lovers.

Once you have descended Lovers Leap, continue north on a steep, descending trail with loose rock and dirt until reaching the boundary of the state park at 1.65 miles. The trail heads due west at the boundary for the next mile through ponderosa pine savanna. Keep an eye out for the white trail posts, as there are several trails through this area, and it is easy to follow another post or footpath. At 2.89 miles, find a white post in a shrubby area to begin the hardest section of the hike.

The next half mile climbs up and down one ridge before climbing to the top of another ridge. The gate at 3.39 miles is the end of the most strenuous climbing, although there remains more ascent but it is more gradual than the previous half mile. Head southeast at 3.75 miles along a forested trail. Wildlife, such as mule deer or even bighorn sheep, might grace your presence as you approach the turn-off for a viewpoint at 4.2 miles. Time your hike to reach this viewpoint at sunset, as the views of Red Cloud Buttes, Giants Coffins Butte, the White River Valley, and the Pine Ridge escarpment to the south are a perfect climax to this spectacular hike.

The remaining portion of the hike descends to the junction below McKenzie Pass, at times traversing loose rock on steep sections of trail. After reaching McKenzie Pass, be sure to look back and relish the epic hike to Lovers Leap and Red Cloud Buttes that you have just done.

Above left: Lovers Leap takes its name from a local Native American legend.
Above right: McKenzie Pass Trailhead is the best of several trailheads giving access to Red Cloud Buttes.
Below: Giants Coffins Butte (right) and Red Cloud Buttes (left).

LOVERS LEAP AND RED CLOUD BUTTES

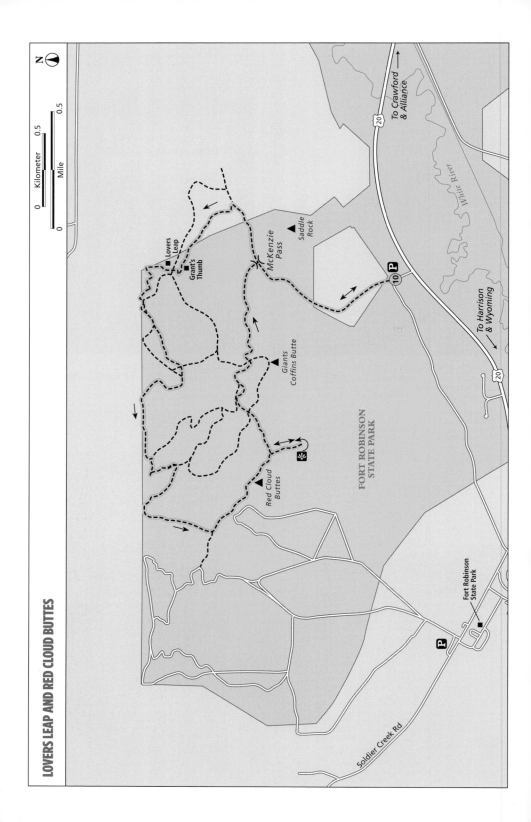

Lovers Leap

Grant's Thumb

Saddle Rock

McKenzie Pass

Giants Coffins Butte

Red Cloud Buttes

FORT ROBINSON STATE PARK

White River

To Crawford & Alliance

To Harrison & Wyoming

Fort Robinson State Park

Soldier Creek Rd

N

0   Kilometer   0.5

0   Mile   0.5

MILES AND DIRECTIONS

0.00 Begin at McKenzie Pass Trailhead and head north.

0.62 McKenzie Pass.

0.69 Continue straight (east) on Wagon Wheel Trail.

0.97 Turn left (west) onto Lovers Leap Trail.

1.34 Reach a fork at the base of a rock formation; keep left.

   Option: The right fork is a steep shortcut that connects with the trail above Grant's Thumb (the hoodoo just past this rock formation).

1.41 Turn right (east) onto East Red Cloud Loop, then keep right to follow Lovers Leap Trail.

1.43 Turn left (north).

1.50 Scramble to the top of Lovers Leap.

1.53 Lovers Leap.

1.61 Keep right (north) onto East Red Cloud Butte Loop.

1.65 Sharp left turn as trail heads west.

2.15 Turn left (south).

2.21 Reach a fork; keep right (west).

2.25 Continue straight (west).

2.84 Sharp right turn to continue west on East Red Cloud Butte Loop.

2.89 Turn left (south) into a shrubby area.

3.08 Turn right (west) to continue on East Red Cloud Butte Loop.

3.20 Continue straight (west).

3.27 Continue straight (west).

3.39 Gate; turn left (south) after closing the gate.

3.75 Turn left (southeast) onto East Red Cloud Butte Loop.

3.88 Continue straight (east).

3.94 Continue straight (east) on East Red Cloud Butte Loop.

3.99 Gate.

4.20 Turn right (south) to reach a viewpoint.

4.35 Viewpoint; turn around.

4.70 Keep right (east) on East Red Cloud Butte Loop.

4.77 Continue straight on East Red Cloud Butte Loop.

4.97 Keep right (southeast) onto Mule Trail / East Red Cloud Butte Loop.

5.58 Turn right (south) toward McKenzie Pass.

6.27 Arrive back at McKenzie Pass Trailhead.

Mule deer on East Red Cloud Buttes Loop

11 ROBERTS LOOP

Roberts Loop provides access to the Pine Ridge National Recreation Area, created in 1986 to provide backcountry recreation opportunities in ponderosa pine environments. Substantial parts of the area were burned by fires in 2006 and 2012, leaving snags and dead timber littering the canyons and uplands. The trail, however, is in good condition and presents the opportunity to experience firsthand an ecosystem regenerating after fire. The east leg of Roberts Loop climbs out of a canyon to upland grassland, while the west leg descends into a wider canyon along a trail that resembles the closest thing to a mountain pass in Nebraska.

Start: Roberts Trailhead Campground
Elevation gain: 3,998 to 4,457 feet
Distance: 3.33-mile lollipop
Difficulty: Difficult due to rugged terrain
Hiking time: 2 hours
Seasons/schedule: Trails open year-round; best in spring and fall to avoid summer heat
Fees and permits: None
Trail contact: Nebraska National Forest Pine Ridge Ranger District, 125 N Main St., Chadron 69337; (308) 432-0300
Dog-friendly: Yes, on leash
Trail surface: Mowed grass and single-track dirt footpaths
Land status: Nebraska National Forest Pine Ridge Ranger District
Nearest town: Chadron 19 miles to the northeast
Maps: USGS Chimney Butte, NE 2021; Forest Service map available at fs.usda.gov/main/nebraska/maps-pubs

Other trail users: Equestrians and mountain bikers
Special considerations: Trail markers are wood posts painted brown and white. The loop section of this lollipop trail can be completed either clockwise or counterclockwise. There is no water and no shade on the entire trail; pack plenty of water and sun protection. There are numerous snags and fire-damaged trees that can be hazardous, especially in windy conditions. Be aware of flash floods after heavy rain. Long pants are recommended due to tall grass and sharp yucca leaves.
Amenities available: Pit toilet, trash bins, water (in season), tent campsites with fire rings and picnic tables at the trailhead.
Maximum grade: 19%
Cell service: At trailhead, full coverage; on trail, reception is inconsistent.

FINDING THE TRAILHEAD

From Chadron, head west on US 20 W / Crazy Horse Memorial Highway / Bridges to Buttes Byway. After 9.8 miles, turn south onto Eleson Road. After 3.2 miles, turn right (west) to stay on Eleson Road, which curves to head south again for 2.5 miles. Immediately after Eleson Road curves to the east, turn right (south) to continue on Eleson Road for 2 miles. Turn left (east) at Bethel Church to follow Bethel Road for 1.8 miles to reach Roberts Trailhead Campground. **GPS:** N42° 40.708' W103° 9.059

Trail Conditions: The trail is well marked and maintained by the Forest Service. However, in some areas the footpath is faint, but always look ahead to find the next trail marker post.

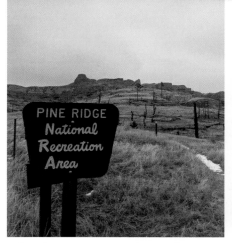

Left: Roberts Loop passes through the Pine Ridge National Recreation Area.
Right: Pine Ridge Trail can be accessed via Roberts Loop.

THE HIKE

Roberts Campground and Trailhead is the original home of Willis Roberts, who with his wife Ita raised nine children here during the Great Depression in the 1930s. The family sold their property to the United States Forest Service in 1974. Remnants of other homesteads are scattered across the Pine Ridge Ranger District of the Nebraska National Forest. Drought and the Great Depression caused many homesteaders to sell their land to the federal government. These parcels became part of the national forest in northwestern Nebraska.

The trail begins behind the riders' ramp next to the campground's vault toilet. Pass through the gate and head south toward a hill following the brown and white trail posts put up by the Forest Service; these will be your trail markers for this hike. Once the posts reach the top of the hill, the trail heads southeast along a ridge. To the east is a great view of a chain of ponderosa-studded buttes. Pine Ridge National Recreation Area is marked by a fence (0.4) and a box with a trail usage survey. The terrain becomes more rugged as the trail enters the recreation area. The footpath in places is faint so always look ahead for the next trail post to stay on the trail.

The trail reaches a fork (0.7) shortly after entering the recreation area. The east leg climbs out of a narrow canyon, while the west leg traverses upland prairie before descending into a wide canyon. Neither leg is significantly steeper than the other, thus Roberts Loop can be completed clockwise or counterclockwise. We will keep left (southeast) onto the east leg to complete the loop clockwise. There are a lot of snags and fire damage in the narrow canyon, so be cautious during high winds. The fires were so recent that there is little to no new ponderosa regrowth at the moment.

Several sections of the east leg have steep sides plunging into the canyon or side ravines but exposure is limited. The trail is more rugged the deeper it reaches into the canyon, including a very steep drop at one point (1.29). Switchbacks (1.46) lead us out of the canyon into upland prairie, where the east and west legs connect (1.55).

Heading west, the views of Pine Ridge are unobstructed due to fire damage and the complete absence of mature ponderosa or even saplings. Continue northwest toward Roberts Campground at the junction with Pine Ridge Trail (1.69). At a trail post (1.99), look northeast to see the canyon you just hiked out of on the east leg. The trail continues

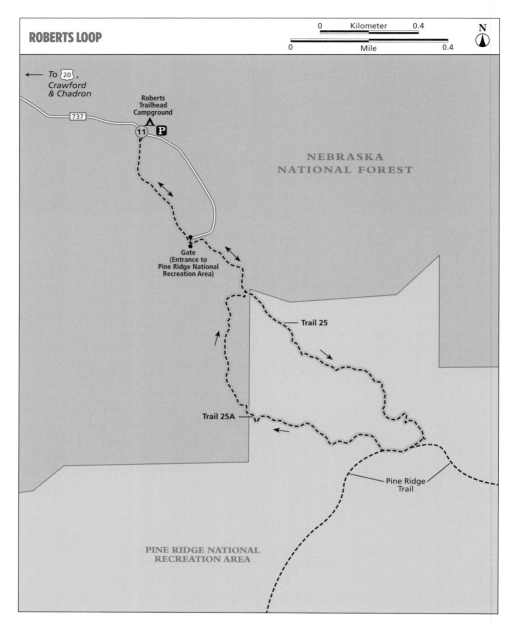

0   Kilometer   0.4

0   Mile   0.4

N

← *To* 20 ,
*Crawford
& Chadron*

737

Roberts
Trailhead
Campground

11   P

**NEBRASKA
NATIONAL FOREST**

Gate
(Entrance to
Pine Ridge National
Recreation Area)

Trail 25

Trail 25A

Pine Ridge
Trail

**PINE RIDGE NATIONAL
RECREATION AREA**

to climb toward another trail post in the notch in the ridge ahead (2.1). This last section of the west leg of Roberts Loop resembles a mountain pass. As you descend, take time to look back at the "pass" and the ridge that, with enough imagination, resembles a glacial cirque. The west leg terminates at the junction with the east leg (2.67); keep left to return to the campground. Before you return to Roberts Trailhead (3.33), turn around to get one final view of the canyon and ridge country of the Pine Ridge National Recreation Area.

Pine Ridge National Recreation Area.

MILES AND DIRECTIONS

0.00 Begin at Roberts Trailhead Campground; go through the gate behind the riders' ramp and follow the brown and white posts heading south up a hillside.

0.20 Reach a barbed wire fence and continue east following the trail marker posts.

0.40 Reach the entrance to Pine Ridge National Recreation Area; continue east following the trail posts.

Fire damage has scarred the rugged Pine Ridge terrain.

0.70 Reach a fork; keep left (southeast) to follow the east leg of Roberts Loop.

0.89 Pass a trail marker post and continue southeast.

1.55 At a trail sign, keep right (west) at the fork to follow the west leg of Roberts Loop.

1.67 Reach a trail marker post and head west toward a trail sign.

1.69 Reach the trail sign and keep right (northwest) toward Roberts Campground.

1.99 Continue west at a trail marker post.

2.10 Reach the crest of a ridge and descend along the trail heading west.

2.67 Reach the junction of the west and east legs of Roberts Loop; keep left (northwest) to return to Roberts Trailhead Campground.

2.94 Reach the boundary of Pine Ridge National Recreation Area; continue northwest.

3.14 Continue northwest at a trail marker post near a barbed wire fence.

3.33 Arrive back at Roberts Trailhead Campground.

12 BLACK HILLS OVERLOOK TRAIL

Black Hills Overlook Trail is a fun and easy out-and-back hike with some of the best views of any trail in Nebraska, including views of the distant Black Hills in South Dakota. The trailhead, located in the Pine Ridge District of the Nebraska National Forest, is accessed via Chadron State Park. Its proximity to the state park allows more experienced hikers the opportunity to explore footpaths along razor ridges that plunge into deep canyons. Hikers can use those footpaths to connect this trail with Steamboat Butte Trail in the state park for an amazing hiking experience.

Start: Black Hills Overlook Trailhead at the end of FR 714-A
Elevation gain: 4,078 to 4,223 feet
Distance: 2.01 miles out and back
Difficulty: Easy
Hiking time: 1 hour
Seasons/schedule: Trails open year-round, sunrise to sunset; best in spring and fall to avoid the heat
Fees and permits: None required if you do not stop in Chadron State Park
Trail contact: Nebraska National Forest Pine Ridge District, 125 N Main St., Chadron 69337; (308) 432-0300; Chadron State Park, 15951 US 385, Chadron 69337; (308) 432-6167
Dog-friendly: Yes, on leash no longer than 6 feet
Trail surface: Dirt and crushed rock
Land status: Nebraska National Forest Pine Ridge Ranger District
Nearest town: Chadron 10 miles to the north
Maps: USGS Coffee Mill Butte, NE 2021; for sections in the Nebraska National Forest, available upon request from Pine Ridge district office; for sections in Chadron State Park, available at outdoornebraska.gov/chadron
Other trail users: Mountain bikers
Special considerations: The trailhead is in the national forest but must be accessed via Chadron State Park. There is another trailhead in the state park but it has limited parking and is unmarked and difficult to find among tent campsites. There is no shade on the majority of the trail, so plan accordingly. The forest service road, FR 714-A, leading to the trailhead is in good condition but it would be prudent to check road conditions with the ranger office beforehand.
Amenities available: Parking only at the trailhead; none on the trail
Maximum grade: 15%
Cell service: At the trailhead, average reception that cannot be relied upon; on the trail coverage is possible on ridges and in clearings

FINDING THE TRAILHEAD

From Chadron, head south on US 385 for approximately 8.4 miles. Turn west at the entrance sign to enter Chadron State Park. Before reaching the park office building, turn left then immediately keep left to head toward the Trading Post. Continue straight on the park road, passing the Trading Post, duplex cabins, and both Spotted Tail Shelter and Soapweed Shelter. After Soapweed Shelter, keep left at the next fork and continue along this road, entering the national forest, for roughly 1.5 miles to arrive at the Black Hills Overlook parking area.

Trail Conditions: The trails in the national forest are generally better maintained and marked than trails in the state park. Utmost care should be taken in wet conditions. Black Hills Overlook Trail receives moderate to heavy traffic.

Black Hills Overlook Trail traverses Nebraska National Forest and Chadron State Park.

THE HIKE

There are a lot of trails in the Pine Ridge region with sweeping, expansive views of the buttes and canyon country. Few, if any, allow hikers to take in those views without breaking a sweat. Black Hills Overlook Trail packs views of the Nebraska National Forest, Chadron State Park, and the Black Hills of South Dakota on the horizon into a short and easy 2-mile out-and-back hike. Multiple connecting trails allow hikers to explore the state park and national forest. Be aware, however, that trails listed on park maps may not be maintained.

The Black Hills Overlook Trailhead can only be accessed by driving through Chadron State Park (a park entry permit is not required if you do not park in the state park). The turn for FR 714-A is near Sawmill Shelter, the trailhead for Steamboat Butte Trail. For the intrepid hiker, Black Hills Overlook Trail and Steamboat Butte Trail can be combined via unofficial footpaths to make a longer, much more difficult hike. Please note, however, that part of the state park is open to hunting, so access may be limited on these side trails, particularly from October 1 to December 31. Additionally, these trails cross rugged terrain and are not maintained, making navigation complicated.

Sticking to official trails, head north from the trailhead on Black Hills Overlook Trail to shortly reach Lookout Point, a flat rocky viewpoint. On clear days, the Black Hills of South Dakota can be seen across the plain to the north. Also note the dead timber littering the north-facing slopes, evidence of the 1973 Dead Horse Fire, which also burned areas around FR 714-A. The most recent fire occurred in 2012, and the area around the lookout suffered the most noticeable damage. The Forest Service replanted some of the burned areas in 2018 to regenerate the pine savanna.

Continue west after leaving the lookout, enjoying the views as you hike along the top of a ridge. The trail enters Chadron State Park after one-half mile, then shortly reenters the national forest after 0.7 mile. The trail heads north before it wraps around the north side of a hill. The trail descends to a junction: left leads to Trailrider Trailhead, while

BLACK HILLS OVERLOOK TRAIL

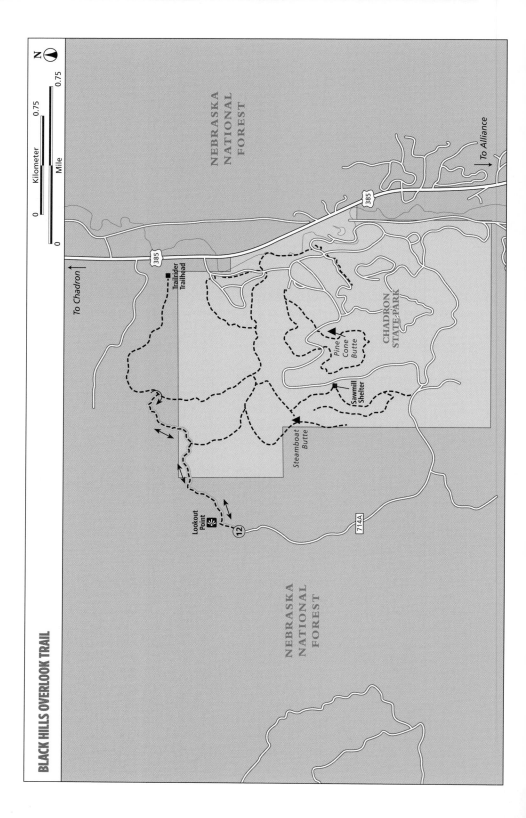

Hikers can venture off the trail via footpaths that descend into rugged canyons.

right descends into Dead Horse Canyon via a special hunting area. If you do not plan to go either direction, turn around and return to the trailhead via the same trail.

MILES AND DIRECTIONS

0.00 Begin at Black Hills Overlook Trailhead.

0.11 Lookout Point.

0.49 Pass through a fence to enter Chadron State Park; continue northeast.

0.60 Continue straight.

Option: Turn right (south) to follow a footpath along the ridge that leads to Chadron State Park with access to Steamboat Butte Trail.

0.70 Pass through another fence to reenter Nebraska National Forest; continue north.

1.00 Reach the end of the trail. Turn around and head toward Black Hills Overlook Trailhead.

Option: Turn left to reach Trailrider Trailhead near US 385.

Option: Turn south to reenter Chadron State Park, with access to Steamboat Butte Trail.

1.90 Lookout Point.

2.01 Arrive back at Black Hills Overlook Trailhead.

Right top: View from the ridge on Black Hills Overlook Trail in winter.
Right bottom: View of Chadron State Park from the ridgetop trail.

13 STEAMBOAT BUTTE TRAIL

The loop trail to Steamboat Butte is a perfect hike for families to explore the ridge and canyon country in Chadron State Park in the Pine Ridge region. The trail is short and relatively easy, with the exception of a few narrow but short sections atop the ridge with steep slopes on both sides. The loop climbs up the ridge via beautiful ponderosa pine savannah and then opens up along the ridge with views of Steamboat Butte, Pine Cone Butte, and the surrounding Pine Ridge.

Start: Steamboat Loop Trailhead near Sawmill Shelter
Elevation gain: 3,980 to 4,184 feet
Distance: 1.41-mile loop
Difficulty: Moderate, due to steep climb up and back down ridge
Hiking time: 1 hour
Seasons/schedule: Trail open year-round, sunrise to sunset; good any time of year
Fees and permits: A park entry permit is required and may be purchased at the park, statewide Game and Parks offices and permit vendors, or online at outdoornebraska.gov.
Trail contact: Chadron State Park, 15951 US 385, Chadron 69337; (308) 432-6167; outdoornebraska.gov/chadron; chadron@nebraska.gov
Dog-friendly: Yes, on leash
Trail surface: Grass and dirt footpaths

Land status: Chadron State Park
Nearest town: Chadron 10 miles to the north
Maps: USGS Coffee Mill Butte, NE 2021; available at outdoornebraska.gov/maps
Other trail users: Mountain bikers; there are also equestrian-only trails in the park
Special considerations: The section of trail along the ridge is exposed to sun and wind. If windy, trees and snags present hazards. Avoid climbing on fragile sandstone buttes.
Amenities available: At trailhead, vault toilets, picnic shelter, parking; in the state park, water pumps, park office, and camping
Maximum grade: 12%
Cell service: At trailhead, reliable and strong coverage; on trail, reliable coverage on ridges and clearings

FINDING THE TRAILHEAD

From Chadron, head south on US 385 for approximately 8.4 miles. Turn west at the entrance sign to enter Chadron State Park. Before reaching the park office building, turn left then immediately right following the sign indicating the sports field and campground. Continue on this park road, passing a tennis court, the turn-off for the campground, and Pine Cone Shelter. The parking area for Sawmill Shelter and Steamboat Loop Trailhead is 0.8 mile after Pine Cone Shelter. **GPS:** N42° 42.558' W103° 1.424

Trail Conditions: The trail descending the ridge (if hiking the loop clockwise) is faint and hard to follow, as the footpath almost disappears in the grass. Look below to find the path heading south that returns to the trailhead. This section is also steep and can be slippery. The section of the trail along the ridge is well defined but exposed to the elements. Take caution around the buttes as the sandstone is delicate; climbing the buttes can contribute to their accelerated erosion.

THE HIKE

Chadron State Park became Nebraska's first state park in 1921. The Civilian Conservation Corps was active in the park in the 1930s. The park offers 6 miles of hiking trails, and when combined with the adjacent Pine Ridge District of the Nebraska National Forest, hikers can explore over 100 miles of trails "among distinctive buttes and canyons of Nebraska's Pine Ridge." The West Ash Fire in August 2012 burned over 58,000 acres in the Pine Ridge. Chadron State Park was threatened, but thanks to backfires set by crews, many structures were saved while 90 percent of the park burned. However, most of the forest survived intact as it was mostly grass fire through the understory.

Steamboat Loop Trail takes hikers from Sawmill Shelter, through beautiful parklike ponderosa savanna, and up to the top of a ridge with excellent views of the park and the surrounding national forest. The trail was an Eagle Scout project dedicated to tenderfoot scout Mark

Parklike ponderosa savanna on Steamboat Butte Trail.

Steamboat Butte (center) from the ridge on Steamboat Butte Trail.

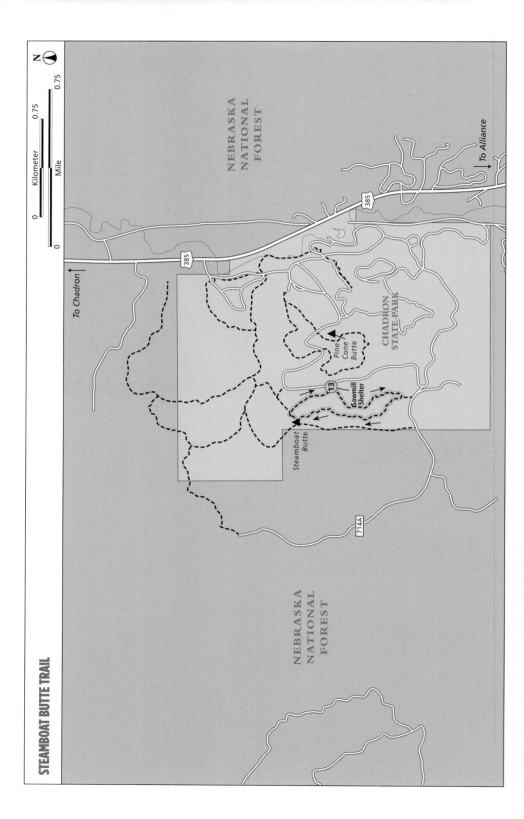

STEAMBOAT BUTTE TRAIL

N

Kilometer
0   0.75

Mile
0   0.75

To Chadron

To Alliance

385

385

714A

NEBRASKA
NATIONAL
FOREST

NEBRASKA
NATIONAL
FOREST

CHADRON
STATE PARK

Pine
Cone
Butte

Steamboat
Butte

Sawmill
Shelter

13

The hike along the ridge passes several sandstone outcrops.

Wigington. The trail sees heavy foot traffic, so it is unlikely that you will encounter some of the Pine Ridge's most notable residents: bighorn sheep, elk, mule deer, and mountain lions. The views and the pristine ponderosa groves are worth the climb up the ridge. This hike is a great introductory trail for children as the climb is not too strenuous and the trail is easy to follow. The only caution is, if hiking the trail clockwise, the descent from the ridge follows a faint footpath down the steep hillside. Otherwise, the trail presents few problems.

Begin at the parking area for Sawmill Shelter and head toward the trailhead sign at the beginning of the loop. Keep left (south) to follow the loop clockwise. The mowed path climbs south through ponderosa pine with a grassy understory until reaching an open field at the top of the ridge. Ahead there is a road that leads to the national forest and the trailhead for the Black Hills Overlook Trail. Follow the mowed path as it bends sharply right to head north along the ridge.

The trail at the beginning is along a wide ridge, but as it continues north the ridge narrows considerably to become a razor ridge. Pass by several sandstone outcrops, some within easy reach to scramble up for better views of the state park and Pine Ridge. The fork at 1.1 miles offers you a chance to hike to the base of Steamboat Butte. Keep right to follow the path as it descends from the ridge to head south back to the trailhead.

MILES AND DIRECTIONS

0.00   Begin at Steamboat Loop Trailhead; take the left fork (south).

0.06   Continue straight (southwest) passing a spur trail on the right.

0.50   Reach a fork in a clearing; turn sharply right to head north along the ridge.

1.10   Reach a fork; keep right (northeast) to descend the ridge.

   Side trip: Keep left at the fork to climb Steamboat Butte.

1.20   Keep right at a trail marker to head south toward the trailhead.

1.30   Reach a fork and keep left (south) toward Sawmill Shelter.

1.41   Arrive back at Steamboat Loop Trailhead.

14 SPOTTED TAIL LOOP

Named after a Brulé Lakota tribal chief whose murder led to a landmark Supreme Court case, Spotted Tail Loop crosses open meadows, steep canyons, and ponderosa pine savanna, much of it burned in the catastrophic 2006 Spotted Tail Fire that reached the edge of Chadron. The trail leads to an overlook with sweeping views of Pine Ridge and the Black Hills of South Dakota to the north. Dispersed camping is allowed along FR 711 near the trailhead, a peaceful location with a great view of the terrain that Spotted Tail Loop traverses.

Start: Spotted Tail Trailhead
Elevation gain: 3,686 to 4,339 feet
Distance: 6.06-mile loop
Difficulty: Difficult due to rugged terrain
Hiking time: 3 hours
Seasons/schedule: Trails open year-round; best in spring and fall to avoid summer heat
Fees and permits: None
Trail contact: Nebraska National Forest Pine Ridge Ranger District, 125 N Main St., Chadron 69337; (308) 432-0300; fs.usda.gov/main/nebraska/home
Dog-friendly: Yes, on leash
Trail surface: Grass and dirt footpaths
Land status: Nebraska National Forest Pine Ridge Ranger District
Nearest town: Chadron 7 miles to the north
Maps: USGS Chadron East, NE 2021; Forest Service maps available at fs.usda.gov/main/nebraska/maps-pubs and at the ranger district office in Chadron
Other trail users: Equestrians and mountain bikers
Special considerations: Trail is marked with wooden posts painted white at the top. Check hunting season dates and dress appropriately if you hike during hunting season. The trail passes through tall grasses, so it is recommended to wear long pants and do a tick check after completing the trail. Google Maps indicates there is a campground near the trailhead. However, there is no campground or facilities near the trailhead; dispersed camping is permitted.
Amenities available: No amenities at the trailhead or on the trail
Maximum grade: 38%
Cell service: Full and reliable coverage at the trailhead and on ridges and in clearings while on the trail

FINDING THE TRAILHEAD

From Chadron, head south on US 385 S / Ash Street / Gold Rush Byway for 5 miles. Turn left (east) onto King Canyon Road. Head east for 0.5 mile, then continue straight onto Spotted Tail Road / FR 733. After approximately 0.9 mile, turn left to stay onto FR 711. After 100 feet, turn right onto a pull-off to arrive at the Spotted Tail Trailhead. **GPS:** N41° 45.375' W102° 59.340

Trail Conditions: The trail is mostly well marked by brown and white posts placed by the Forest Service. There are some areas where you need to look ahead to find the next trail marker to ensure that you are on the correct track. Portions of the trail are slightly exposed on steep canyon sides but there is never any danger. Please make sure you close any gates that you pass through. Trail receives light use.

Ponderosa pine savanna.

THE HIKE

The Spotted Tail Fire of 2006 burned over 68,000 acres in Dawes and Sioux Counties. Prolonged drought had created extremely dry conditions in the Nebraska National Forest near Chadron. On July 26, 2006, a lightning strike ignited the grasslands 7 miles south of town. Like most ponderosa pine forests in the west, the Pine Ridge was untouched by fire for nearly 100 years, growing dense with young seedlings and older trees alike. Drought conditions and high winds pushed the all-engulfing fire to the campus of Chadron State College. The beloved pine forest on C-Hill was destroyed, but the fire line on the hill saved the campus and town—a commemorative stone marks the line, dedicated to the local residents and fire crew and volunteers from seven states that battled the blaze. Three homes were destroyed, but no lives were lost. The fire sparked a change in forest management, as forest thinning, grazing, logging, and prescribed burns became preferred techniques to prevent the accumulation of heavy fuel loads that dense forests produce. Ponderosa saplings planted in 2008 promise a hopeful and healthier future for this fire-scarred land.

The trailhead off FR 711 has expansive views west of the bare hills with clusters of pines that survived the fire. Spotted Tail Trail climbs to the top of those hills, crossing a saddle between two buttes before climbing to the top of one and following its ridge to FR 733 and then Pine Ridge Trail to return to the trailhead. The route described here follows the loop counterclockwise; clockwise has less elevation gain but ends on a dour note with a long slog through fire ravaged country.

From the trailhead, head southeast at the trail distance sign. The trail climbs gently yet steadily through new ponderosa growth. Notice the stand of tall pines that escaped the fire, as well as the shorter ponderosa that has taken hold after the 2006 fire. After nearly 1 mile, the trail crosses FR 733 at 0.88 mile; you can take the forest road as a shortcut, but you will miss the views south of Strong Canyon and Chadron State Park. Continue south climbing through a meadow, passing through a gate, and then heading southeast along the side of a hill with views of the aforementioned canyon and state park.

After the trail bends to head north, reach a gate and cross FR 733 again at 1.43 miles. Here the trail follows the spine of a ridge heading north. The first half mile is relatively flat, allowing you to enjoy the sweeping views of Pine Ridge, and on a clear day, the

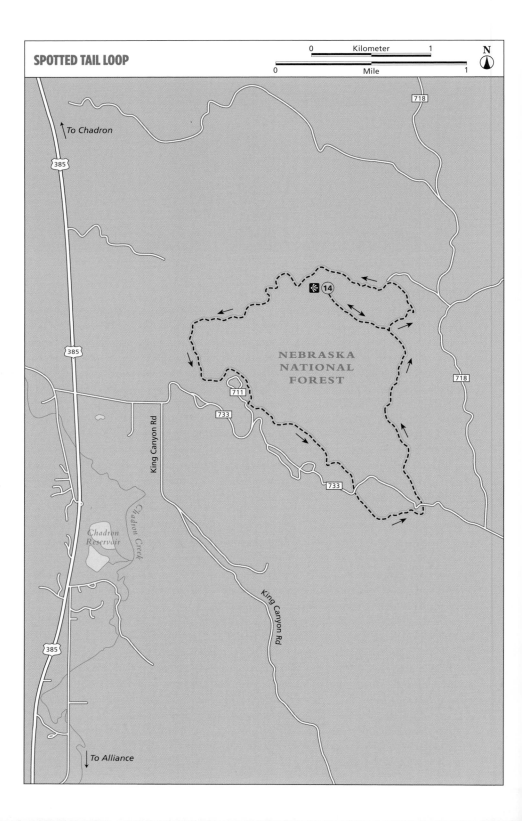

SPOTTED TAIL LOOP

0   Kilometer   1

0   Mile   1

N

718

↑ To Chadron

385

385

14

NEBRASKA
NATIONAL
FOREST

718

King Canyon Rd

711

733

733

Chadron Creek

Chadron
Reservoir

King Canyon Rd

385

↓ To Alliance

Black Hills of South Dakota on the northern horizon. The trail climbs steeply at 1.97 up an incline with a maximum grade of 38 percent; the climb is strenuous but short.

At 2.56 miles, take the 0.4-mile spur trail that leads to an overlook with more impressive views of the surrounding national forest. At the edge of the cliff, marked by three dead trees, look down to see the pass between two hills that the trail takes on the second half of the loop. Return to the overlook trail junction and head northeast. After a steep descent through a rugged section of trail, reach an area with views to the east of pristine ponderosa pine savanna. After taking in the views, continue northwest as the trail meanders through summer grazing pastures for cattle. The trail posts here can be difficult to find among the pines, so always look ahead for the next post.

The trail crosses through a fence to enter Pasture 30A at 4.17 miles, then climbs to reach the pass between the two hills. Look above to your left to recognize the three dead trees hanging on the cliff atop the overlook. Most of the remaining hike is downhill, with two more notable climbs. The creek bottom at 5.3 miles is overgrown with tall grasses in summer, so once you reach the trailhead at 6.06, make sure you check for ticks and other hitchhikers.

MILES AND DIRECTIONS

0.00 Begin at Spotted Tail Trailhead; at the trail distance sign, keep right (southeast).

0.44 Pass through a gate and continue southeast.

0.88 Cross FR 733 and continue southeast uphill through a meadow toward a gate at the crest of the hill.

Option: Turn left (east) to follow FR 733 for 0.5 mile until it crosses Spotted Tail Trail.

1.03 Reach a gate; cross through it and continue southeast.

1.11 Reach a fork; keep left (east) to continue on Spotted Tail Trail.

1.39 Trail bends to head north.

1.43 Pass through a gate, cross FR 733, and continue north following the trail marker posts.

2.19 Pass through a gate and continue northeast.

2.56 Reach a trail distance sign at a fork; keep left (northwest) to follow the Overlook Trail.

Spotted Tail Trailhead.

3.00 Reach the overlook; turn around and return to the Overlook Trail junction.

3.48 Reach the Overlook Trail junction; turn left (northeast) onto Spotted Tail Trail.

3.70 Trail reaches the bottom of steep descent; the trail turns sharply north.

4.17 Reach a fence; continue northwest into Pasture 30A.

4.34 Reach the top of the pass between two hills.

5.00 Cross through a gate and continue south.

5.71 Keep left (east) at a trail marker post.

6.06 Arrive back at the Spotted Tail Trailhead.

15 THE CLIFFS

The Cliffs is named for the cliff face that rises above the national forest trailhead and popular recreation area along Big Bordeaux Creek. There are numerous trails in this area of canyon country on the southern edge of Pine Ridge. This hike makes use of national forest roads and trails to climb out of the Big Bordeaux Creek watershed into upland prairie to Table Road, the southern boundary of the national forest. The second half of the loop descends back into the meandering bed of Big Bordeaux Creek and follows it as it passes more impressive cliff faces.

Start: The Cliffs Trailhead
Elevation gain: 3,793 to 4,328 feet
Distance: 8.09-mile loop
Difficulty: Difficult due to length
Hiking time: 3–5 hours
Seasons/schedule: Trails open year-round; best in spring and summer for wildflowers in open meadows and fall for colors along Big Bordeaux Creek
Fees and permits: None
Trail contact: Nebraska National Forest Pine Ridge Ranger District, 125 N Main St., Chadron 69337; (308) 432-0300; fs.usda.gov/main/nebraska/home
Dog-friendly: Yes, on leash
Trail surface: Dirt and grass
Land status: Nebraska National Forest Pine Ridge Ranger District
Nearest town: Chadron 13 miles to the north

Maps: Kings Canyon, NE 2021; Forest Service maps available at fs.usda .gov/main/nebraska/maps-pubs
Other trail users: Equestrians and mountain bikers; also motorized users on sections
Special considerations: Hunting is allowed on national forest land, so check hunting season dates and wear appropriate clothing. Road conditions are poor after precipitation, so check with the ranger district before making travel plans. Water obtained from Big Bordeaux Creek should be filtered or purified.
Amenities available: There is a vault toilet, 1 picnic table, and 2 fire rings at the trailhead. Dispersed camping is allowed.
Maximum grade: 11.5%
Cell service: Coverage possible in open meadow sections and at the trailhead

FINDING THE TRAILHEAD

From the intersection of US 385 and US 20 in Chadron, travel 5 miles east on US 20 to Bordeaux Road. Head south 7 miles on Bordeaux Road to FR 723. Drive west 1.4 miles to Cliffs Trailhead. **GPS:** N42° 43.037' W103° 55.842

Trail Conditions: The trail is waymarked with white diamonds and occasional white-tipped wood posts. There are also signs for specific trail and road numbers. The trail is well marked and maintained by the Forest Service. Trails can get slick and muddy after precipitation. There are numerous spur trails and loop combinations, so pick a route and take a physical copy of a map in addition to a digital version.

THE HIKE

There are numerous trails and forest roads that branch out from The Cliffs Trailhead, a popular camping spot set along Big Bordeaux Creek with numerous vertical cliff faces rising from the creek bed. A map from the Forest Service of the national forest or the

The Cliffs takes its name from the cliffs at the recreation area and along the Big Bordeaux Creek.

USGS topographical map would be handy to explore all the trails in the area, as both list the forest roads and trails. The loop described here heads south out of the creek bottom into upland prairie, before turning back north to follow Big Bordeaux Creek back to the trailhead, passing underneath the impressive sandstone and clay cliffs. There are plenty of options to extend or shorten this loop if you so desire.

Heading west on FR 723 from The Cliffs Trailhead, turn south onto Trail 209 and follow it along the creek momentarily before it climbs south up a ridge with the creek on your right (west). Trail 209 climbs 300 feet over the next 1 mile until it reaches upland prairie (1.55). The open grasslands here, surrounded by ponderosa-studded canyons, would be a great place for wildflowers during the spring and summer. Trail 209 turns into FR 728, a double-track road open to motorized vehicles. Continue south on FR 728 for approximately 1 mile.

At the junction of FRs 728 and 776 (2.65), keep right (southwest) on FR 728 as it begins to descend into ponderosa forest. Veer right onto Trail 208 (2.98), which traverses the bottom of a forested ravine heading south. Many of the pines here are marked with orange paint, likely part of a forest-thinning management plan for this dense section of forest. The climb out of this ravine to FR 727 is the steepest climb of this hike.

Once you reach FR 727, turn north to follow the forest road for 1 mile through upland prairie. Another option is to turn south onto FR 727 to hike to Table Road, where you can take Trail 209 north following a tributary of Big Bordeaux Creek until reaching a junction with FR 727 and Trail 24. We continue north on FR 727, passing a windmill (4.38) and then reaching the junction with Trail 24 (5.14) that takes us down into the Big Bordeaux watershed.

The trail along the creek bottom is a prime wildlife habitat: In winter, the trail is full of animal tracks, including those of bobcat, raccoon, and deer. At the confluence of several streams (6.1), head north on Trail 24 as it follows Big Bordeaux Creek for the next 2 miles. The trail crosses the creek several times and passes numerous vertical cliff faces on both the west and east banks of the creek. With the eponymous cliffs in sight, Trail 24 joins Trail 209 (7.83) and shortly after FR 723 (7.98), leading us back to the recreation area and trailhead.

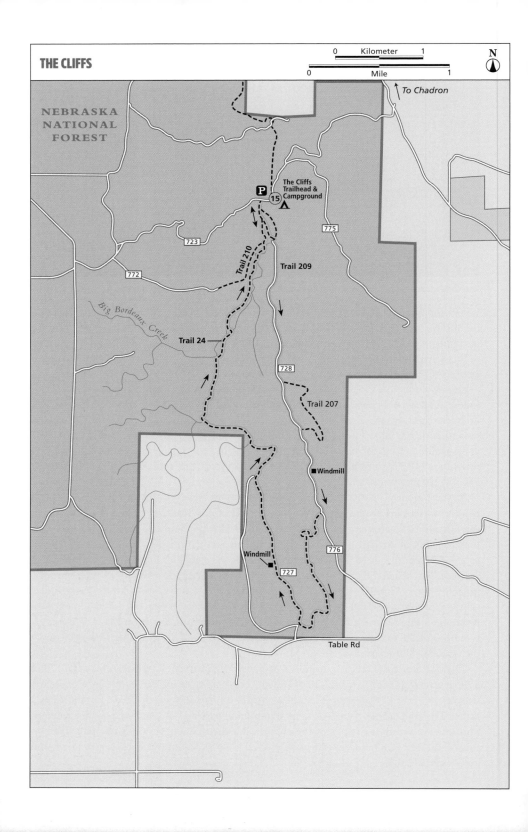

THE CLIFFS

0   Kilometer   1
0   Mile   1

N

To Chadron

NEBRASKA
NATIONAL
FOREST

P

15

The Cliffs
Trailhead &
Campground

775

723

772

Trail 210

Trail 209

Big Bordeaux Creek

Trail 24

728

Trail 207

Windmill

Windmill

776

727

Table Rd

MILES AND DIRECTIONS

0.00 Begin next to the vault toilets at The Cliffs Trailhead; head west on FR 723.

0.08 After crossing a cattle grid, turn left (south) onto Trail 209.

0.12 Reach a fork; keep left to pass through a gate and continue on Trail 209.

0.27 Reach another fork; keep left (southeast) on Trail 209.

0.41 Creek crossing.

0.46 Cross an elevated cattle grid; keep right to head southwest.

1.11 Continue south along the ridge after crossing an elevated cattle grid.

1.30 Trail 209 becomes FR 728; continue south on FR 728.

1.55 Continue south on FR 728.

Option: Veer left onto Trail 207 to follow it for roughly 0.5 mile until it rejoins FR 728.

A windmill in an open meadow in the Nebraska National Forest.

1.85 Continue south on FR 728.

Bailout: Turn right (west) onto Trail 24B, which will take you to Trail 24 that you can take north following Big Bordeaux Creek back to the trailhead.

2.04 Trail 207 comes in on your left; continue south on FR 728.

2.65 Reach a fork; keep right (southwest) on FR 728.

2.98 Reach a sign for Trail 208; veer right (south) onto Trail 208.

3.94 Reach a junction; turn right (north) onto FR 727.

Option: Turn left (south) onto FR 727 until you reach Table Road and the junction with Trail 209. Take Trail 209 north until it connects with FR 727 (see mile 5.14).

4.38 At a windmill, keep left (north) at the fork on FR 727.

5.14 Reach a junction; continue straight (northeast) on Trail 24.

6.00 Reach a junction; continue straight (north) on Trail 24 as it follows the creek.

6.09 Cross a cattle grid.

6.39 Cattle grid.

6.57 Reach a junction; keep right to stay on Trail 24.

6.62 Cattle grid.

6.92 Creek crossing and cattle grid.

7.05 Cross the creek twice.

7.50 Creek crossing.

7.83 At the junction of Trails 24 and 209, continue straight (north) on 209.

7.98 Pass through a gate, then turn right (east) onto FR 723.

8.09 Arrive back at The Cliffs Trailhead and recreation area.

B **PINE RIDGE TRAIL**

The best backcountry experience in Nebraska, the Pine Ridge Trail spans 40 miles of the Nebraska National Forest south of Chadron. Test your backpacking skills traversing a region rich in natural and cultural history while enjoying sweeping views of ponderosa pine forest and eroded buttes that challenge the stereotypical flat Nebraska landscape. Devastating fires in 2006 and 2012 scarred large tracts of this long-distance trail, yet some stands of ponderosa survived intact.

Start: Spotted Tail Trailhead (east trailhead); West Ash Trailhead (west trailhead)

Elevation gain: Variable depending on starting and ending point

Distance: 40-mile point-to-point

Difficulty: Difficult due to length, rugged terrain, sun exposure, and unreliable water sources during summer

Hiking time: Multiple days

Seasons/schedule: Open year-round; best outside of summer to avoid heat and ticks

Fees and permits: None

Trail contact: Nebraska National Forest Pine Ridge Ranger District, 125 N Main St., Chadron 69337; (308) 432-0300; fs.usda.gov/nebraska

Dog-friendly: Yes, on leash

Trail surface: Grass and dirt footpath

Land status: Nebraska National Forest Pine Ridge Ranger District

Nearest town: Chadron and Crawford to the north

Maps: USGS Belmont, Chadron East, Chimney Butte, Coffee Mill Butte SW, Coffee Mill Butte, Kings Canyon; 2′x 3′ map available for purchase at ranger district office, by phone, or online; digital map also available to purchase using the Avenza application

Other trail users: Mountain bikers, equestrians

Special considerations: If starting at the Spotted Tail Trailhead, you will go about 10 miles before reaching Chadron State Park with water. From there, your next sources of water, which the trail directly crosses, are Deadhorse Creek, Cunningham Creek, East Ash Creek, and West Ash Creek. Transportation, or parking 2 cars at opposite trailheads, should be arranged before undertaking the hike.

Amenities available: None; some amenities, such as water and toilets, can be found on or near the trail at Chadron State Park and Roberts Tract Campground and Trailhead

Maximum grade: Variable

Cell service: Coverage may be present in areas along the trail but cannot be relied upon for the entirety of the hike.

FINDING THE TRAILHEAD

From Chadron to Spotted Tail Trailhead, head south on US 385 S / Ash Street / Gold Rush Byway for 5 miles. Turn right (east) onto King Canyon Road. Head east for 0.5 mile, then continue straight onto Spotted Tail Road / FR 733. After approximately 0.9 mile, turn left to stay onto FR 711. After 100 feet, turn right onto a pull-off to arrive at the Spotted Tail Trailhead.

From Crawford to West Ash Trailhead, at the intersection of US 20 and NE 71, head north on US 20 for 0.4 mile. Turn right (east) onto West Ash Creek Road. Continue east for 11 miles until reaching West Ash Trailhead.

Ponderosa pine savanna and sandstone buttes characterize the Pine Ridge region.

GPS (Spotted Tail Trailhead): N42° 45.376' W102° 59.340'
GPS (West Ash Trailhead): N42° 37.610' W103° 14.773'
Trail Conditions: The trail is waymarked with brown posts and signs at important points; some trail markers might be dislodged due to cattle, wind, or other reasons. Snags in fire-damaged areas are hazardous in windy conditions. Sun exposure, unreliable water sources, and ticks are of genuine concern during the summer months. The trail receives light to medium usage.

C COFFEE MILL BUTTE

Rising above Deadhorse Road, Coffee Mill Butte's name is a nod to its resemblance to an old hand-operated coffee grinder. This hike explores the canyons and ridges west of the butte. There are several options to either shorten or lengthen this hike. The terrain is rugged, with steep climbs into and out of canyons and along narrow razor ridges; navigation can be difficult at times. The second half of the loop follows Pine Ridge Trail as it traverses the central part of Pine Ridge. There is extensive fire damage, but the ponderosa pines in the deep, isolated canyons were largely spared.

Start: Coffee Mill Trailhead on FR 702
Elevation gain: 3,880 to 4,350 feet
Distance: 4.87-mile loop
Difficulty: Difficult due to rugged terrain
Hiking time: 3 hours
Seasons/schedule: Trails open year-round; best in spring and fall due to cooler weather
Fees and permits: None
Trail contact: Nebraska National Forest Pine Ridge Ranger District, 125 N Main St., Chadron 69337; (308) 432-0300; fs.usda.gov/recarea/nebraska/recarea/?recid=10615
Dog-friendly: Yes, on leash
Trail surface: Grass and dirt footpaths and double-track forest road
Land status: Nebraska National Forest Pine Ridge Ranger District

Nearest town: Chadron 15 miles to the north
Maps: USGS Coffee Mill Butte, NE 2021; Forest Service maps available at fs.usda.gov/main/nebraska/maps-pubs and the ranger district office in Chadron
Other trail users: Equestrians and mountain bikers
Special considerations: The trail is marked with brown posts with white tips. Hunting is allowed in season on national forest lands; check hunting season dates and wear appropriate clothing during hunting season.
Amenities available: No amenities at the trailhead or on the trail
Maximum grade: 17%
Cell service: There is full coverage at the trailhead. On the trail, coverage is available on ridges and in clearings.

FINDING THE TRAILHEAD

From Chadron, head west on US 20 W / Bridges to Buttes Byway. After 4.5 miles, turn south onto Deadhorse Road. Follow this road for 10 miles. Keep right, leaving Deadhorse Road, to follow a double-track dirt road that runs south parallel to Deadhorse Road. This is FR 702. After it bends to the west you will arrive at the Coffee Mill Butte Trailhead. **GPS:** N42° 40.748' W103° 4.850

Trail Conditions: The trail is well marked with posts in most places. Always look ahead for the next trail marker post. If you cannot see a post, don't divert from the trail until you find the next trail marker. The area suffered severe damage from wildfires in 2006 and 2012; burnt trees and snags can be hazardous in windy conditions. There is no shade or water on the entire route, so pack accordingly. Flash floods are a significant hazard immediately after heavy precipitation. The trail receives light traffic.

Coffee Mill Butte rises above Deadhorse Road.

D STRONG CANYON

Easy access from US 385 makes Strong Canyon an excellent hike to do any time of the year. The climb up a grassy hillside during spring will reward the effort with wildflowers and expansive views of Pine Ridge and Chadron State Park to the west. The grasses on the rolling landscape turn copper and gold in autumn, while in winter numerous animal tracks can be spotted in the snow as you hike along the forested bottom of Strong Canyon.

Start: Strong Canyon Trailhead
Elevation gain: 3,746 to 4,131 feet
Distance: 5.48-mile loop
Difficulty: Moderate due to steep climb up a ridge
Hiking time: 2–3 hours
Seasons/schedule: Trails open year-round; due to easy access, loop can be done at any time of the year to enjoy in different seasons
Fees and permits: None
Trail contact: Nebraska National Forest Pine Ridge Ranger District, 125 N Main St., Chadron 69337; (308) 432-0300; fs.usda.gov/main/nebraska/home
Dog-friendly: Yes, on leash
Trail surface: Dirt and grass
Land status: Nebraska National Forest Pine Ridge Ranger District
Nearest town: Chadron 10 miles to the north

Maps: USGS Coffee Mill Butte, NE 2021; USGS Kings Canyon, NE 2021; Forest Service maps available at fs.usda.gov/main/nebraska/maps-pubs; NW Nebraska Trails Association maps available at http://www.nwnebraskatrails.com/trails-guide.html
Other trail users: Equestrians and mountain bikers; also motorized vehicles on national forest roads
Special considerations: Hunting is allowed on national forest land, so check hunting season dates and wear appropriate clothing.
Amenities available: Parking at trailhead; dispersed camping off FR 719
Maximum grade: 17%
Cell service: Full coverage at trailhead and on ridges and in clearings; no reception in the canyon

FINDING THE TRAILHEAD

From Chadron take US 385 south at the intersection with US 20 for approximately 8 miles. Turn east opposite the entrance to Chadron State Park, then immediately take the left fork for FR 719. Continue about 0.2 mile on FR 719 to a small parking area at the Strong Canyon Trailhead. **GPS:** N42° 42.869' W103° 0.441

Trail Conditions: The trail is waymarked with posts with either specific trail or road numbers, white-tipped posts, or white diamonds nailed to trees or posts. Where the trail is faint or nonexistent, look for the next trail post or white diamond to continue following the trail. Be cautious of tree hazards in fire-damaged and forested sections of the trail. The trail receives light traffic.

Strong Canyon provides excellent views of the surrounding Pine Ridge region.

A typical scene in the Sandhills.

SANDHILLS

The largest dune complex in the western hemisphere, the Sandhills are vast and wild—an estimated 85 percent of the nearly 20,000-square-mile region is intact habitat, much of it never plowed. It is the largest remaining grassland ecosystem in the United States, and its biodiversity has largely been preserved due to a lack of land fragmentation. The region sits atop the Ogallala Aquifer, and many streams and rivers like the Loup system originate in the Sandhills. Migratory birds make use of the numerous lakes, marshes, fens, and ephemeral ponds that dot the rolling mixed-grass prairie. Distances are vast, and services are limited, but rewards await intrepid visitors seeking solitude and serenity.

Prickly pear flowering underneath ponderosa pine.

16 SANDHILLS NATURE TRAIL

Crescent Lake National Wildlife Refuge is 30 miles from the nearest services on sandy roads that can become impassable under inclement weather conditions, yet the diversity of wildlife and tranquility of the lakes, marshes, and sandhill prairie make it more than worth the journey. The constant trill of red-winged and yellow-headed blackbirds provides the soundtrack for the Sandhills Nature Trail, an easy 2-mile loop and bird-watchers' delight that passes Gimlet Lake and Mallard Arm, two of the roughly thirty lakes within the refuge. In April, the refuge is home to thousands of migratory waterfowl, marsh birds, and shorebirds. Fall is another great time to visit as the big bluestem and switchgrass grow taller than 6 feet in wet meadows.

Start: Trailhead south of refuge headquarters
Elevation gain: 3,836 to 3,856 feet
Distance: 2.10-mile loop
Difficulty: Easy due to level terrain and short distance
Hiking time: 1 hour
Seasons/schedule: Open year-round, sunrise to sunset; best in April for migratory birds
Fees and permits: None
Trail contact: Crescent Lake National Wildlife Refuge, 10630 Rd. 181, Ellsworth 69340; (308) 762-4893; fws.gov/refuge/crescent-lake
Dog-friendly: Dogs are not allowed on Sandhills Nature Trail
Trail surface: Mowed grass

Land status: Crescent Lake National Wildlife Refuge
Nearest town: Oshkosh 30 miles to the south
Maps: USGS Mumper, NE 2021; refuge map available online and at kiosks throughout the refuge
Other trail users: None
Special considerations: The nearest services are 30 miles away, so plan accordingly. The sandy roads can be problematic. Spring is the best time to visit but the weather is also unpredictable and roads can become impassable.
Amenities available: None
Maximum grade: 2%
Cell service: Weak to nonexistent for most carriers

FINDING THE TRAILHEAD

From Oshkosh, head north on W 2nd Street / Road 179. After approximately 13 miles, keep left (north) onto Road 181. Continue on Road 181 for 15 miles until reaching the refuge headquarters. Turn left (west) to reach the parking area and trailhead. **GPS:** N41° 45.657' W102° 26.234'

Trail Conditions: The trail is not waymarked but easy to follow. High water levels can affect sections of the trail. The trail receives light traffic.

THE HIKE

Since 1936, 279 species of birds have been observed at Crescent Lake National Wildlife Refuge, the second largest local bird list in Nebraska. The refuge was created to protect habitat and breeding grounds for birds and wild animals. A visit to Crescent Lake will provide plentiful evidence that the refuge's mission has been a success and may include the following encounters: pronghorn grazing in the grasslands adjacent to the road at the refuge's entrance; a red-tailed hawk perched on a fence post; or, a squadron of American

Gimlet Lake at Crescent Lake National Wildlife Refuge.

white pelicans serenely gliding onto Island Lake, perhaps part of the pelican colony of nearly one hundred nests discovered in June 2021 at the lake.

The wildlife spectacle does not stop once you arrive at the refuge headquarters and trailhead. A cacophony of the musical "o-ka-leeee" from red-winged blackbirds and the harsh "oka-wee-wee" of yellow-headed blackbirds will be ever present on the hike, especially at the Gimlet Overlook, a small platform overlooking Gimlet Lake in a marshy area surrounded by cattails and other marsh vegetation. The overlook is visible from the trailhead, as it is only 0.2 mile from the beginning of the hike. This is a great place to study the refuge's bird list, which can be obtained at the information kiosk at the refuge entrance south of Island Lake. The list includes neotropical migrants that spend the summer in the Sandhills and the rest of the year in tropical habitats in Central and South America.

After the overlook, the trail heads east through a marsh north of Gimlet Lake. Standing water can be encountered along this section depending on the water level and recent precipitation. A short loop leads to a bench at 0.45 mile, then the trail runs directly alongside the northeastern shore of the lake with standing water again a possibility. With the refuge road on your left, turn right (south) at an intersection at 0.71 mile to head south onto Mallard Arm Loop.

The trail continues south with Gimlet Lake to the west for 0.2 mile, at which point it leaves the lake behind and heads into sandhill prairie before reaching Mallard Arm at 1.17 miles. The bench here is a good place to rest and bird-watch. Continue north along Mallard Arm to complete the loop at 1.57 miles and turn left to head northwest at 1.63 miles to return to the trailhead via Sandhills Nature Trail.

Even though your hike is complete, continue to keep an eye out for wildlife. Marsh wrens, blue-winged teal, and perhaps trumpeter swans can be seen in the wetland complexes that make up Crescent Lake National Wildlife Refuge. In the grassland sections of the park, burrowing owls, upland sandpipers, and long-billed curlews offer more opportunities to add species to your wildlife list.

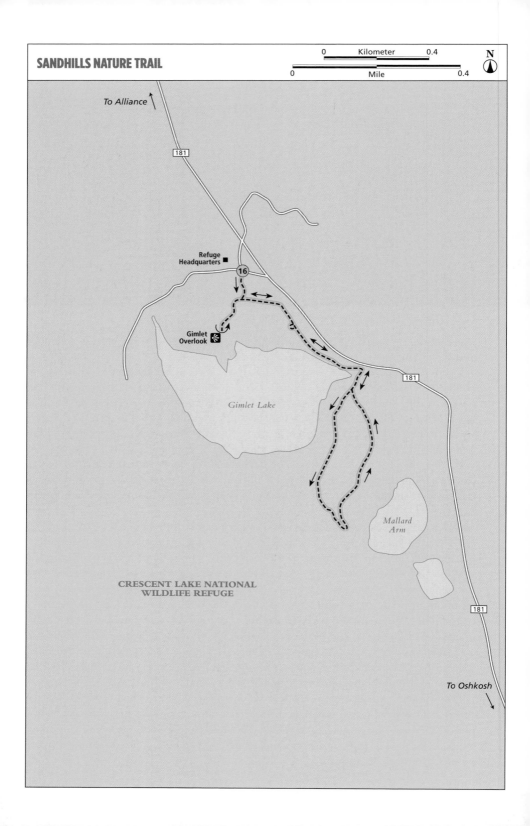

0   Kilometer   0.4

0   Mile   0.4

N

To Alliance

181

Refuge
Headquarters ■

16

Gimlet
Overlook

Gimlet Lake

181

*Mallard
Arm*

CRESCENT LAKE NATIONAL
WILDLIFE REFUGE

181

To Oshkosh

Top left: Yellow-headed blackbird (*Xanthocephalus xanthocephalus*).
Top right: White-faced ibis (*Plegadis chihi*) in a tree on Gimlet Lake.
Bottom: Gimlet Lake overlook.

MILES AND DIRECTIONS

0.00   Begin at the trailhead south of the refuge headquarters and head south.

0.10   Keep right (southwest) toward Gimlet Overlook.

0.20   Gimlet Overlook; turn around and return to the previous junction.

0.30   At the fork, keep right (east) onto Sandhills Nature Trail.

0.45   Reach a short loop leading to a bench overlooking Gimlet Lake.

0.71   At the junction, turn right (south) onto Mallard Arm Loop.

1.17   Near a bench, Mallard Arm Loop bends on itself to head north.

1.57   Turn right (north).

1.63   Turn left (northwest) to return to trailhead via Sandhills Nature Trail.

2.10   Arrive back at the trailhead.

17 BLUE JAY TRAIL

Blue Jay Trail meanders under the shade of a ponderosa pine forest planted in the early 1900s, one of two forest preserves created in Nebraska's Sandhills by a 1902 proclamation by President Theodore Roosevelt. Of the 116,000 acres that comprise Samuel R. McKelvie National Forest, only 2,500 are forested, hand-planted in 1903. Blue Jay Trail begins and ends at Steer Creek Campground, a campsite that feels more like the American West than Midwest. The trail is short and easy, so best to take your time and inhale the sweet aroma of ponderosa pine bark in the warm summer sun.

Start: Trailhead next to campsite 16 at Steer Creek Campground
Elevation gain: 3,101 to 3,061 feet
Distance: 1.18-mile loop
Difficulty: Easy due to level terrain and short distance
Hiking time: Less than 1 hour
Seasons/schedule: Open year-round; there are viewing blinds available in the national forest to view the sharp-tailed grouse mating displays each April
Fees and permits: None (unless camping)
Trail contact: Nebraska National Forest Bessey Ranger District; 40637 River Loop, Halsey 69142; (308) 533-2257; fs.usda.gov/nebraska
Dog-friendly: Yes, on leash
Trail surface: Dirt and grass footpaths

Land status: Samuel R. McKelvie National Forest
Nearest town: Valentine 44 miles to the northeast
Maps: USGS Spring Lake, NE 2021; forest visitor map available online or by mail via the United State Forest Service online store
Other trail users: None
Special considerations: Hunting is permitted during rifle deer season (mid-November), so dress and plan accordingly.
Amenities available: Water, vault toilets, picnic tables, fire rings, and campsites and horse corrals available at Steer Creek Campground
Maximum grade: 3%
Cell service: Weak to no coverage at the campground and on the trail

FINDING THE TRAILHEAD

From Valentine, head south on NE 97 for approximately 26 miles. Turn right (west) onto Merritt Dam Road and cross the dam. Continue west for 15 miles, then turn left (southwest) onto NE 16F Spur. Continue for 2 miles until reaching Steer Creek Campground. Alternatively, from Valentine head west on US 20. After 30 miles, turn left (south) onto NE 16F Spur. Continue south for 18 miles until reaching Steer Creek Campground. **GPS:** N42° 41.371' W101° 41.371'

Trail Conditions: The northern half of the loop is clearly waymarked and easy to follow. The southern half of the loop has fewer trail markers and is confusing in several segments; always be looking for the next trail marker. If the trail is overgrown with grass, look for the next trail markers. Snags and standing trees can become hazards in high winds. Ticks are common during the spring, summer, and early fall. The trail receives light foot traffic.

THE HIKE

Originally called the Niobrara Reserve when it was created by a proclamation in 1902 by Theodore Roosevelt, Samuel R. McKelvie National Forest totals 116,000 acres of

A bench on Blue Jay Trail offers a place to contemplate the beauty of a man-made forest.

grasslands and hand-planted ponderosa pine forest. The vast majority of the preserve is grasslands, as only 2,500 acres are forested. Luckily for hikers, the only maintained hiking trail is under the shade of pine trees and not on the sun-baked prairie. Hunting, fishing, horseback riding, and bird-watching are other popular outdoor recreation activities at McKelvie National Forest. Visitors can camp among the ponderosa pine at Steer Creek Campground. The campground offers twenty-three campsites with tables and fire rings, as well as vault toilets and one hand pump for water.

There are two trailheads to access Blue Jay Trail within the campground. At the time of publication, the trailhead between campsites 19 and 20 was blocked by a large tree pile from dead and dying trees that needed to be cut down as they were hazardous to campers. The other trailhead, next to campsite 16, was still accessible. Beginning here, head west past the trailhead sign toward a fence. After passing through the gate, head west along a barbed wire fence. The resin produced by ponderosa pine creates an acidic soil environment, inhibiting understory growth. Thus, there is not much of a discernible footpath through the pine cones and needles. Instead, follow the helpful trail markers placed by the United States Forest Service. There are two different trail markers along the way: wooden posts with a small brown sign with a hiker icon on it; and orange flexible posts with a trail sticker attached. The first half of Blue Jay Trail, from the campsite 16 trailhead to NE 16F Spur, is well waymarked and easy to follow. However, the second, southern half of the loop has less trail markers that makes navigation more difficult.

Near a trail marker at 0.26 mile, take a seat on a nearby bench to do some bird-watching or aromatherapy as the sun warms the pine needles. After leaving the bench, Blue Jay Trail enters a clearing in the forest. The footpath is faint through the grass so pay heed to the next trail marker. Also, there can be standing water here in the meadow, so watch your step. The trail continues west for a quarter mile through more forest and clearings until it bends south to approach the highway.

Pass through a gate, ensuring that you close it behind you, and cross the highway at 0.48 mile. There is another fence on the other side of the road but instead of a gate that

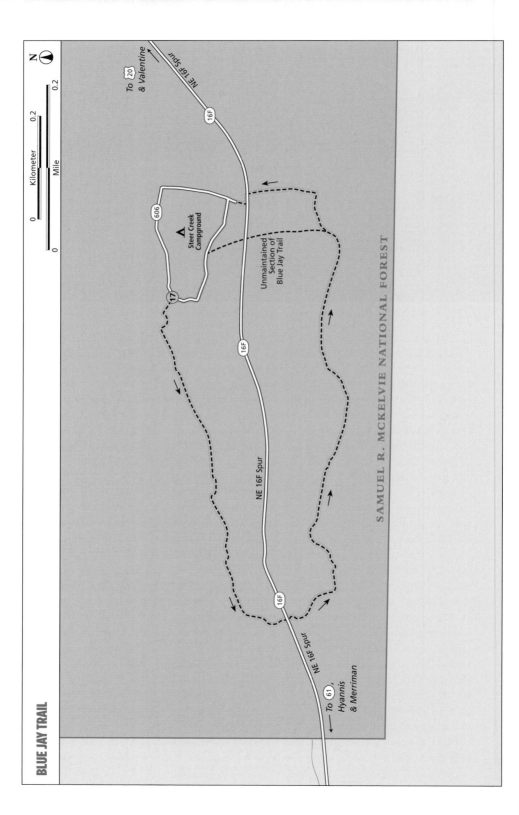

BLUE JAY TRAIL

N

Kilometer
0   0.2   0.2
Mile

To 20
& Valentine

NE 16F Spur

16F

606

Steer Creek
Campground

17

Unmaintained
Section of
Blue Jay Trail

16F

NE 16F Spur

NE 16F Spur

16F

To 61,
Hyannis
& Merriman

SAMUEL R. MCKELVIE NATIONAL FOREST

Steer Creek Campground has twenty-three campsites surrounded by aromatic ponderosa pine.

needs to be closed, this fence has a kissing gate that allows humans but not livestock to pass through. The southern half of the loop begins here and navigation becomes more difficult. After the gate, keep left (southeast) at the fork at 0.52 mile to enter the forest once again. From here until you return to the campground, find the next trail marker at each marker you pass; some markers might have been knocked over by wildlife or wind.

Blue Jay Trail continues east through forest until reaching a clearing at 0.83 mile. Continue east through more forest until reaching a bench at the 1-mile point of the hike. Shortly after the bench, the original trail heads north. However, at the time of publication, several trail markers on this section had been knocked over, making navigation difficult. Additionally, the kissing gate before the highway was overgrown with grass and weeds. As a detour, continue east at 1.1 miles to head toward an unnamed forest road. Once you have reached the road, turn left (north) at 1.12 miles. Reach NE 16F Spur at 1.18 miles, crossing it to return to Steer Creek Campground.

MILES AND DIRECTIONS

- **0.00** Begin at the trailhead next to campsite 16; head west.
- **0.03** After passing through the gate, head west along a barbed wire fence, then cross a small footbridge over a creek.
- **0.05** After crossing the creek, turn left (west) at the trail sign on a narrow footpath; ahead you will see a trail sign with a hiker on it.
- **0.26** Bench.
- **0.43** Trail bends south to approach the highway; reach a gate and cross through it heading south.
- **0.48** Continue straight (south) crossing NE 16F Spur; pass through another gate after crossing the highway.
- **0.52** Reach a fork and keep left (southeast) to head into the forest.
- **1.00** Bench and trail sign.
- **1.10** Keep right (east) to head toward the forest road.
- **1.12** Turn left (north) onto an unnamed forest road.
- **1.18** Reach NE 16F Spur; cross it heading north to arrive back at Steer Creek Campground.

18 CCC FIRE TOWER TRAIL

One of two dedicated hiking trails at Valentine National Wildlife Refuge, the CCC Fire Tower Trail climbs nearly 200 feet in less than 1 mile to reach a decommissioned fire tower built by the Civilian Conservation Corps during the Great Depression. The viewing deck on the fire tower offers views of the rolling Sandhills prairie and Hackberry Lake and Dewey Lake, where one of the few remaining Sandhills fens is protected as part of the Charles L. Wiseman Natural Area. The Marsh Lakes Overlook Trail, an easy 0.13-mile out-and-back hike, is the only other dedicated hiking trail at the refuge.

Start: CCC Fire Tower Trail Trailhead
Elevation gain: 2,940 to 3,125 feet
Distance: 1.31 miles out and back
Difficulty: Easy but with a climb of 183 feet over 0.6 mile to the CCC Fire Tower
Hiking time: 1 hour
Seasons/schedule: Open year-round, dawn to dusk; best in April for sharp-tailed grouse in viewing blinds on refuge land; May and September–October for migratory birds; August for sunflowers
Fees and permits: None
Trail contact: Valentine National Wildlife Refuge, 39679 Pony Lake Rd., Valentine 69201; (402) 376-1889; fws.gov/refuge/valentine
Dog-friendly: Yes, on leash
Trail surface: Mowed grass

Land status: Valentine National Wildlife Refuge
Nearest town: Valentine 31 miles to the north, Thedford 63 miles to the south
Maps: USGS Simeon, NE 2021; refuge map available at kiosks on refuge land or the refuge website
Other trail users: None
Special considerations: There is no shade along the entirety of the trail. The viewing deck at the fire tower is accessed via 33 stairs.
Amenities available: None at the trailhead; there are toilets nearby at the refuge sub-headquarters on NE 16B Spur
Maximum grade: 8%
Cell service: Coverage is available at the trailhead and along the trail.

FINDING THE TRAILHEAD

From Valentine, head south on US 20 / US 83 / Blue Star Memorial Highway. After 4.3 miles and crossing the Niobrara River, turn right (southwest) onto US 83. Continue south on US 83 for 11.4 miles. Then, turn right (west) onto NE 16B Spur and drive west, passing the road south to Big Alkali State Wildlife Management Area, then south and finally west, driving between Watts Lake to the north and Hackberry Lake to the south. After 13.8 miles, turn left (south) into the parking area for the CCC Fire Tower Trail Trailhead. Shortly before the trailhead pull-off, there is an access road on the south side of the highway that leads to the refuge sub-headquarters where there are publicly accessible toilets. **GPS:** N42° 34.069' W100° 42.477'

Trail Conditions: The trail is not waymarked and not needed, as there are no intersecting trails or navigational issues. There are multiple interpretive panels along the trail explaining the local flora and fauna. Sun exposure and ticks are hazards during the summer. The trail receives light traffic.

Top: CCC Fire Tower.
Bottom: One of the last remaining fens in the Sandhills is at Dewey Lake.

THE HIKE

Nebraska's largest of seven publicly accessible national wildlife refuges, Valentine National Wildlife Refuge was created in 1935 by Congress as a "breeding ground" for wildlife. The refuge has been named an Important Bird Area by Nebraska Audubon; 270 species of birds have been identified here. Notable species include long-billed curlew, greater prairie chicken, sharp-tailed grouse, and black tern, while northern shoveler, American bittern, upland sandpiper, and American tree sparrow are commonly sighted at the refuge. Viewing blinds are available on a first-come, first-served basis in spring to witness the fascinating mating rituals of greater prairie chickens and sharp-tailed grouse.

The refuge totals nearly forty small lakes, most shallow and marshy. Dunes rise out of these lakes, some as high as 200 feet, and the valleys between them are natural basins for

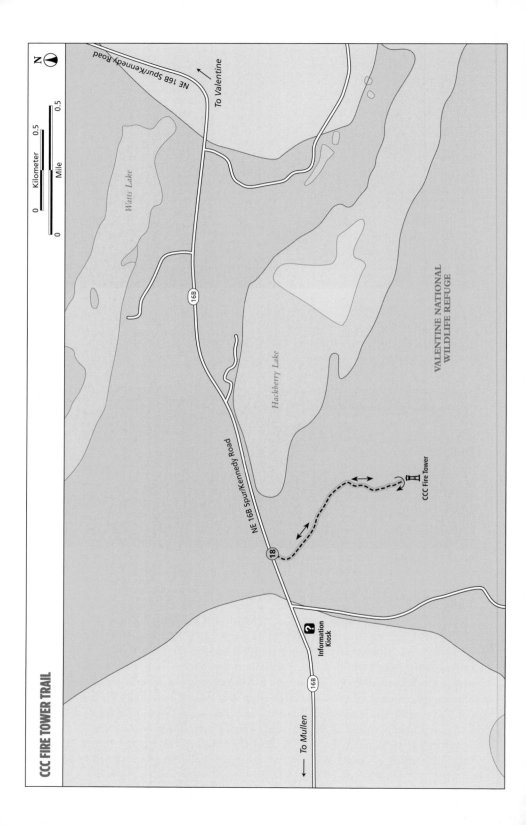

CCC FIRE TOWER TRAIL

N

0 Kilometer 0.5

0 Mile 0.5

NE 16B Spur/Kennedy Road

To Valentine

Watts Lake

16B

Hackberry Lake

NE 16B Spur/Kennedy Road

18

CCC Fire Tower

Information Kiosk

16B

To Mullen

VALENTINE NATIONAL
WILDLIFE REFUGE

lakes, marshes, and fens. The dunes are quite young; they were formed 10,000 years ago by wind. Low rainfall encouraged the growth of drought-resistant plants that stabilized the dunes into the Sandhills of today.

While short at under one and a half miles, the CCC Fire Tower Trail includes all of the previously mentioned ecosystems: marshes, Sandhills prairie, lakes, and a rare Sandhills fen. The trailhead is off NE 16B Spur and just west of the refuge sub-headquarters, where toilets are available. There are no amenities at the trailhead, but there is shade. The trail immediately crosses a footbridge over a small marsh. The entirety of Hackberry Lake, with the exception of the shoreline that borders the highway, is ringed by this marsh. At a bench at 0.09 mile, the trail begins to head southeast running parallel to a grove of eastern redcedar. Sandhills prairie extends south of the trail and the contrast in vegetation from the marsh to the prairie is stark.

A bench at 0.43 mile marks the trail's departure from the cedar grove, as it

Trailhead for CCC Fire Tower Trail.

heads due south to climb to the CCC Fire Tower. The tower is reached at 0.65 mile; thirty-three steps lead to a viewing deck. The stairs to the fire lookout atop the tower have been removed, but the view from the deck is great nonetheless. Hackberry Lake lies to the northeast with Watts Lake beyond it; to the east is Dewey Lake. A plaque 20 yards south of the stairs notes that the area between Hackberry Lake and Dewey Lake is the Charles L. Wiseman Natural Area, named after a former manager of the refuge and closed to public entry. One of the last Sandhills fens not drained and converted to a hay meadow is at Dewey Lake. Sandhills fens, similar to peatlands but fed by groundwater and not rain, contain plants typically found farther north in Minnesota and Canada. There is a binocular tower viewer on the viewing deck to get a closer view of the fen, Dewey Lake, and Hackberry Lake before heading back to the trailhead.

MILES AND DIRECTIONS

0.00 Begin at the CCC Fire Tower Trail Trailhead; head south passing through a gate.

0.09 Bench.

0.43 Bench.

0.65 CCC Fire Tower; turn around.

1.31 Arrive back at the trailhead.

19 SCOTT LOOKOUT NATIONAL RECREATION TRAIL

The Western hemisphere's largest hand-planted forest is located in the Bessey Ranger District of the Nebraska National Forest. Co-located with the District, the Bessey Nursery provides seedlings for western forests killed by wildfires as well as for windbreaks and wildlife plantings. The hand-planted forest provides a plethora of recreation opportunities in the heart of the Sandhills, the largest grass-stabilized dune complex in the western hemisphere. Scott Lookout National Recreation Trail winds through pine and cedar forest to Scott Fire Lookout, still used to this day to spot fires. Climb the ninety-three steps to the top of the lookout for splendid views of the forest and the rolling Sandhills prairie. **(Note: During this writing, the author learned that the tower burned down [2022], but Nebraska National Forest hopes to rebuild it in the future.)**

Start: Scott Tower Trailhead on FR 223 south of Bessey Campground

Elevation gain: 2,778 to 2,946 feet

Distance: 5.55 miles out and back

Difficulty: Moderate due to length and sandy trail

Hiking time: 2–3 hours

Seasons/schedule: Trail is open year-round, sunrise to sunset; good any time of year

Fees and permits: None. Parking in the main parking lot at the Bessey Recreation Complex costs $5 per day, or purchase an annual pass for $20 per year. Parking in the forest is free; however, vehicles must be parked within 30 feet of a road designated on the motor vehicle use map.

Trail contact: Bessey Ranger District, 40637 River Loop, Halsey 69142; (308) 533-2257; fs.usda.gov/nebraska

Dog-friendly: Yes, on 6-foot leash

Trail surface: Sand with some areas of wood chips

Land status: Nebraska National Forest Bessey Ranger District

Nearest town: Broken Bow 55 miles to the southeast, Thedford 15 miles to the northwest

Maps: USGS Halsey, NE 2021; trail map available at self-register kiosk at Bessey Campground; mobile, interactive, and hard copy maps available online at www.fs.usda.gov/main/nebraska/maps-pubs

Other trail users: None

Special considerations: There is no water source on the trail; water is available at Bessey Campground in season and at the recreation building in winter.

Amenities available: None at the trailhead; there are toilets, water, parking, picnic areas, tent camping, and a developed campsite at Bessey Campground. Dispersed camping is allowed in the national forest.

Maximum grade: 10%

Cell service: Weak to no reception on the trail; good reception at the fire tower

FINDING THE TRAILHEAD

From Halsey, head west on NE 2; from Thedford head east on NE 2. Turn south at the entrance to Nebraska National Forest. After crossing the railroad tracks and Middle Loup River, continue south past the Bessey Ranger District headquarters and the day-use parking area for the Bessey Recreation Complex. At the

Views of Nebraska National Forest and the Sandhills from Scott Fire Lookout.

self-registration kiosk, turn left (east), then turn right (south) onto FR 223. Continue on FR 223 past the Hardwood Loop camping sites. The Scott Lookout Trail Trailhead is located shortly after the Hardwood Loop turn-off. **GPS:** N41° 53.966' W100° 18.074'

Trail Conditions: The trail has waymarks at each half mile. There are three crossings with forest roads and OHV trails, so cross with caution. Ticks and poison ivy are present on the trail. The trail receives light foot traffic.

THE HIKE

The story of the creation of the Nebraska National Forest is straight from a movie script. Charles E. Bessey came to Nebraska in 1884 to serve as dean of the Industrial College of the University of Nebraska. A botanist, academic, and conservationist, Bessey was concerned with deforestation, and his idea for the Sandhills was unorthodox because there was no forest to replant—rather, he wanted to create a forest where there had not been one. Bessey finally obtained approval from the Department of Agriculture in 1891 and oversaw the planting of over 13,000 seedlings. However, government officials resisted further experiments, and Bessey never visited the site in Holt County again, assuming the trees had died in the dry and windy Sandhills conditions.

However, in 1901 William L. Hall, a government official in the Bureau of Forestry, visited the Holt County site and returned to Lincoln to inform Bessey of his astonishing discovery. "I have seen them!" Hall exclaimed. Hall had encountered pine trees towering 20 feet high in a forest on the Sandhills prairie. The unexpected success of the experimental plantings led President Theodore Roosevelt in 1902 to create two forest reserves in Nebraska, the Niobrara Reserve in Cherry County (now the Samuel R. McKelvie National Forest) and the Dismal River Reserve in Blaine and Thomas Counties (now the Nebraska National Forest Bessey Ranger District). The forest at the Bessey Ranger District is the world's largest hand-planted forest and the only human-created forest existing in the National Forest System. The nursery has provided hundreds of millions of seedlings that have been used across the Great Plains.

In 1965, the Plum Fire burned over a third of the forest. The wooden steps of Scott Fire Lookout, built in 1942, did not survive the fire but the lookout itself survived and is

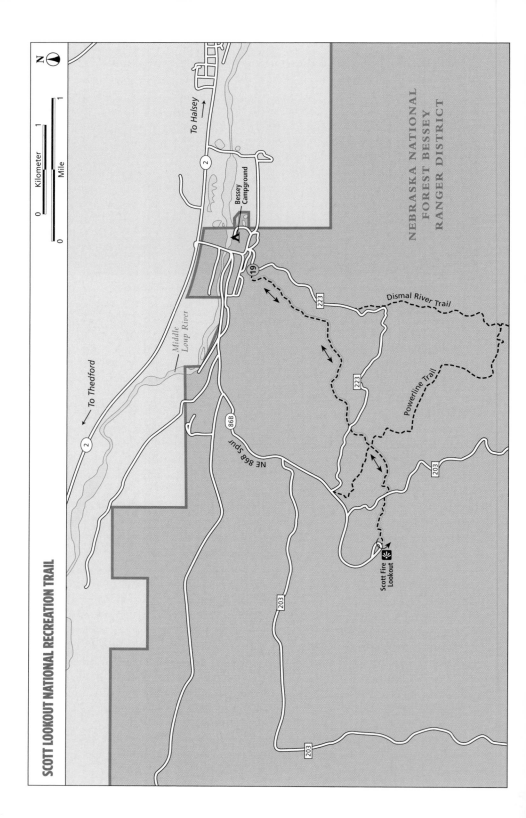

SCOTT LOOKOUT NATIONAL RECREATION TRAIL

NEBRASKA NATIONAL
FOREST BESSEY
RANGER DISTRICT

To Halsey

To Thedford

Middle
Loop River

Bessey
Campground

Dismal River Trail

Powerline Trail

NE 868 Spur

Scott Fire
Lookout

N

Kilometer

Mile

still used to this day as a fire lookout. The public can climb the ninety-three metal steps to the top to take in the sweeping views of the pine forest and rolling Sandhills prairie. The trailhead is located just south of the Bessey Recreation Complex. At 0.13 mile, the Scott Lookout National Recreation Trail passes through an area included in a 2011 prescribed burn, used to lessen overall fire danger and lessen the risk of a severe event like the 1965 fire. The trail continues in a southwesterly direction along a sandy footpath through ponderosa pine and eastern redcedar. Cross a footbridge at 1.15 miles and then pass by a wildlife water tank and picnic table at 1.24 miles.

There is not much for views for the entirety of the trail until the fire lookout as the dense forest and the topography of the Sandhills preclude expansive views typical of the Great Plains. The shade and sweet smell of pine more than make up for lack of views. Furthermore, incredible views await atop the Scott Fire Lookout. The trail continues southwest, crossing FR 223 at 1.61 miles and the Powerline Trail at 1.83 miles. Cross another forest road, FR 203, at 2.27 miles before reaching the Scott Fire Lookout at 2.71 miles. Climb the ninety-three steps to reach the top of the lookout and take in the incredible views of the forest and Sandhills before returning via the same trail to the trailhead.

MILES AND DIRECTIONS

0.00 Begin at the Scott Tower Trailhead heading west.

1.15 Cross a footbridge.

1.61 Continue straight (southwest) crossing FR 223.

1.83 Continue straight (southwest) after crossing Powerline Trail.

2.17 Indicated by a trail sign, turn left (south).

2.27 Cross FR 203 and continue northwest on Scott Lookout Trail.

2.55 Continue straight (west).

2.67 Reach the loop road around the fire tower; cross the road and continue west to climb the stairs on the hillside.

2.71 Reach the Scott Fire Lookout Tower; turn around.

3.14 Continue straight (east) crossing FR 203.

3.25 Indicated by the trail sign, turn right (east).

3.60 Continue straight (east) crossing Powerline Trail.

3.82 Cross FR 223; continue straight (northeast).

4.15 Reach the picnic table and stock tank; continue northeast.

4.25 Footbridge.

5.55 Arrive back at the trailhead.

Top: Scott Fire Lookout.
Bottom: Ninety-three stairs lead to the top of Scott Fire Lookout.

20 OLSON NATURE PRESERVE

Tucked into 112 acres on the eastern edge of the Sandhills, Olson Nature Preserve includes several interesting ecosystems to explore via its trail system. Tallgrass prairie, wetlands, and a cottonwood grove border the half-mile stretch of Beaver Creek that crosses the preserve. Bur oak forest covers the steep escarpment that gives way to Sandhills prairie in the upland section of the preserve. The trail system, and the preserve itself, is the fruit of labor by PPRI staff, ONP land stewards, volunteers, and scouts, making it an exemplary wildlife preserve.

Start: Footbridge over Beaver Creek
Elevation gain: 1,818 to 1,930 feet
Distance: 2.18-mile loop
Difficulty: Easy but with 1 steep 100-foot climb
Hiking time: 1 hour
Seasons/schedule: Trails open year-round, sunrise to sunset; best any time of year
Fees and permits: None
Trail contact: Prairie Plains Resource Institute; 1307 L St., Aurora 68818; (402) 694-5535; prairieplains.org
Dog-friendly: Yes, on leash
Trail surface: Mowed grass
Land status: Prairie Plains Resource Institute

Nearest town: Albion 10 miles to the south
Maps: USGS Petersburg, NE 2021; there is no trail map available online or at the trailhead
Other trail users: None
Special considerations: Prescribed burns are conducted on occasions; contact Prairie Plains Resource Institute or check their website for updates.
Amenities available: Portable toilet and picnic shelter at the trailhead
Maximum grade: 12%
Cell service: Moderate to good coverage by most carriers

FINDING THE TRAILHEAD

From Albion, head north on NE 14 for 8 miles. Turn left (northwest) onto Y Road and continue for 1 mile to the entrance gate. After closing the entrance gate, continue west until reaching the parking area and bridge over Beaver Creek. **GPS:** N41° 47.996' W98° 6.629'

Trail Conditions: The trails are well maintained and mowed frequently. There are no trail waymarks and no trail map available online or at the trailhead. Tree snags are potential hazards in high winds and ticks are a nuisance in summer. The trail receives light to moderate traffic.

THE HIKE

In 1992, a group of citizens asked the estate of Grant and Berenice Olson to set aside a portion of their ranch for conservation and public use, stressing the ecological value of the land. On the extreme eastern edge of the Sandhills, the Olson ranch encompassed not only Sandhills prairie but also oak woodland, riparian forest, and wetlands that are part of the Loup River watershed. The estate agreed to an arrangement and in 1995 Prairie Plains Resource Institute (PPRI) undertook ownership of the land, later adding another tract for a total of 112 acres.

Left: The entrance to Olson Nature Preserve on Y Road in Boone County.
Right: The trail climbs through the oak woodland to reach views of Sandhills prairie stretching to the west.

Despite its small area, Olson Nature Preserve is home to several different ecosystems. Beaver Creek crosses the preserve from north to south along the eastern edge of the preserve, carving a sandy canyon where plants and animals common in the Loup River watershed are found. A grove of cottonwoods and a tallgrass prairie provide habitat on the western bank of the creek. A small outdoor classroom is used for environmental education on the southern end of the cottonwood grove. There are also some wetlands areas on both sides of the creek. A steep, wooded slope of bur oaks divides the lowland area of the preserve from the upland Sandhills prairie, where typical Sandhills flora such as yucca grow along the mowed trails.

The current condition of Olson Nature Preserve (ONP) as a pristine wildlife habitat and excellent outdoor recreation site is due to the efforts of PPRI staff, ONP land stewards, and volunteers. Prescribed burns and grazing are used as land management tools, while trail design and construction of benches and shelters have been the result of various projects led by Scouts and volunteers. There are nearly 3 miles of trails on the preserve and the following hike takes hikers through each ecosystem on a short 2-mile hike.

Beginning at the parking area, head west and cross the short footbridge over Beaver Creek. Shortly after crossing the bridge there is an outdoor classroom with several benches. Keep to the left on the mowed path that follows Beaver Creek heading south. The trail follows the creek as it heads south, with tallgrass prairie on your right. Upon reaching the southern boundary of the preserve, the path bends to the west shortly before heading north once it reaches the oak woodland that clings to the steep slope. The twisted limbs of bur oaks provide welcome shade as you hike north with the tallgrass prairie now on your right.

OLSON NATURE PRESERVE

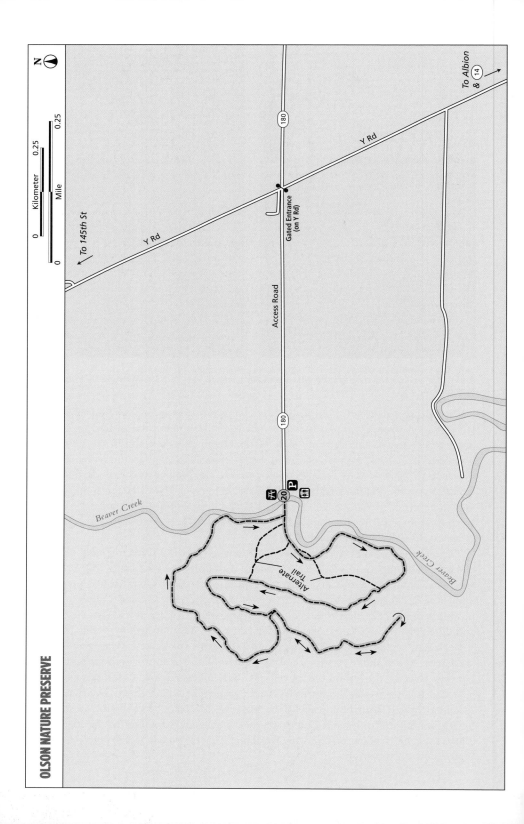

Left: Beaver Creek and the cottonwood grove on the right, bur oak woodland on the left.
Right: The limb of a large bur oak spreads across the trail.

After 0.75 mile, the trail bends on itself as it climbs up the steep escarpment through the oak woodland. The climb, about 100 feet in roughly one-half mile, is strenuous but soon levels out and heads south with Sandhills prairie to the west and the oak woodland to the east. Continue straight (south) at the fork at 0.91 mile; the hike to the southern boundary and back to this fork is about 0.7 mile. Once you reach the boundary, turn around and head back to the fork with wind turbines and farmland on the horizon to the north.

The trail descends from the ridge and then heads east toward Beaver Creek. The right fork at 1.9 miles passes along the cottonwood grove; instead, keep left to return to the footbridge by following the mowed path alongside Beaver Creek.

MILES AND DIRECTIONS

0.00 Begin at the parking area; head west and cross the footbridge over Beaver Creek.

0.07 Keep left at the fork.

0.10 Keep left (southwest) to follow the mowed path along Beaver Creek.

0.14 Reach a fork; keep left (south).

0.36 Trail reaches a barbed wire fence at the southern boundary of the preserve; continue west.

0.43 Keep left (north) to follow the mowed path with the oak woodland on your left (west).

0.70 Reach a fork and keep left (north) to continue along the edge of the oak woodland.

0.73 Bench.

0.75 At the fork, keep left (northwest) to head uphill through the oak woodland.

0.91 Keep left at the fork to continue south with the oak woodland to the east and Sandhills prairie to the west.

0.94 Bench.

1.07 Keep right (south).

1.13 Bench.

1.24 Southern boundary of the preserve; turn around and head north on the same path.

1.67 Head west on the mowed path through Sandhills prairie.

1.90 Keep left (east) to follow the trail alongside Beaver Creek.

2.10 Turn left (east) and cross the footbridge over Beaver Creek.

2.18 Arrive back at the trailhead and parking area.

E ISLAND LAKE LOOP

If you want to explore more of Crescent Lake National Wildlife Refuge, the 7-mile loop around Island Lake is an excellent choice. The loop follows a sandy two-track path primarily used by primitive vehicles that, along with the final section via the refuge road, circumnavigates Island Lake. American white pelicans and other wildlife can be seen near the lake, which is surrounded by low grass-covered dunes. Unlike the Sandhills Nature Trail near the refuge headquarters, dogs are allowed on the trails that comprise Island Lake Loop.

Start: Small parking area and boat launch on the south end of Island Lake
Elevation gain: 3,792 to 3,835 feet
Distance: 7.27-mile loop
Difficulty: Easy due to level terrain
Hiking time: 3 hours
Seasons/schedule: Open year-round, sunrise to sunset; best in Apr for migratory birds
Fees and permits: None
Trail contact: Crescent Lake National Wildlife Refuge, 10630 Rd. 181, Ellsworth 69340; (308) 762-4893; fws.gov/refuge/crescent-lake
Dog-friendly: Yes, on leash
Trail surface: Sandy two-track
Land status: Crescent Lake National Wildlife Refuge

Nearest town: Oshkosh 20 miles to the south
Maps: USGS Mumper, NE 2021; refuge map available online and at kiosks throughout the refuge
Other trail users: Motor vehicles
Special considerations: The nearest services are 30 miles away, so plan accordingly. The sandy roads can be problematic. Spring is the best time to visit but the weather is also unpredictable and roads can become impassable.
Amenities available: None
Maximum grade: 6%
Cell service: Weak to nonexistent for most carriers

FINDING THE TRAILHEAD

From Oshkosh, head north on W 2nd Street / Road 179. After approximately 13 miles, keep left (north) onto Road 181. Continue on Road 181 for approximately 15 miles until entering the wildlife refuge. Turn right (east) on the sandy two-track and continue until reaching a small parking area. **GPS:** N41° 43.589' W102° 24.017'

Trail Conditions: Much of the trail follows a sandy two-track primitive trail, while the last section follows the main refuge road. The trail is not waymarked, but both the primitive vehicle trail and the refuge road are listed on the refuge map. The trail receives light traffic.

American white pelicans
on Island Lake.

F EAST END ACCESS TRAIL

The East End Access road, beginning on the west end of Center Lake and then following its northern shore, is a beautiful two-track trail to hike during the summer. The trailhead is easily accessed east of the refuge headquarters on Pony Lake Road. A summer hike offers the opportunity to encounter some of the 270 birds, 59 mammals, and 22 reptiles and amphibians at Valentine National Wildlife Refuge.

Start: East End Access Trailhead between Pony Lake and Center Lake
Elevation gain: 2,891 to 2,910 feet
Distance: 6.20 miles out and back
Difficulty: Easy due to flat terrain
Hiking time: 2–3 hours
Seasons/schedule: Open year-round, dawn to dusk; best in May and Sept–Oct for migratory birds
Fees and permits: None
Trail contact: Valentine National Wildlife Refuge, 39679 Pony Lake Rd., Valentine 69201; (402) 376-1889; fws.gov/refuge/valentine
Dog-friendly: Yes, on leash
Trail surface: Primitive two-track road

Land status: Valentine National Wildlife Refuge
Nearest town: Valentine 31 miles to the north, Thedford 63 miles to the south
Maps: USGS Simeon, NE 2021; refuge map available at kiosks on refuge land or the refuge website
Other trail users: None
Special considerations: There is no shade along the entirety of the trail.
Amenities available: None at the trailhead; there are toilets at the refuge headquarters west of the trailhead on Pony Lake Road
Cell service: Coverage is available at the trailhead and along the trail

FINDING THE TRAILHEAD

From Valentine, head south on US 83; from Thedford, head north on US 83. Turn east onto Pony Lake Road and keep right at the turn-off for the refuge headquarters. Continue east on Pony Lake Road for approximately 1 mile until reaching the East End Access Trail sign between Pony Lake and Center Lake. **GPS:** N42° 28.848′ W100° 29.905′

Trail Conditions: The trail follows a public use trail that is open to 4WD vehicles. There are no waymarkings, but the out-and-back trail is simple. The trail can be overgrown, especially in summer, and ticks will be a nuisance. The trail receives light traffic.

A tranquil Center Lake reflecting the grassy dunes of the Sandhills.

The Niobrara River near Norden Chute.

NIOBRARA VALLEY

"There is perhaps no single river, or indeed any 100-mile stretch of river in all of North America, that is more interesting biologically than the Niobrara," wrote Paul Johnsgard in *The Nature of Nebraska*. The Niobrara River is so unique that Johnsgard wrote an entire book about its ecology and natural history. Not only is the river valley a major transition zone from eastern plant and animal species to western species, but there are several plants found in the Niobrara Valley that are found nowhere else in Nebraska, for example paper birch in the cool spring-branch canyons. Beginning in Valentine and heading east, the 76-mile stretch of the Middle Niobrara has been designated a National Scenic River because of its biodiversity and recreation opportunities. Waterfalls, rapids, and steep pine-covered slopes offer hikers adventures only found in this part of Nebraska.

View of Niobrara Valley.

21 GOVERNMENT CANYON

Government Canyon is a hidden gem tucked away at the Valentine State Fish Hatchery. Outside of hunting season, you will likely only encounter birds, deer, and other animals on the trail despite its proximity to the town of Valentine. The trail travels up the pine-studded canyon for over two and a half miles, the first section with open views of the canyon rim before traversing along a wooded stream and through open meadows. The turnaround of this out-and-back hike is at the northern boundary of the reserve, a beautiful ponderosa pine savanna with excellent birding opportunities.

Start: Government Canyon Trailhead
Elevation gain: 2,457 to 2,584 feet
Distance: 5.20 miles out and back
Difficulty: Moderate due to length
Hiking time: 2–3 hours
Seasons/schedule: Open year-round, dawn to dusk
Fees and permits: None
Trail contact: Valentine State Fish Hatchery, 90164 Hatchery Rd., Valentine 69201; (402) 376-2244
Dog-friendly: Yes, on 6-foot leash
Trail surface: Sandy two-track
Land status: Valentine State Fish Hatchery (Nebraska Game and Parks Commission)

Nearest town: Valentine to the southwest
Maps: USGS Valentine North, NE, SD 2021
Other trail users: Bikers and hunters
Special considerations: Firearm and archery hunting for deer and turkey is permitted on select portions of the area. Ticks are abundant during the summer.
Amenities available: None
Maximum grade: 5%
Cell service: Yes, adequate coverage at the trailhead and in open sections of the canyon

FINDING THE TRAILHEAD

From the Cherry County Hospital in Valentine, head north on N Green Street for 1.3 miles. After entering the Valentine State Fish Hatchery, continue past the ponds until Hatchery Road bends to the north. Take the first left, then keep right to reach the parking area at the Government Canyon Trailhead. **GPS:** N42° 53.584' W100° 31.850'

Trail Conditions: The trail is not waymarked but is easy to follow for most of the hike. As you venture farther north up the canyon, the trail is not mowed as frequently, leading to knee-high or taller grass along and on the trail, which means a high probability of ticks. Light trail traffic.

THE HIKE

Government Canyon, managed by the Nebraska Game and Parks Commission, totals 720 acres that includes a portion of adjacent Fishberry Canyon. Dams were constructed in both canyons in 1984 to prevent soil erosion and flooding of the streams that feed the Valentine State Fish Hatchery. The Valentine State Fish Hatchery is one of five in the state of Nebraska. It produces millions of eggs annually and stocks nearly 700,000 fish in the lakes of Cherry County.

The publicly accessible area of Government Canyon is popular with deer and turkey hunters, but bird-watching, mountain biking, and hiking are other activities that provide

Climbing north into Government Canyon.

Hatchery ponds in Government Canyon.

recreation opportunities for outdoor enthusiasts. The trail begins by passing a maintenance and storage area for the Valentine State Fish Hatchery. Soon after, the canyon opens
up with views of both the west and east canyon rims. The canyon bottom is forested
with cottonwood, ash, elm, and boxelder, while ponderosa pine dots the upper reaches
of the canyon's sides. After 0.5 mile the trail gently climbs out of the wooded canyon
bottom to follow the two-track path along the drier, west-facing canyonside. The trail
here is largely treeless with Great Plains yucca dotting the hillside. There are a lot of snags
along the trail here, remains of either a previous fire or windstorm.

At 1 mile the trail reaches the southern end of a series of ponds created by damming
the Fishberry Creek to prevent soil erosion and flooding. Be mindful if you leave the
trail here, as poison ivy is present along both sides of the trail. The two-track forks at

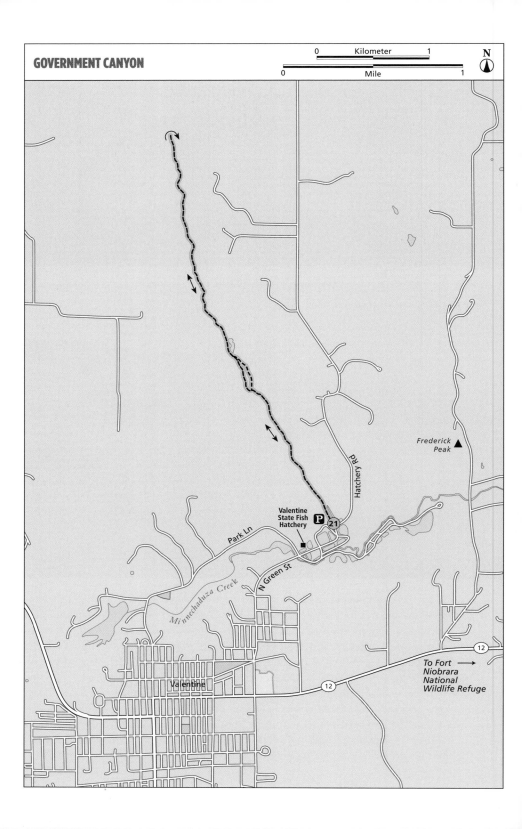

0   Kilometer   1

0   Mile   1

N

Frederick
Peak ▲

Hatchery Rd

Valentine
State Fish
Hatchery   P 21

Park Ln

N Green St

Minnechaduza Creek

Valentine

To Fort
Niobrara
National
Wildlife Refuge

12

12

Northern boundary of Government Canyon.

0.9 mile but reconnects at the northern end of the first pond at 1.2 miles. If you wish to cut the hike short, this is the perfect place to take the other fork south to return to the trailhead. Continuing north, the trail passes two more ponds and then passes over a rock levee at 1.34 miles.

The trail meanders along the wooded canyon bottom, crossing the stream several times until reaching a fence at 1.68 miles. The two-track climbs gently through an open meadow bordered by ponderosa to the east and a wooded ravine to the west. As the trail penetrates deeper into the canyon, the grass along the trail becomes longer and denser. Open meadows alternate between oak and ash forest to ponderosa savanna as the trail continues due north. The northern boundary of Government Canyon, marked by a sign and fence, is set in a beautiful open meadow with ponderosa pine climbing the slopes of the canyon. This is an excellent area to have a picnic or grab a pair of binoculars to spot some ponderosa savanna bird species such as orioles, grosbeaks, sparrows, and nuthatches. The hike back to the trailhead is a gentle 2.6-mile descent along the same two-track road.

MILES AND DIRECTIONS

0.00 Begin at the Government Canyon Trailhead and head north on the two-track path.

0.10 Continue north as the trail passes a maintenance yard to the west.

0.93 Reach a pond; keep right (north).

1.16 Turn left (west) to cross an earthen dam between two ponds.

1.17 Turn right (north) to follow the track on the west bank of another pond.

2.61 Reach the northern boundary of Government Canyon; turn around and return via the same track.

4.02 Keep right (south).

4.28 Reach the southern end of a pond; continue straight (southeast).

5.20 Arrive back at Government Canyon Trailhead.

22 FORT FALLS TRAIL

East and West converge along the Niobrara River, creating biologically unique ecosystems where different animal species hybridize and plants found nowhere else in Nebraska, such as paper birch, thrive in the cool spring-branch canyons. Fort Falls Trail is an easy, short trail that takes hikers past one of the tallest waterfalls in the state, then along a beautiful stretch of the federally designated Niobrara National Scenic River popular with kayakers, canoeists, and floaters.

Start: Fort Falls parking lot
Elevation gain: 2,327 to 2,446 feet
Distance: 0.90-mile loop
Difficulty: Easy except the steep descent to the falls and subsequent climb out the river valley
Hiking time: 1 hour
Seasons/schedule: Open year-round, dawn to dusk; excellent birding in late spring
Fees and permits: None
Trail contact: Fort Niobrara National Wildlife Refuge, 39983 Refuge Rd., Valentine 69201; (402) 376-3789; fws.gov/refuge/fort-niobrara
Dog-friendly: Yes, on leash
Trail surface: Dirt footpath, metal stairs, concrete path
Land status: Fort Niobrara National Wildlife Refuge

Nearest town: Valentine 5.5 miles to the southwest
Maps: USGS Cornell Dam, NE, SD 2021; refuge map available online and at park visitor center
Other trail users: None
Special considerations: There is no winter maintenance on any trails in the refuge; Fort Falls Trail is hazardous or even impassable in the winter. An alternate trailhead avoids the steep descent via the stairs to the falls, but instead follows the trail along the river with less elevation change.
Amenities available: Toilets at the refuge visitor center and at the alternate trailhead
Maximum grade: 13%
Cell service: Yes, coverage is weak but present on the trail

FINDING THE TRAILHEAD

From downtown Valentine head north on N Main Street and take a right on E 5th Street; E 5th Street becomes NE 12. Drive about 4.5 miles to 16D / County Road, and turn right over Cornell Bridge. Follow Refuge signs to Fort Falls Trail. **GPS:** N 42° 54.047' W 100° 27.988'

Trail Conditions: The trail is waymarked with interpretive panels; short but steep inclines and declines can be slippery even when dry; moderate to heavy trail traffic.

THE HIKE

"There is perhaps no single river, or indeed any 100-mile stretch of river in all of North America, that is more interesting biologically than the Niobrara. The narrow Niobrara Valley is indeed where the East ends and the West begins," wrote biologist Paul A. Johnsgard in *The Nature of Nebraska*. Johnsgard wrote an entire book, *The Niobrara: A River Running through Time*, about the biological diversity and uniqueness of the Niobrara River.

The Niobrara Valley is a transitional zone where eastern and western plant and animal species meet their range limits. In some instances, species hybridize in contact zones along the valley, such as Baltimore orioles and Bullock's orioles. Additionally, the spring-branch

Left: Fort Falls.
Right: Niobrara River from Fort Falls Trail.

canyons on the south side of the river create cool, moist microclimates where paper birch and quaking aspen still survive, long since disappeared from the dry Great Plains. The only places to see these ice age relics in Nebraska are along the Niobrara Valley in temperate enclaves, such as Fort Niobrara National Wildlife Refuge.

The refuge was originally established to protect bison and other large game animals, such as elk, and also to protect habitat for native birds. Confined herds of bison and elk range on the preserve and 230 species of birds have been reported. Much of the wildlife refuge is Sandhills prairie, about two-thirds, while the rest is mixed riparian hardwood forest. Fort Falls Trail loops through the latter, taking hikers past the eponymous 60-foot waterfall and along a beautiful stretch of the Niobrara River through a forest of ash, basswood, birch, hackberry, and oak.

The trail has two trailheads—for quick access to the waterfall, begin at the upper trailhead near the corrals. Concrete stairs eventually lead to a metal staircase that takes you 100 feet down to the Niobrara River. Before the river, however, the trail passes by Fort Falls, a 60-foot waterfall that is only surpassed by nearby Smith Falls as the highest in Nebraska. As you descend down the staircase, take notice of the temperature change. Fort Falls is located in one of the many spring-branch canyons on the south side of the

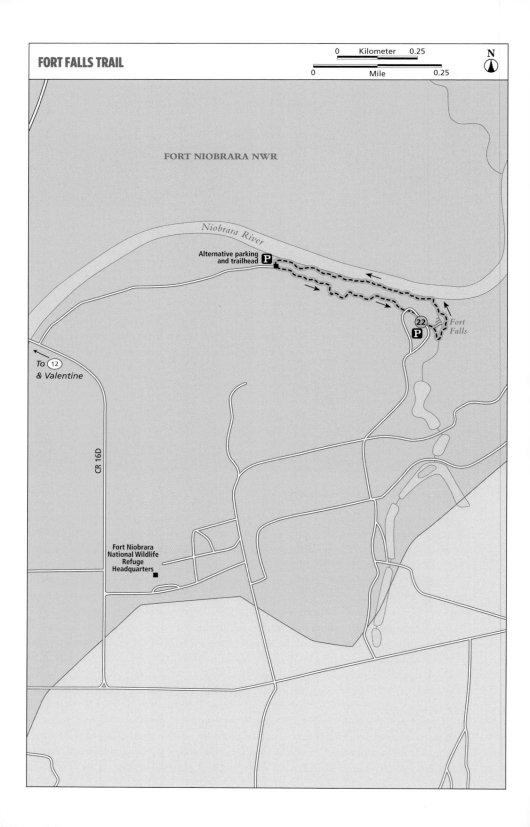

0   Kilometer   0.25

0   Mile   0.25

N

FORT NIOBRARA NWR

Niobrara River

Alternative parking
and trailhead   P

22
P

Fort
Falls

To 12
& Valentine

CR 16D

Fort Niobrara
National Wildlife
Refuge
Headquarters

Alternate trailhead to the falls avoids the steep descent and ascent to the falls, instead following an uneven path along the Niobrara River.

river, which create a microclimate where paper birch survives along with other plant species that disappeared when the glaciers receded at the end of the last ice age. The cool, moist microclimate has conserved these ice age relics, and these canyons are the only place in Nebraska where trees like paper birch can still be found.

Once Fort Falls Trail reaches the river, the trail heads west upstream through hardwood forest with ash, basswood, birch, hackberry, ironwood, and oak. Helpful interpretive panels explain the different flora and fauna encountered along the trail. After 0.53 mile, the trail reaches an alternative trailhead and parking area. Continue east following signs directing you to the main parking lot. The trail climbs out of the canyon and levels out once it reaches a bench at 0.72 mile with a view of the northern bank of the Niobrara River. Take a seat on the bench to spot an indigo bunting or another of the 230 bird species on the Fort Niobrara bird list. The last section of the trail passes through a grove of sumac before reaching the main parking area and trailhead.

MILES AND DIRECTIONS

0.00 Begin at trailhead and descend concrete steps and then a metal staircase.

0.07 Reach the top of Fort Falls.

0.10 Reach the bottom of Fort Falls.

0.17 Turn left (west) to continue on Fort Falls Trail as it follows the river against its current.

0.48 Pass a bench and cross a footbridge.

0.53 Reach an alternative trailhead for Fort Falls Trail; continue straight (east).

0.62 Cross a footbridge.

0.65 Stairs climbing up the hillside.

0.72 Bench.

0.90 Arrive back at the upper parking area and trailhead.

23 SMITH FALLS TRAIL AND JIM MACALLISTER NATURE TRAIL

A visit to Smith Falls is one of the highlights of a trip to the 76-mile stretch of Niobrara River east of Valentine that was designated a National Scenic River by the United State Congress in 1991. While many paddlers and floaters stop at Smith Falls State Park to stand underneath Nebraska's tallest waterfall, Smith Falls Trail gives hikers easy access to the cool, spring-branch canyon via a boardwalk. Jim MacAllister Nature Trail allows hikers to explore the wooded southern bank of the river as well as upland prairie.

Start: Smith Falls State Park East Campground
Elevation gain: 2,305 to 2,496 feet
Distance: 2.05 miles out and back
Difficulty: Moderate due to elevation gain on Jim MacAllister Nature Trail
Hiking time: 1–2 hours
Seasons/schedule: Open year-round, dawn to dusk; Smith Falls Trail is good any time of year, including winter, while Jim MacAllister Nature Trail is more difficult in winter with snow and ice
Fees and permits: A park entry permit is required and may be purchased at the park, statewide Game and Parks offices and permit vendors, or online at outdoornebraska.gov.
Trail contact: Smith Falls State Park, 90195 Smith Falls Rd., Valentine 69201; (402) 376-1306; outdoornebraska.gov/smithfalls
Dog-friendly: Yes, on leash no longer than 6 feet

Trail surface: Crushed rock, boardwalk, dirt footpath
Land status: Smith Falls State Park (privately owned and leased to Nebraska Game and Parks Commission)
Nearest town: Valentine 19 miles to the west
Maps: USGS Sparks, NE, SD 2021; park map available at park headquarters and online at outdoornebraska.gov/smithfalls
Other trail users: None
Special considerations: ADA accessible from trailhead to Smith Falls
Amenities available: Toilets, water, information, and concession stand at the visitor center; camping sites are available upon reservation or on a first-come, first served basis
Maximum grade: 15%
Cell service: Sufficient reception at trailhead, while coverage might be weak in the canyon and at the falls

FINDING THE TRAILHEAD

From Valentine, head east on NE 12 for 14.7 miles. Turn right (south) onto Smith Falls Road. After 3.5 miles, turn left (east) to reach the visitor center. Parking is available here or at the campground on the riverbank below the visitor center. The trailhead begins at a footbridge crossing a drainage ditch that empties into the Niobrara River. **GPS:** N42° 53.460′ W100° 18.704′

Trail Conditions: The trail is not waymarked but is well maintained and easy to follow. There are sections on the Jim MacAllister Nature Trail with tree snags that may pose dangers in high winds. There is heavy trail traffic to Smith Falls, while traffic is light on the Jim MacAllister Nature Trail.

Smith Falls, the highest waterfall in Nebraska.

THE HIKE

Smith Falls Trail begins in the east campground at the bottom of the stairs below the visitor center. After crossing a footbridge over a ditch, continue west through the west campground until arriving at the Verdigre Bridge that spans the Niobrara River. This bridge was originally constructed in 1910 in the town of Verdigre, then moved to nearby Verdigre Mill to carry traffic on NE 14 before it was put in storage in 1993. The Nebraska Game and Parks Commission reassembled the bridge in 1996 at Smith Falls State Park, and people from all over the world have since passed underneath as they float down the Niobrara River.

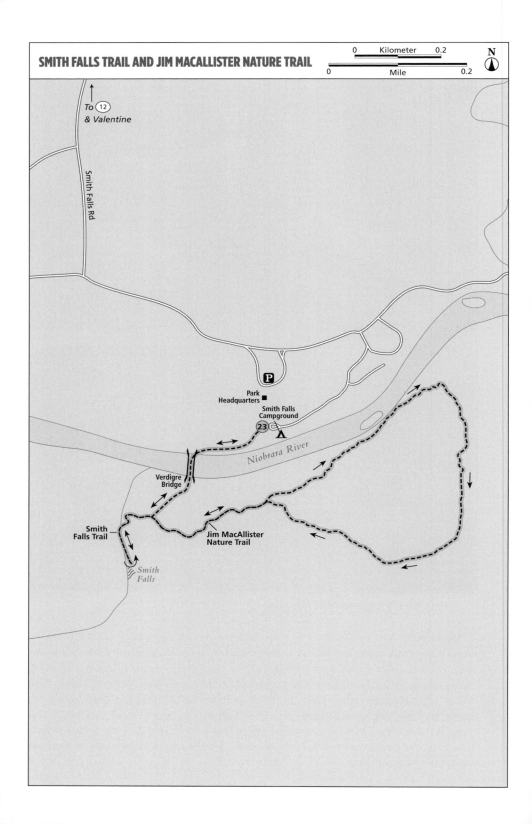

0   Kilometer   0.2

0   Mile   0.2

N

To 12
& Valentine

Smith Falls Rd

P

Park
Headquarters

Smith Falls
Campground

23

Niobrara River

Verdigre
Bridge

Smith
Falls Trail

Jim MacAllister
Nature Trail

Smith
Falls

Top: Verdigre Bridge was reassembled at Smith Falls State Park in 1996.
Bottom: The Niobrara River from Verdigre Bridge.

The trail continues southwest through a day-use area of the state park before reaching the Frederick Krzyzanowski Memorial Walkway at 0.3 mile. This is the only access to the falls as venturing off-trail is prohibited to prevent erosion and protect rare plants in the cool, spring-branch canyon. The boardwalk receives heavy traffic not only from day hikers visiting the park but also people floating or paddling the Niobrara during the summer. Smith Falls is reached after a short walk from the beginning of the boardwalk.

At 63 feet, Smith Falls is the tallest waterfall in Nebraska. Known by early settlers as Arikaree Falls, the falls gets its current name from the Smith family, who filed the first homestead on the surrounding land. The canyon carved by the spring-fed stream contributes

Upland prairie on Jim MacAllister Nature Trail.

to a cool microclimate that has allowed paper birch and a hybrid of quaking aspen and bigtooth aspen to survive. Both tree species are relics of the last ice age, and when the glaciers retreated the boreal forest that it supported also almost disappeared. North-facing spring-branch canyons, including Smith Falls, are the only places in Nebraska to find these and other locally uncommon plant species.

After snapping a picture of Smith Falls, return to the beginning of the Frederick Krzyzanowski Memorial Walkway boardwalk to access the Jim MacAllister Nature Trail. This is a 1-mile lollipop trail that traverses the wooded southern bank of the Niobrara River before climbing south into upland prairie. There are remnants of prescribed burns and muddy areas, so the hiking is more difficult than the easy Smith Falls Trail. Keep left (east) at 0.71 mile to continue following the trail with the Niobrara River on your left. At 1.1 miles, the trail heads south away from the river and climbs steeply through ponderosa pine before reaching an open meadow at 1.3 miles. The rolling Sandhills prairie extends to the south beyond the southern boundary of Smith Falls State Park. The trail begins to descend at 1.5 miles with wooden steps and posts placed in the ground to prevent erosion and help hikers manage the steep slope. At 1.59 miles, continue west to reach the day-use area, where you can wade into the Niobrara River before heading back to the trailhead.

MILES AND DIRECTIONS

0.00 Begin at the east campground at the bottom of the stairs below the visitor center; head west and cross a footbridge over a stream.

0.12 Cross Verdigre Bridge over the Niobrara River.

0.30 Boardwalk to Smith Falls.

0.40 Smith Falls; turn around.

0.50 Turn east onto Jim MacAllister Nature Trail.

0.89 Cross a footbridge.

1.10 Trail heads south and begins to climb the hillside.

1.59 Keep right to descend the stairs. At the bottom of the stairs, keep left to head west.

1.90 Turn right (north) to head toward Verdigre Bridge and the Niobrara River.

2.05 Arrive back at the Smith Falls East Campground.

24 NIOBRARA VALLEY PRESERVE

The Niobrara Valley Preserve lies in the heart of the transition zone between western coniferous and eastern deciduous forests. The ecological importance of the area is illustrated in the fact that the preserve is one of the largest managed by The Nature Conservancy in the United States. A staggering 581 plant species have been identified on the preserve's 56,000 acres. A hiking trail, offering a 1.5-mile or 2.5-mile loop, offers spectacular views of the wild Niobrara River. Nearby, Norden Chute is the perfect place to relax after hiking the preserve.

Start: Trailhead at small parking pull-off west of the mailbox and access road to The Nature Conservancy headquarters
Elevation gain: 2,158 to 2,355 feet
Distance: 2.63-mile loop
Difficulty: Moderate due to strenuous climb at the beginning and end of the hike
Hiking time: 1.5–2 hours
Seasons/schedule: Open year-round; best in late summer for wildflowers
Fees and permits: None
Trail contact: The Nature Conservancy Niobrara Valley Preserve, 42269 Morel Rd., Johnstown 69214; (402) 722-4440; nature.org/nebraska
Dog-friendly: No

Trail surface: Mowed grass and two-track sandy road
Land status: The Nature Conservancy
Nearest town: Valentine to the west, Ainsworth to the southeast, Springview to the northeast
Maps: USGS Norden, NE 2021; trail map posted at trailhead kiosk
Other trail users: None
Special considerations: The Niobrara Valley Preserve is in a remote location; prepare appropriately with adequate fuel, water, and other supplies in case of emergency.
Amenities available: None
Maximum grade: 14%
Cell service: Weak to no coverage on most of the trails

FINDING THE TRAILHEAD

From Valentine, travel east on NE 12 for approximately 29 miles. Turn left (south) onto Norden Road. Continue for 7 miles, crossing the Norden Bridge over the Niobrara River before reaching the trailhead pull-off just west of the mailbox and access road to the preserve's headquarters. **GPS:** N42° 46.962' W100° 2.123'

Trail Conditions: Trails are waymarked with signs. Ticks and poison ivy are potential hazards. Light trail traffic.

THE HIKE

The Niobrara Valley Preserve lies at an ecological crossroads on the Great Plains, with six ecosystems contributing to the biodiversity of the region: northern boreal forest, eastern deciduous forest, rocky mountain pine forest, Sandhills prairie, northern mixed–grass prairie, and tallgrass prairie. Biologists have identified 581 plant species, 213 birds, 86 lichen and mosses, 70 butterflies, 44 mammals, 25 fish, 17 reptiles, and 8 amphibians at the preserve. The facilities at the preserve host researchers, students, ranchers, and conservation professionals as they learn about and share their knowledge of the biodiversity of the region.

Top: Bench overlooking the Niobrara Valley Preserve.
Bottom: Norden Chute (public access at Norden Bridge).

A wildfire in 2012 burned over half of the preserve (29,842 acres), however, The Nature Conservancy has taken advantage of this natural event to monitor how the different ecosystems recover and also by hosting fire trainings to educate land managers and others in the best land management techniques. Bison and cattle grazing are other land management techniques being used to mimic the natural conditions and influences that have shaped the Niobrara River Valley and Sandhills prairie. Two bison herds graze two large grasslands, while other pastures are leased to local ranchers to graze their cattle herds.

The hike begins on the west side of Norden Road, opposite a mailbox and entrance road to The Nature Conservancy headquarters. Head southwest from the trailhead kiosk, then turn northwest at 0.13 mile to reach a viewpoint with expansive views of the Niobrara River. The views are epic in scale, with nothing but wilderness extending to

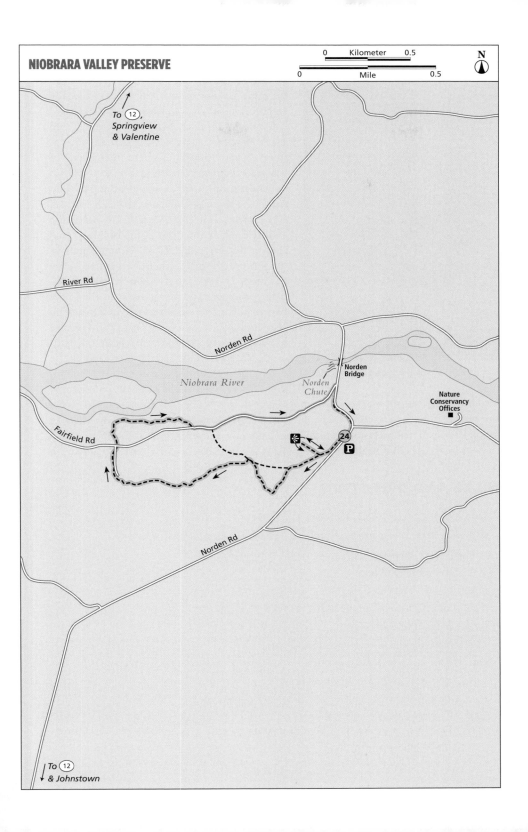

NIOBRARA VALLEY PRESERVE

0   Kilometer   0.5

0   Mile   0.5

N

To (12),
Springview
& Valentine

River Rd

Norden Rd

Niobrara River

Norden
Chute

Norden
Bridge

Nature
Conservancy
Offices

Fairfield Rd

24

P

Norden Rd

To (12)
& Johnstown

the north and west. Return to the main trail and continue southwest. Upon reaching a fork at 0.42 mile, keep left (southwest) to climb to the highest point on the trail at 2,355 feet; the right fork avoids the climb up to this point.

Continue along the trail as it descends, with excellent views again of the Niobrara Valley in front of you. Shortly after the trail bends to the west you will arrive at the turn-off for the short loop to the north; continue straight (west) for the next half mile through bur oak forest. Cross Fairfield Road at 1.4 miles and continue north, then east as the trail runs parallel to the Niobrara River with wetlands to the left (north) of the trail. The mowed grass trail ends at 1.81 miles, where it meets Fairfield Road again. Continue east on the sandy two-track for over one-half mile until reaching Norden Road at 2.41 miles. Turn right (south) to return to the trailhead, or head north to reach Norden Bridge and Norden Chute.

Pincushion cactus flowering in early June. One of the most impressive natural features in the state of Nebraska, Norden Chute is protected by The Nature Conservancy and, as part of the Niobrara National Scenic River, the National Parks Service. A hydraulic feature, not a waterfall, Norden Chute requires floaters and paddlers to portage around the dangerous and turbulent waters. If you'd like to cool off in the river, head to the east side of the bridge where the water is calmer.

MILES AND DIRECTIONS

0.00 Begin at the trailhead and head southwest.

0.13 Turn right (northwest) to follow an out-and-back spur trail to a viewpoint.

0.21 Viewpoint; turn around.

0.31 Turn right (southwest).

0.42 Keep left (southwest).

0.56 Highest elevation on the hike (2,354 feet).

0.78 Continue straight (west).

1.40 Cross Fairfield Road and continue north.

1.81 Continue east on Fairfield Road.

2.41 Turn right (south) onto Norden Road.

   Side trip: Turn left (north) for Norden Bridge and Norden Chute.

2.63 Arrive back at the trailhead.

25 LONG PINE CREEK AND DALE MUNDORF MEMORIAL NATURE TRAIL

Known as Nebraska's Oasis, the crystal-clear waters of Long Pine Creek offer some of the best trout fishing in the state. Inextricably linked to the railroad, the town of Long Pine's current claim to fame is the tallest bridge in Nebraska, now part of the nearly 200-mile Cowboy Trail. At the nearby state recreation area, a 1-mile out-and-back trail leads hikers alongside Lone Pine Creek through cedar forest and underneath US 20 to an idyllic fishing hole. The Dale Mundorf Memorial Nature Trail explores a side canyon in the recreation area with interpretive displays to learn about the local flora and fauna.

Start: Trailhead is located next to campsite #6 and a picnic shelter
Elevation gain: 2,245 to 2,375 feet
Distance: 1.40 miles out and back
Difficulty: Easy
Hiking time: 1 hour
Seasons/schedule: Trails open year-round, sunrise to sunset; good any time of year
Fees and permits: A park entry permit is required and may be purchased at the park, statewide Game and Parks offices and permit vendors, or online at outdoornebraska.gov.
Trail contact: Long Pine State Recreation Area, 87770 Willow Ridge Ave., Long Pine 69217; (402) 684-2921; outdoornebraska.gov/longpine
Dog-friendly: Yes, on leash

Trail surface: Mowed grass and dirt footpaths
Land status: Long Pine State Recreation Area
Nearest town: Long Pine 2.5 miles to the south, Ainsworth 8.5 miles to the west
Maps: USGS Long Pine, NE 2021; park map available online (trails not listed)
Other trail users: None
Special considerations: Long sleeves and pants are recommended in the summer to prevent ticks.
Amenities available: Vault toilets and hand pump hydrants throughout the recreation area
Maximum grade: 12%
Cell service: Moderate reception for most carriers in the recreation area

FINDING THE TRAILHEAD

From Ainsworth, head east on US 20; from Bassett, head west on US 20. Turn south onto Long Pine State Recreation Road, then turn east to enter the park. At the next two forks, keep right to follow the one-way signs. Continue southwest past campsites #2 and #3 before arriving at the camper registration kiosk. The trailhead is next to campsite #6 and a picnic shelter. **GPS:** N42° 32.674′ W99° 42.617′

Trail Conditions: There are no waymarkings on the trail. The trail following Long Pine Creek north from the camping area can be overgrown with vegetation. Sections of the Dale Mundorf Memorial Nature Trail can be slippery and muddy after recent precipitation. Ticks in summer are a nuisance. The trail receives light traffic.

THE HIKE

As you are driving on US 20, between the towns of Ainsworth and Basset, the road plunges down into the forested watershed of Long Pine Creek. The canyon formed by the creek, which empties into the Niobrara River 13 miles to the north, is an oasis on the northern reaches of the Nebraska Sandhills. The town of Long Pine was created in 1876 and grew quickly after it was linked in 1881 with the Chicago and North Western railroad line, known as the Cowboy Line. Railroaders, rustlers, and other frontier icons passed through Long Pine throughout its history as a railroad hub. The last train passed through the town in 1992, however the abandoned line was turned into the Cowboy Trail that begins in Chadron in northwestern Nebraska and runs for nearly 200 miles to Norfolk. The railroad bridge, the tallest in Nebraska, is southwest of the town and is part of the Cowboy Trail.

Top: The Dale Mundorf Memorial Nature Trail begins on the west side of the creek, while another trail heads downstream along the east bank.
Bottom: The trail leads to a tranquil bend in the creek near the parking area for the wildlife management area.

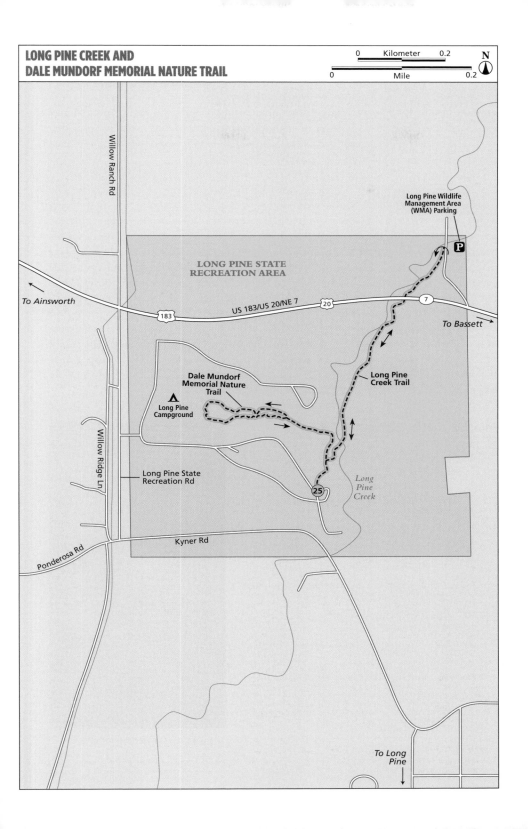

0   Kilometer   0.2

0   Mile   0.2

N

LONG PINE STATE
RECREATION AREA

Long Pine Wildlife
Management Area
(WMA) Parking

P

To Ainsworth

US 183/US 20/NE 7

183   20   7

To Bassett

Long Pine
Creek Trail

Dale Mundorf
Memorial Nature
Trail

Long Pine
Campground

Willow Ranch Rd

Willow Ridge Ln

Long Pine State
Recreation Rd

25

Long
Pine
Creek

Ponderosa Rd

Kyner Rd

To Long
Pine

Long Pine State Recreation Area lies northwest of the town along US 20. The park is popular with campers and anglers, as Long Pine Creek has some of the best trout fishing in the state. The crystal clear, shallow water is also a pleasure to wade through on a hot summer day. The Dale Mundorf Memorial Nature Trail is another good activity in the summer heat, as it explores a cool, shady canyon to the west of the creek. Another trail runs parallel to Long Pine Creek on its eastern bank, passing through cedar and pine forest. While the Long Pine area is part of the Sandhills, the creek empties into the Niobrara and thus has been included in the Niobrara Valley section.

Begin at the trailhead next to campsite #6 and head north. Cross the footbridge and look for a narrow footpath as it heads north along the eastern bank of the creek. The grass grows tall here, so it's best to wear long pants and sleeves to avoid ticks and thorny plants. There are several points along this trail that provide access to the creek. Continue north until reaching a clearing before the highway. There is a steep path underneath the overpass; follow it and continue north until it joins an unnamed road at 0.41 mile. This road leads to a parking area for the Long Pine Creek Wildlife Management Area. The parking area is the terminus of the trail, but before heading back to the footbridge, take the narrow footpath at 0.42 mile that leads to a beautiful bend in Long Pine Creek, a secluded spot to take a refreshing dip or cast a fishing line.

Once you have returned to the footbridge over Long Pine Creek at 0.8 mile, cross it, then turn left to access the Dale Mundorf Memorial Nature Trail. The trail climbs 125 feet over a short distance to a viewpoint on the western edge of the recreation area. Follow the loop as it snakes through a deep and narrow ravine to return to the Dale Mundorf trailhead at 1.3 miles and then campsite #6 at 1.4 miles.

MILES AND DIRECTIONS

0.00 Begin at the Long Pine Creek trailhead next to campsite #6 and head north.

0.10 Turn right (east) and cross the footbridge over Long Pine Creek, then follow the footpath north along the creek.

0.32 Continue north underneath US 20.

0.41 Unnamed road.

0.42 Turn left (west) onto a narrow footpath.

0.44 Long Pine Creek; turn around and return via the same path to the footbridge.

0.80 Cross the footbridge over the creek, then turn left (north).

0.90 Head west onto the Dale Mundorf Memorial Nature Trail.

0.95 Keep right and climb up the stairs.

1.10 Viewpoint.

1.20 Keep right to head toward Long Pine Creek.

1.30 Turn right (south).

1.40 Arrive back at the trailhead.

The hike passes underneath US 20.

HONORABLE MENTION

G COWBOY TRAIL

The Cowboy Trail is a 195-mile path that follows the abandoned Chicago and North Western railroad from Norfolk to Valentine, dubbed the "Cowboy Line." There are plans to extend the trail to Chadron, which would make it the longest rails-to-trails path in the United States at 321 miles. This easy and short section of the Cowboy Trail uses a trailhead near Valentine to cross the 148-foot Cowboy Trail Bridge that spans the Niobrara River, offering expansive views of the Niobrara Valley and plenty of bird-watching opportunities.

Start: Cowboy Trail State Recreation parking area
Elevation gain: 2,522 to 2,560 feet
Distance: 1.70 miles out and back to Valentine Bridge
Difficulty: Easy
Hiking time: 1 hour
Seasons/schedule: Trail open year-round; best in spring and fall
Fees and permits: None
Trail contact: Nebraska Game and Parks Commission Recreational Trails; outdoornebraska.gov/cowboytrail/
Dog-friendly: Yes, on leash
Trail surface: Crushed limestone
Land status: Nebraska Game and Parks Commission

Nearest town: Valentine 3.5 miles to the northwest
Maps: USGS Valentine South, NE 2021; interactive trail map available at outdoornebraska.gov/cowboytrail
Other trail users: Equestrians and cyclists
Special considerations: There is no shade or water along the trail. People with a fear of heights or vertigo may find the bridge crossing difficult.
Amenities available: Parking at the trailhead
Maximum grade: 0%
Cell service: Full coverage at the trailhead and on the trail

FINDING THE TRAILHEAD

From Valentine, drive south on US 20. After 3.6 miles, turn left (east) after the sign for Cowboy Trail State Recreation Parking Area.
GPS: N42° 50.040' W100° 31.065

Trail Conditions: Level-grade trail that follows an old railroad bed. The crushed limestone trail is wide and well maintained. There are no intersecting trails. The trail to the bridge receives moderate traffic.

The Cowboy Trail crosses the Niobrara River over an old rail bridge.

Hundreds of thousands of sandhill cranes stop along the Central Platte Valley from mid-February to mid-April every spring.

PLATTE VALLEY

The Platte is unassuming as rivers go: flat, shallow, and often dry in summer. In fact, Nebraska gets its name from the Platte, which the Otoe called Ñí Brásge, meaning "flat water."

Annual bird migrations, however, turn the Platte River Valley into an epic landscape every spring. The Big Bend Reach of the Central Platte Valley lies within the Central Flyway, an important migratory route for birds, most famously sandhill and whooping cranes. While hiking during the spring migration is discouraged to protect the birds, summer is an excellent time to hike the numerous prairies and wet meadows along the Platte as wildflowers bloom and native grasses like big bluestem grow to more than 6 feet tall. Thanks to conservation efforts led by The Nature Conservancy, National Audubon Society, and other organizations, future generations will be able to witness the annual migrations and wonders of the prairies.

The sandy beach allows access to the North Platte River at Buffalo Bill State Recreation Area.

26 NORTH PLATTE RIVER TRAIL

The North Platte River Trail follows the west bank of the North Platte River near Scout's Rest, the home ranch of Buffalo Bill Cody from 1886 to 1913. The trail takes hikers right along the North Platte River, offering scenic views of the river and wildlife including songbirds, shorebirds, waterfowl, deer, and migrating cranes in the spring.

Start: North end of campground
Elevation gain: 2,679 to 2,871 feet
Distance: 1.86 miles out and back
Difficulty: Easy
Hiking time: 1 hour
Seasons/schedule: Trails open year-round, sunrise to sunset; best in spring during the sandhill crane migration
Fees and permits: A park entry permit is required and may be purchased at the park, statewide Game and Parks offices and permit vendors, or online at outdoornebraska.gov.
Trail contact: Buffalo Bill State Recreation Area, 2921 Scouts Rest Ranch Rd., North Platte 69101; (308) 535-8035; outdoornebraska.gov/buffalobillsra/

Dog-friendly: Yes, on leash
Trail surface: Mostly grass and sand
Land status: Buffalo Bill State Recreation Area
Nearest town: North Platte
Maps: USGS North Platte West, NE 2021; available online at outdoornebraska.gov
Other trail users: None
Special considerations: The park map lists other trails that explore the floodplain to the southeast of the campground.
Amenities available: Vault toilets and water at the parking area for the beach and trailhead
Maximum grade: 0%
Cell service: Good coverage by most carriers

FINDING THE TRAILHEAD

From exit 177 on I-80, head north on US 83 for 1.3 miles. Turn west onto US 30 and drive for 1.6 miles until reaching N Buffalo Bill Avenue. Turn north and continue for 1 mile. Keep right to enter the state recreation area. Continue north on the park road until reaching the campground. The day-use parking area and trailhead are on the northern end of the campground. **GPS:** N41° 10.372′ W100° 47.338′

Trail Conditions: The trail is not waymarked and oftentimes the trail itself is hard to distinguish in the tall grasses alongside the river. Ticks are common in summer. Areas can be muddy or wet. The trail receives light to moderate traffic.

THE HIKE

William F. Cody was born in eastern Iowa on the Mississippi River in 1846, then moved to Kansas with his family when he was seven years old. After the death of his father, Cody found work supplying buffalo meat to railroad workers, then served as a scout for the Union Army in the Civil War. In 1868, Cody won a hunting contest in Kansas, earning the nickname that would become famous across the United States and Europe.

Buffalo Bill Cody's fame skyrocketed after the publication of a dime novel fictionalizing his adventures in the Wild West—over 1,500 dime novels propagated tall tales about him over the course of his life. Cody continued to hunt buffalo, leading wealthy clients and dignitaries on hunting trips. He also began to perform in theater productions in the

Buffalo Bill's ranch is located nearby at Buffalo Bill State Historical Park.

1870s but stopped briefly to participate in the United States' war against the Sioux. His return to the stage in New England was met with shock and controversy after he displayed the scalp of a Cheyenne warrior he killed in a duel. Cody later spoke for Native American rights when he visited Wounded Knee shortly after the 1890 massacre.

Cody became one of the nation's first pitchmen, appearing in advertisements for cigars, bourbon, rifles, and western clothing. He was portrayed in more than thirty films and received the Medal of Honor from the US Army. He gained most notoriety, however, from his traveling exhibition about the American frontier. The first Buffalo Bill's Wild West show took place in 1883 and ran for thirty years, touring across the country and even Europe. Noted figures from the American West joined the exhibition such as Annie Oakley, Black Elk, Calamity Jane, and Sitting Bull.

Scout's Rest, located on the river near North Platte, became Cody's base of operations for 17 years and his base of operations during the Wild West period. The show paid for the two-story "Mansion on the Prairie" and the large barn where Cody kept his ranch horses. The state recreation area lies to the east of the ranch along the North Platte River, which this hike follows downstream for over half a mile. The trailhead is located on the north end of the campground loop. There is no trailhead signage, so head southeast along the beach. Pass a large cottonwood on your right, then look for a footpath through the

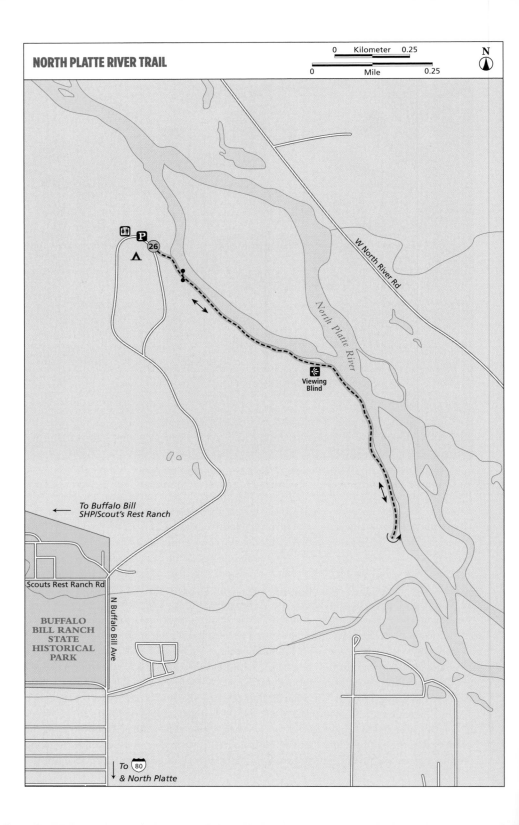

NORTH PLATTE RIVER TRAIL

0   Kilometer   0.25

0   Mile   0.25

N

W North River Rd

North Platte River

Viewing
Blind

26

P

To Buffalo Bill
SHP/Scout's Rest Ranch

Scouts Rest Ranch Rd

N Buffalo Bill Ave

BUFFALO
BILL RANCH
STATE
HISTORICAL
PARK

To 80
& North Platte

The North Platte River Trail follows the shallow river.

grass alongside the river. Pass through the gate at 0.13 mile and continue southeast along the river. The lack of trail developments gives a wild feeling to the hike and it is not uncommon to see a variety of birds and other wildlife. The viewing blind at 0.48 mile is an ideal spot to see wildlife.

Continue for nearly one–half mile before reaching a marshy area where the footpath disappears in the mud and reeds. Turn around to return to the campground via the same path alongside the river.

MILES AND DIRECTIONS

0.00 Begin at the beach and head southeast along the river bank.

0.13 Pass through the gate and continue south-east along the river bank.

0.48 Viewing blind.

0.93 Turn around and return via the same path along the river.

1.74 Gate.

1.86 Arrive back at the beach and parking area.

Goldenrod blooming at the end of summer at the campground.

27 DERR HOUSE PRAIRIE

Derr House Prairie is part of a chain of grasslands and wetlands, known collectively as the Platte River Prairies, between Grand Island and Kearney. The Nature Conservancy owns and manages the prairies, using prescribed burns and grazing to maintain plant diversity. Derr House Prairie offers a 3-mile saunter via the West Trail and East Trail loops. Both trails traverse restored prairies, while the East Trail includes native sandhills prairie. The proximity to I-80 makes this hike an ideal spring or summer stroll when the prairie is ablaze with wildflowers such as blazing star, purple prairie clover, prairie larkspur, wild bergamot, and more.

Start: West Trailhead next to Derr House
Elevation gain: 1,959 to 2,040 feet
Distance: 3.02-mile double loop
Difficulty: Easy due to flat terrain
Hiking time: 1–2 hours
Seasons/schedule: Trails open year-round, sunrise to sunset; best in spring for prairie wildflowers
Fees and permits: None
Trail contact: The Nature Conservancy, 13650 S Platte River Dr., Wood River 68883; (402) 694-4191; nature.org/en-us/get-involved/how-to-help/places-we-protect/platte-river-prairies/
Dog-friendly: No
Trail surface: Mowed grass
Land status: The Nature Conservancy

Nearest town: Grand Island 23 miles to the northeast
Maps: USGS Prosser, NE 2021; paper trail guide at Derr House (if available) and at The Nature Conservancy website (see trail contact)
Other trail users: None
Special considerations: There is no shade or water available at the Derr House or along the trail. Cattle might be present grazing on portions of the prairie. Ticks are common during the summer.
Amenities available: None
Maximum grade: 6%
Cell service: Full coverage at the Derr House and along all sections of the trails

FINDING THE TRAILHEAD

At exit 300 on I-80, take NE 11 south for 2 miles. As NE 11 curves sharply east, turn south onto Platte River Drive. Shortly after turning, veer right onto a gravel driveway leading to Derr House. The West Trailhead is on the south side of Derr House. **GPS:** N40° 44.011' W98° 34.711

Trail Conditions: The mowed grass trails are not waymarked, but they are easy to follow. Cattle may be present during the year grazing on sections of the prairie; be respectful and do not approach cattle. There are tall grasses along most of the trail, so it is recommended to wear long pants during tick season. The trails receive light foot traffic.

THE HIKE

The Nature Conservancy owns six parcels of land and has five easements along the Platte River, all comprising the Platte River Prairies complex. The Nature Conservancy has restored some of the cropland to prairie and uses prescribed burns and grazing to manage the land. Derr House Prairie, located just south of I-80 at the Wood River exit, contains significant upland and wetland habitat for migratory birds as well as native plants and animals. The property includes two trails divided by Platte River Drive, West Trail and East Trail.

West Trail crosses lowland grasslands that were restored and seeded from 1999 to 2002. Big bluestem, indiangrass, Canada milkvetch, purple prairie clover, and wild bergamot are just some of the many plant species found on West Trail. Cross the road to the trailhead for East Trail. This section of Derr House Prairie contains both native and restored prairie. The native prairie is located on the southern half of this tract of land and contains sandhills prairie. Sand lovegrass, sand dropseed, needle-and-thread, stiff sunflower, blazing star, spiderwort, and more can be found along East Trail on this prairie, which was restored and seeded in 2002.

Derr House Prairie is part of the Platte River Prairies managed by The Nature Conservancy.

Derr House Prairie also provides habitat for numerous grassland bird species. Grasshopper sparrows, bobolinks, dickcissels, upland sandpipers, bobwhite quail, sedge wrens, and eastern and western meadowlarks can all be seen and heard on the prairie. Its proximity to the Platte River also makes Derr House an attractive destination during the crane migration in the spring.

Sunflowers in early fall near Derr House.

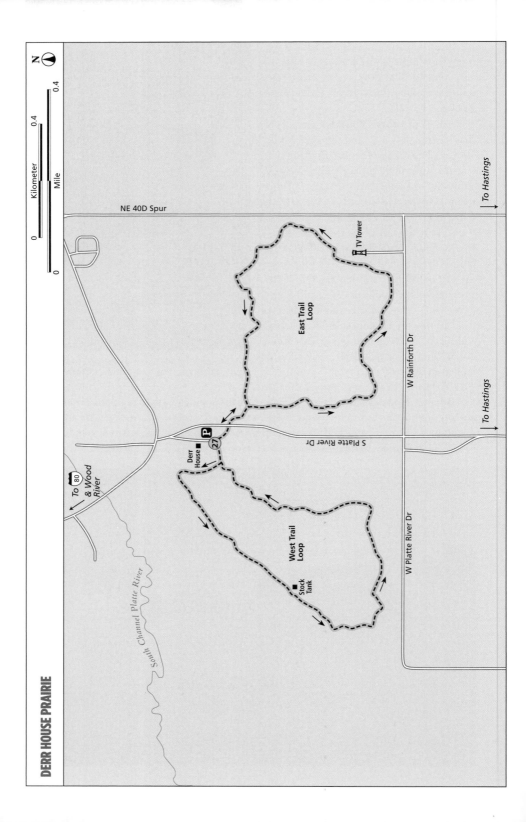

DERR HOUSE PRAIRIE

N

Kilometer
0   0.4

Mile
0   0.4

South Channel Platte River

To 80 & Wood River

NE 40D Spur

Derr House

P

27

East Trail Loop

TV Tower

West Trail Loop

Stock Tank

S Platte River Dr

W Rainforth Dr

W Platte River Dr

To Hastings

To Hastings

Left: West Trail winding through the prairie in winter.
Right: East Trail traverses a sandhill prairie.

Combine West and East Trails to make an easy yet enjoyable 3-mile hike. The mailbox outside Derr House has an informative booklet to browse before you begin your hike. Begin from Derr House at the gate for West Trail. The 1.45-mile loop follows a mowed path in the grass through the wet meadow. There are some faint trails that intersect with West Trail, so just continue on the same mowed path until returning to the trailhead. Cross Platte River Drive at 1.51 miles to reach the trailhead for East Trail. This loop is slightly longer and also has slightly more elevation change, as the trail climbs a hill near the tower. The southern half of the loop passes through Sandhills prairie; try to notice the subtle differences between it and the wet meadow to the west.

MILES AND DIRECTIONS

0.00   Begin at West Trailhead and head south.

0.05   Keep right (northwest) at the fork.

0.48   Cross a two-track trail and continue heading south on a mowed path.

1.21   Cross a two-track trail; continue north.

1.41   Reach a fork and keep right to return to West Trailhead.

1.45   Reach the West Trailhead; turn south onto the gravel driveway and head toward the road.

1.51   Cross Platte River Drive heading east to access East Trailhead at the gated entrance.

1.58   Reach a fork; keep right (south).

1.69   Cross a two-track trail; continue heading south.

2.01   Heading east, cross a mowed path and continue heading east.

2.75   Continue west.

2.97   Reach a fork, keeping right to return to East Trailhead.

3.02   Arrive at the East Trailhead.

28 CRANE TRUST PRAIRIE TRAIL

Located on the Big Bend of the Central Platte River, the most important staging area for sandhill cranes along the Central Flyway, Crane Trust is a bird-watchers' mecca. Endangered species also make a stopover during their migration, including whooping cranes, interior least terns, and piping plovers. In addition to guided experiences during migration season, Crane Trust offers 10 miles of trails. This hike makes use of the trail system for a 4.5-mile loop, bordering riparian woods along the Platte River before wandering through the grasses and wildflowers of Ruge Prairie. A small herd of bison graze on the pastures; trails on these pastures are closed when bison are present.

Start: Behind the Nature Center on its south side
Elevation gain: 1,925 to 1,982 feet
Distance: 4.54-mile loop
Difficulty: Easy due to flat terrain
Hiking time: 2–3 hours
Seasons/schedule: Trails open from 9 a.m. to 4 p.m., Mon to Sat; trails are closed during holidays (including from Dec 25 to Jan 1). Trail hours change during migration season; check with the Nature Center.
Fees and permits: None
Trail contact: Crane Trust, 9325 S Alda Rd., Wood River 68883; (308) 382-1820; cranetrust.org
Dog-friendly: No
Trail surface: Mowed grass
Land status: Crane Trust
Nearest town: Grand Island 14 miles to the northeast

Maps: USGS Alda, NE 2021; available inside the Nature Center and online at cranetrust.org
Other trail users: None
Special considerations: Check with the Nature Center for trail closures during migration season; the trails are closed until the sandhill cranes have left Crane Trust property, usually around 10 a.m. Additionally, the bison herd is moved to different pastures throughout the year and trails may be closed to protect the bison and the public. Call the center before visiting to check the status of the trails.
Amenities available: Water, rest rooms, and information available at the Nature Center
Maximum grade: 1%
Cell service: Full coverage at the Nature Center and on the trails

FINDING THE TRAILHEAD

At exit 305 on I-80, head south on S Alda Road. The Crane Trust Nature and Visitor Center is immediately south of the interstate. **GPS:** N40° 47.759' W98° 29.531

Trail Conditions: There is no shade along most of the trail. The trails are not marked, but with the map provided at the visitor center (or online) they are easy to follow. The trails are mowed grass and maintain their general location each year. Long pants are recommended during tick season as the trail passes through tall grasses.

THE HIKE

Beginning in mid-February and lasting into April, the skies over the Central Platte River are darkened by millions of geese, cranes, and waterfowl, the din of nearby I-80 drowned out by their cacophony of honks, quacks, and rattles. Crane Trust owns several tracts along this stretch of the north channel of the Platte River, where it restores and

A windmill on Ruge Prairie in late winter.

Crane Trust offers spectacular guided tours during the annual spring sandhill crane migration.

manages critical habitat for sandhill cranes, whooping cranes, and other migratory birds. The Crane Trust Nature and Visitor Center near Alda operates a gift shop and art gallery and offers guided experiences during the crane migration in spring. If you wish to hike the trails during the migration season, check with the Nature and Visitor Center before as the trails are closed until the cranes have left after the morning roost (usually by 10 a.m.). Additionally, Crane Trust manages a small herd of bison that graze the prairies and pastures on their land. To protect the bison and the public, the land management team closes trails on areas where bison are ranging. Always call the Crane Trust before visiting to inquire about the status of the trails.

The hike to Ruge Prairie begins behind the center in a butterfly garden. There are several interpretive panels along the Nature Trail, an asphalt path leading to two foot-bridges spanning the north channel of the Platte River. There is also a 35-foot observation tower offering sweeping vistas of the braided river valley and a chance to see where the bison herd are ranging.

After crossing the bridge, turn left at 0.31 mile to head west on River Trail. The mowed grass path divides the riparian woodland from the rolling grasslands to the south. Crane Trust's trail map lists a spur named Wooded Trail that meanders for three-tenths of a mile through the riparian forest. Continue east on River Trail, which runs parallel to the Platte River for a leisurely mile and a half before reaching Gate D at 1.66 miles; head south through Gate D on Prairie Trail.

The entire system of trails within Ruge Prairie total over 5 miles, of which this hike uses nearly 3 miles; feel free to create your own hike to explore the prairie. After walking south along a fence, Prairie Trail bends southwest at 1.89 miles through open prairie

CRANE TRUST PRAIRIE TRAIL

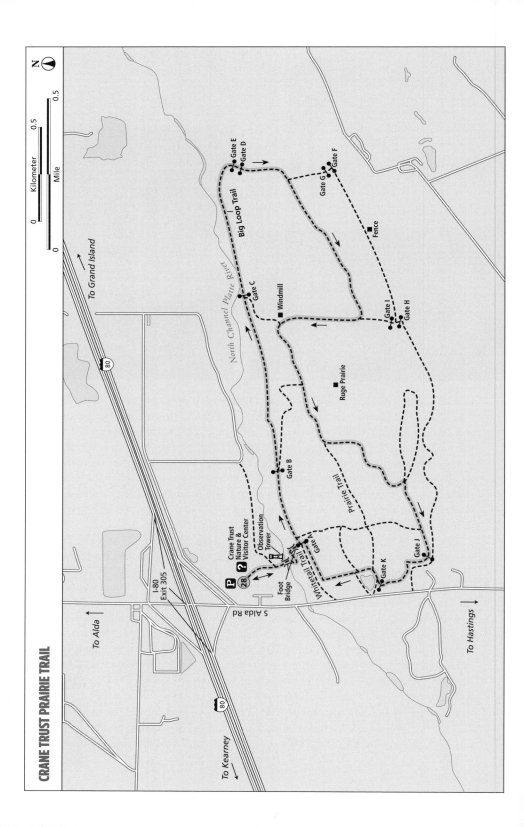

N

Kilometer
0   0.5   0.5

Mile
0   0.5

To Grand Island

To Alda

To Kearney

To Hastings

I-80
Exit 305

80

80

S Alda Rd

North Channel Platte River

Crane Trust
Nature &
Visitor Center

Observation
Tower

Foot
Bridge

P

28

Whitetail Trail

Prairie Trail

Big Loop Trail

Gate A

Gate B

Gate C

Gate D

Gate E

Gate F

Gate G

Gate H

Gate I

Gate J

Gate K

Windmill

Fence

Ruge Prairie

dotted with the occasional tree. Many of these trees are surrounded by dense shrubs, such as serviceberry and sumac, which provide ideal shelter for whitetail deer.

Turn north at 2.42 miles to hike toward a windmill, then turn at 2.67 miles and head west through the middle of Ruge Prairie. There are several bison wallows along the trail as it heads southwest through the prairie. Take the left at a fork after 3.12 miles and follow Prairie Trail to the southwest corner of Ruge Prairie. A lone, large cottonwood at 3.49 miles marks a junction: to the east, a short loop returning to this junction; to the left, Prairie Trail continues west. Head that direction, reaching Gate J at 3.77 miles and turning north to follow Whitetail Trail along the western boundary of Ruge Prairie. Reach the footbridges over the north channel of the Platte River at 4.34 miles and then continue along Nature Trail until reaching the Nature Center.

MILES AND DIRECTIONS

0.00 Begin on the south side of the Nature Center and head south on the Nature Trail.

0.11 Pass an observation tower on your left; continue south toward the bridges.

0.13 Cross two walking bridges across the Platte River.

0.31 Turn left (east) onto River Trail.

0.61 Reach a junction; continue straight (east) on River Trail.

1.18 Reach a junction; continue straight (east) on River Trail.

1.66 Reach Gates D and E; pass through Gate D heading south on Prairie Trail.

1.89 Reach a junction; continue straight (southwest) on Prairie Trail.

2.42 Reach a junction; turn right (north) to continue on Prairie Trail toward a windmill.

2.67 Reach a fork at the windmill; keep left (west) on Prairie Trail.

2.92 Continue straight (west) on Prairie Trail.

3.12 Reach a fork; keep left (southwest).

3.49 At a large cottonwood, turn sharply right (west) to continue on Prairie Trail.

> **Side trip:** Veer left at the junction to complete a short loop that returns to this junction.

3.70 Continue straight (west) on Prairie Trail.

> **Option:** Turn right (north) to return to Gate A and the footbridges.

3.77 Reach Gate J; turn right to head north on Whitetail Trail.

3.99 Reach a junction near Gate K and a pond; keep right (east) to go around the pond.

4.02 Turn left to head north with the pond on your left (west).

4.09 Reach a junction; continue straight (north).

4.34 Turn left (north) at Gate A and cross over the Platte River on the walking bridges.

4.54 Arrive back at the Nature Center.

The trails on Ruge Prairie may be closed due to the presence of bison.

29 GJERLOFF PRAIRIE

Managed by Prairie Plains Resource Institute, Gjerloff Prairie's "open vistas, intimate small valleys and draws, steep cliffs, ravines, and Platte River frontage" make it one of the best examples of loess hills prairie in central Nebraska. Prescribed burns and grazing are used to restore the prairie bluffs to their former pre-settlement state. The prairie explodes with blooming wildflowers in spring and summer and copper-colored grasses in autumn. The Institute offers many educational and recreational events, such as guided hikes to view wildlife or identify wildflowers.

Start: Charles L. Whitney Education Center
Elevation gain: 1,709 to 1,847 feet
Distance: 2.32-mile loop
Difficulty: Easy
Hiking time: 1 hour
Seasons/schedule: Open year-round, sunrise to sunset; best in spring and summer for wildflowers
Fees and permits: None
Trail contact: Prairie Plains Resource Institute; 1307 L St., Aurora 68818; (402) 694-5535; prairieplains.org
Dog-friendly: Yes, on leash
Trail surface: Mowed grass
Land status: Prairie Plains Resource Institute
Nearest town: Central City to the north, Aurora to the south

Maps: USGS Central City West, NE 2021; available online at prairieplains .org/preserves/gjerloff-prairie.html
Other trail users: None
Special considerations: Check the Prairie Plains Resource Institute website for events like guided wildflower hikes. Only trails north of the education center are frequently mowed. The southern part of the preserve is open to explore but the trails may not be visible.
Amenities available: Portable toilet at the parking area next to the education center
Maximum grade: 8%
Cell service: Unreliable coverage; alternates between weak and adequate

FINDING THE TRAILHEAD

From Grand Island, head northeast on US 30 for 9.2 miles. Turn right (east) onto F Road for 2.1 miles until reaching 8th Road / Bader Park Road. Turn right (south) onto 8th Road. After crossing the Platte River, keep left (east) onto W 21 Road. Turn left (north) onto N M Road. After 0.9 mile, keep left (north) to continue on N M Road for 0.6 mile until reaching the Charles L. Whitney Education Center. From I-80, take exit 332 and head north on NE 14 for 12 miles. Turn left (west) onto Highway 41C / E 22 Road and pass through the town of Marquette. After almost 4 miles, turn right (north) onto N M Road and drive until you reach the Charles L. Whitney Education Center. **GPS:** N41° 0.720′ W98° 4.380

Trail Conditions: Low to moderate foot traffic. The mowed grass trails are not way-marked but are mostly easy to follow; in some areas the grass is short due to cattle grazing but the path is visible. Be respectful and cautious if cattle are present grazing on the prairie.

THE HIKE

Prairie Plains Resource Institute was founded in 1980 in Aurora to preserve, maintain, and restore native prairies and wetlands. The sites managed by Prairie Plains offer

Left: Thistles and other wildflowers that bloom throughout the summer.
Center: Charles L. Whitney Education Center at Gjerloff Prairie.
Right: Copper hues of big bluestem in winter.

community education, recreation, and sustainable economic development. Prairie Plains purchased Gjerloff Prairie in 2002 and over subsequent years have managed 390 acres of native and restored prairie bluffs along the Platte River. The large, refurbished barn was transported from another nearby farm and fulfills one of the founding principles of Prairie Plains: "To provide a center where persons of mutual interest in the natural history, horticulture, agriculture, human culture, sociology, development and the welfare of the Plains may exchange ideas for the benefit and welfare of the members thereof and the state and the nation." Check their website as Prairie Plains offers many wonderful events open to the public, such as hikes to identify the many wildflowers seen on the prairie, including Carolina anemone, purple prairie clover, and larkspur.

The trailhead to the northern trails is located near a fire ring north of the education center. Head north until the trail bends west at 0.13 mile and then north again to pass through a fence. There is a wooden ladder to cross the fence in case the gate is closed to keep cattle confined on the prairie. The trail heads north for almost a half mile through the undulating prairie bluffs. Reach the Platte River via a gate at 0.5 mile where there are several logs to sit on near the riverbank. Spend time viewing wildlife along the riverbank before returning to the loop.

The trail runs northeast parallel to the river for another half mile until it reaches a grove of eastern redcedar in the northeastern corner of the preserve. Here you have the option of taking a shortcut after 1.15 miles into the prairie bluffs, however, we will continue south along the eastern boundary of the preserve following the line of a barbed wire fence. Notice the density of eastern redcedar on the east side of the fence while the prairie itself is largely free of this aggressive native species thanks to land management by Prairie Plains. The trail winds through breaks in the prairie bluffs before it turns west

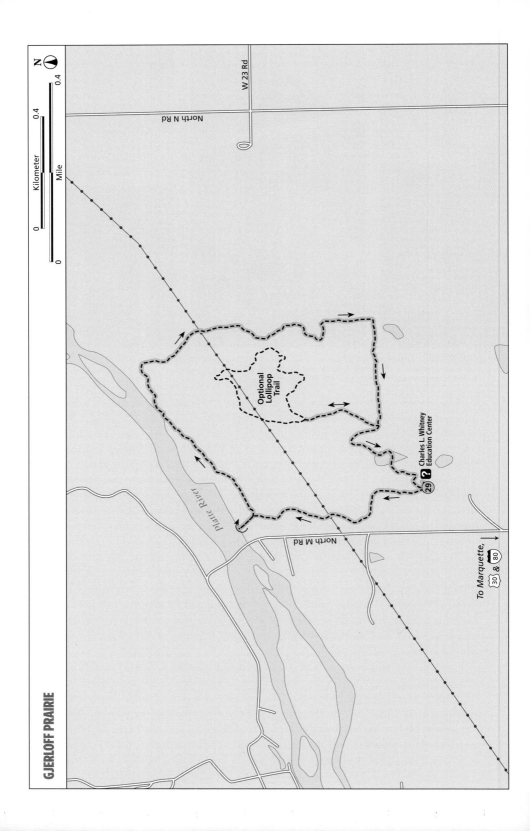

GJERLOFF PRAIRIE

Charles L. Whitney
Education Center

Optional
Lollipop
Trail

Platte River

North M Rd

North N Rd

W 23 Rd

To Marquette,
30 & 80

29

N

Kilometer
0   0.4   0.4

Mile
0   0.4

toward the education center. Before reaching the center, reach a junction at 1.98 miles where you can take a nice side trip on a 1-mile lollipop loop that winds around the top of the prairie bluffs with excellent views of the Platte River. The final jaunt to the education center requires climbing down to a pond and then back up to the education center.

MILES AND DIRECTIONS

0.00 Begin on the west side of Charles L. Whitney Education Center; head north past the north deck and toward a fire ring; take the mowed path heading north into the prairie bluffs and toward the river.

0.10 Reach a fork; keep left (north).

0.13 Trail bends to the left (west).

0.20 Pass through a fence heading north into prairie bluffs.

0.22 Reach a fork; keep right (north).

0.30 Reach a fork; keep right (north).

0.42 Continue straight (north) toward the river.

0.47 Reach a junction; continue straight toward the river (return here after exploring the river).

0.50 Pass through the gate to reach the river bank.

0.62 Return to the junction; turn left (east) to follow the trail parallel to the river.

0.72 Pass a stock tank on the left; continue east.

0.84 Reach a fork; keep left (east) to follow the mowed path running parallel to a barbed wire fence and river on the left (the right fork leads into the hills but is not marked on the map available online).

0.98 Reach a fork; keep right (east).

1.09 Reach a fork; keep right (south).

1.15 Reach a fork; keep left (south).

Option: Right fork is a shortcut to climb up into prairie bluffs.

1.26 Reach a junction; keep left (south).

Option: Right fork leads into prairie bluffs.

1.73 Reach a junction; turn right (west), to follow the path parallel to an electric fence.

1.98 Reach a junction; continue straight (west) to return to the education center. The trail descends north, then bends to climb south up a hill to the education center.

Option: Turn right (north) to complete a 1-mile lollipop trail that winds along the top of the prairie bluffs with views of the river.

2.10 Pass through a fence; continue south through an ungrazed portion of prairie with the education center in front on the hill.

2.20 Reach a fork; keep left.

2.25 Reach the education center; keep right.

2.28 Reach the fire ring and turn left to return to the parking lot.

2.32 Arrive back at the parking area.

30 HACKBERRY TRAIL AND RED CEDAR TRAIL

With its convenient location between Omaha and Lincoln, Schramm Park State Recreation Area is a popular family destination for outdoor activities. Families can spend the day enjoying the aquarium, fish hatchery ponds, and picnic areas while also exploring 3 miles of trails that loop through cedar and oak woodlands along the Platte River. Spring is an excellent time to visit as the woodlands teem with migrating warblers. A meditation shelter on Hackberry Trail offers a peaceful retreat, while the suspension bridge is a highlight on Red Cedar Trail. Don't forget the River View Trail across the highway for a splendid view of the Platte River.

Start: Nature Trail west entrance near the Fish Hatchery Museum
Elevation gain: 1,007 to 1,189 feet
Distance: 2.12-mile loop
Difficulty: Easy due to short distance and excellent trail system
Hiking time: 1 hour
Seasons/schedule: Trails are open year-round, sunrise to sunset; best in spring for warbler migration
Fees and permits: Valid park permit; available for purchase at the Schramm Education Center, kiosks near the park entrance, and online at outdoornebraska.gov.
Trail contact: Schramm Park State Recreation Area, 21502 W NE 31, Gretna 68028; (402) 332-3901 outdoornebraska.gov/schramm
Dog-friendly: Yes, on leash
Trail surface: Dirt and rock
Land status: Schramm Park State Recreation Area

Nearest town: Gretna 9 miles to the north
Maps: USGS Ashland East, NE 2021 and USGS Springfield, NE 2021; trail map posted at the trailhead and available online on the park's website (see trail contact)
Other trail users: Bikers and runners
Special considerations: Avoid hiking on muddy trails to prevent trail degradation.
Amenities available: Restrooms, water, and information at the Schramm Education Center; restrooms near the Fish Hatchery Museum
Maximum grade: 13%
Cell service: Good reception for most carriers at the Schramm Education Center and parking area; limited coverage on the trails underneath the forest canopy

FINDING THE TRAILHEAD

From I-80 exit 432, head south on NE 31 for approximately 5 miles. At the entrance to Schramm Park State Recreation Area, turn left (north) to access the parking area in front of the Schramm Education Center. A trail on the east side of the education center heads toward the historic fish hatchery; Hackberry Trail begins at a trail bulletin board before the Fish Hatchery Museum and Ponds. **GPS:** N41° 1.375' W96° 15.191'

Trail Conditions: The trails are superbly maintained and waymarked. The trail map available at kiosks and online is helpful. The trails receive heavy traffic.

The excellent trail system makes hiking the park easy.

THE HIKE

Schramm Park State Recreation Area began as a fish hatchery in 1882. The hatchery produced fish for state waters but was also a popular family picnic spot. Families enjoyed the rolling hills and woodlands along the Platte River, and after 1974 when the fish hatchery ceased operations, the area was transferred to the state parks department to continue as a recreation area open to the public. The Hatch House Museum, constructed in 1914, is open to the public during the summer months from Memorial Day to Labor Day with interpretive displays about fish management. The surrounding ponds hold rainbow trout and are an excellent area for picnics. The Schramm Education Center has renovated and expanded aquariums displaying the natural aquatic habitats found in Nebraska.

The 3-mile trail system at Schramm Park explores the wooded canyons and bluffs north of the Schramm Education Center. Hackberry Trail is a short nature loop with interpretive displays about the local flora and fauna. Red Cedar Trail explores the northern reaches of the park and crosses a creek several times, with one crossing via a suspension bridge. The park map lists the aforementioned names for the two trails, while signage on the trails refer to Hackberry Trail as Nature Trail #1 and Red Cedar Trail as Nature Trail #2 and Backwoods Trail #2. Navigation is easy on the trails but be aware of mountain bikers and trail runners, as the trails are popular with both.

The longer loop using both Hackberry and Red Cedar Trails can be hiked in either direction; the hike described here follows the loop in a clockwise direction beginning at the trail bulletin board west of the fish hatchery museum on a park road. Head north on Hackberry Trail as it follows a small creek with maintenance buildings on the other side. A short spur trail at 0.25 mile leads to a meditation shelter in the middle of the woods where you can bird-watch or contemplate the serene forest.

To continue on the long loop, leave Hackberry Trail at 0.35 mile by turning left (northwest) at the sign for Nature Trail #2 (Red Cedar Trail). There is a large bur oak at the beginning of the trail. Cross the creek via the suspension bridge at 0.61 mile, then

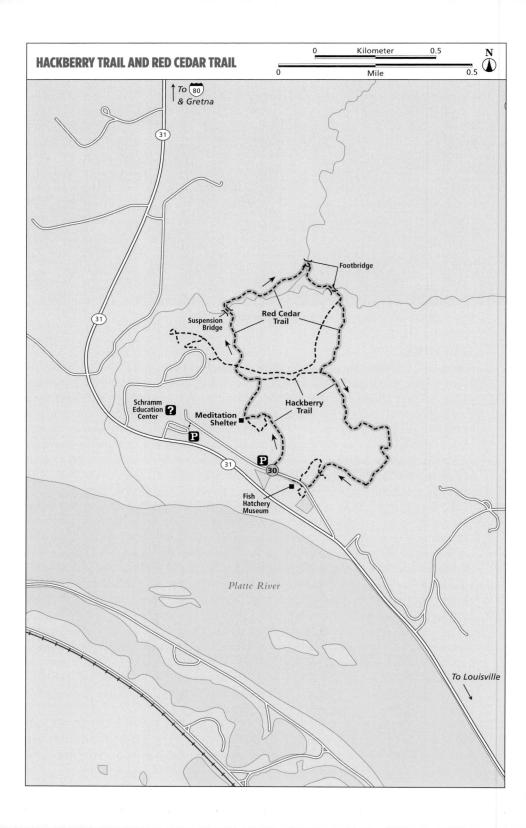

HACKBERRY TRAIL AND RED CEDAR TRAIL

Kilometer

0   0.5

Mile

0   0.5

N

To 80 & Gretna

31

31

Footbridge

Red Cedar Trail

Suspension Bridge

Hackberry Trail

Schramm Education Center

Meditation Shelter

P

P

31

30

Fish Hatchery Museum

Platte River

To Louisville

continue east on Backwoods Trail #2 (Red Cedar Trail). Pass two Adirondack shelters to the north of the trail at 0.78 mile and continue heading east. Cross another bridge at 0.9 mile and a second bridge at the 1-mile mark of the hike. The trail along this northern section of the park is mostly level with small ascents and descents.

Shortly after passing a bench at 1.09, stop at the northern red oak with a tag that displays its scientific name, *Quercus rubra*. A large basswood tree stands in the middle of the trail at 1.16 miles. Red Cedar Trail joins Hackberry Trail at 1.31 miles, where you turn left to continue on the latter. Around 1.6 miles, the trail climbs up stairs bypassing a rutted section of trail. Shortly after there are wooden planks in the ground placed by a Boy Scout troop to prevent trail erosion. The final leg of the hike passes through a picnic and playground area and follows a park road to the east trailhead for the nature trails. Head northwest on the park road to pass the fish hatchery museum and return to the west trailhead.

MILES AND DIRECTIONS

0.00 Begin at the bulletin board at the Nature Trail west entrance and head north on Hackberry Trail.

0.09 Continue straight (north).

0.16 Continue straight.

0.24 Turn right (northeast).

0.25 Spur trail leading to a meditation shelter; continue straight (north).

0.35 Turn left (northwest) onto Nature Trail #2 (Red Cedar Trail).

      Bailout: Turn right (east) if you want to hike the shorter nature loop.

0.60 Bench.

0.61 Suspension bridge.

0.65 Keep right (east) onto Backwoods Trail #2 (Red Cedar Trail).

0.86 Continue straight (east).

0.90 Bridge.

1.03 Cross another bridge.

1.09 Bench.

1.31 Turn left (southeast) onto Nature Trail #1 (Hackberry Trail).

1.39 Pass two benches on the left (east) of the trail.

1.60 Reach stairs to the left of a steep path with exposed tree roots.

1.65 Keep right onto the dirt footpath instead of taking the stairs on the left.

1.71 Bench and picnic shelter.

1.80 East entrance to the Nature Trail; turn right (northwest) onto the park road.

1.95 Reach a parking area, playground, picnic area, vault toilets; continue southwest on the park road.

2.00 Reach the Edward Owen Picnic Area; turn right (northwest) onto the park road passing Canyon Ponds and Waterfowl Display on the right and Gretna Fish Hatchery Museum on the left.

2.12 Arrive back at the trailhead.

31 STONE CREEK FALLS

The trails at Platte River State Park are popular with mountain bikers, and as a result, there is a maze of trails that can prove frustrating for hikers. However, the highlight of the park is Stone Creek Falls, a small, picturesque waterfall that is beautiful any time of the year. The falls can be reached via a short out-and-back hike via two trailheads: a parking lot west of the park headquarters or next to the Walter Scott Jr. Lodge. The former is an easy, flat trail to the falls, while the latter involves a steep descent to the creek but offers the opportunity to climb to the top of the Lincoln Journal Tower with views of the Platte River.

Start: Lincoln Journal Tower (an alternative trailhead is located at the parking lot west of the park headquarters)
Elevation gain: 1,072 to 1,211 feet
Distance: 1.25 miles out and back
Difficulty: Easy
Hiking time: 1 hour
Seasons/schedule: Open year-round, dawn to dusk; Stone Creek Falls is beautiful any season of the year and is often frozen in winter (the alternative trailhead allows easier access in winter)
Fees and permits: Valid park permit; available for purchase at the Schramm Education Center, kiosks near the park entrance, and online at outdoornebraska.gov.
Trail contact: Platte River State Park, 14421 346th St., Louisville 68037; (402) 234-2217; outdoornebraska .gov/platteriver
Dog-friendly: Yes, on leash
Trail surface: Dirt footpaths

Land status: Platte River State Park
Nearest town: Louisville 5 miles to the east, Ashland 11 miles to the northwest
Maps: USGS Manley, NE 2021; park map available at outdoornebraska .gov/platteriver
Other trail users: Mountain bikers
Special considerations: The trails are popular with mountain bikers, so be aware of riders. As a result of the popularity of mountain biking, there is a maze of trails with no waymarking, so hiking the trails can become frustrating if you are accustomed to dedicated hiking trails with signage.
Amenities available: Vault toilets, water, and picnic areas throughout the state park
Maximum grade: 14%
Cell service: Reliable coverage at the trailheads and away from trees; coverage can be limited under the dense tree canopy

FINDING THE TRAILHEAD

From I-80 exit 426, head south on NE 66 for 6.3 miles. Turn north onto 346th Street and continue for 0.5 mile. After passing the park entrance, turn right (east) onto a park road and shortly pass the park headquarters. Keep left at the next fork and continue until reaching the Walter Scott Jr. Lodge. **GPS:** N40° 59.447' W96° 12.794'

Trail Conditions: Park staff are slowly adding more trail signage as their budget permits. Additionally, there is a maze of trails for mountain bikers that can become confusing and frustrating for hikers. Be aware of bikers, especially on blind curves. Ticks are an ever-present concern during the summer months. The trails receive heavy traffic due to the park's location between Omaha and Lincoln.

Stone Creek Falls is a popular hiking destination at Platte River State Park any time of year.

THE HIKE

Located halfway between Omaha and Lincoln, Platte River State Park attracts a variety of outdoor recreationists. Campers can enjoy a weekend at a traditional campsite or glamping cabins located among bur oak, hackberry, American elm, and green ash. Kayakers and canoeists have access to the Platte River Water Trail near the mouth of Decker Creek on the east end of the park. Crawdad Creek allows children to explore the wonders of a freshwater ecosystem while anglers can fish nearby Jenny Newman Lake.

One of the more popular activities at the state park is mountain biking. The far east end of the park has a trail system open only to mountain bikers. The trails west of Decker Creek are open to both mountain bikers and hikers. As a result, there is a maze of trails that are perfect for bikers but can be confusing for hikers. The trails are worth exploration, especially in the fall as the forest turns from dark green to brilliant yellow. Deer take shelter in the cedar forest west of Stone Creek and the observation tower at Mallet Lodge is a great location to bird-watch. Trail traffic, especially mountain bikers, decreases dramatically in winter, and hiking the forest through fresh snow is a quiet and peaceful experience. The trails can become quite muddy as snow melts, so it's best to hike soon after snowfall, especially if the snow is light and dry.

Due to the maze of trails and lack of trail signage, creating a loop can be frustrating. However, park staff are adding more trail signage as funding permits. One of the highlights of Platte River State Park, Stone Creek Falls is easily accessible and one of the best family hikes in the state of Nebraska. There are two trailheads that lead to the small waterfall, which can be visited any time of year, even in winter when the waterfall freezes

A wintery Platte River from atop the Lincoln Journal Tower.

STONE CREEK FALLS

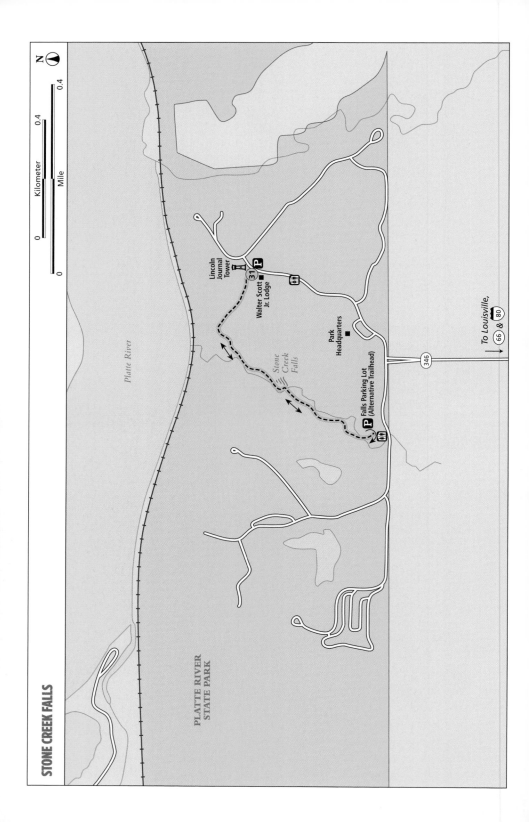

N

0   Kilometer   0.4

0   Mile   0.4

Platte River

Lincoln
Journal
Tower

Walter Scott
Jr. Lodge

31

Stone
Creek
Falls

Park
Headquarters

PLATTE RIVER
STATE PARK

Falls Parking Lot
(Alternative Trailhead)

346

To Louisville,
66 & 80

and creates wonderful photography opportunities. The trail from Falls Parking Lot is a flat, easy 0.3-mile hike to Stone Creek Falls. Beginning at the Walter Scott Jr. Lodge is another option that allows hikers to climb the Lincoln Journal Tower to take in the views of the forest canopy and the Platte River.

After descending the observation tower, head west past the teepee. The trail enters the forest and descends over 100 feet to reach Stone Creek near its confluence with the Platte River. The trail crosses a bridge at 0.21 mile and heads southwest upstream with the creek on your right. This section of the trail is more rugged than the portion from the Falls Parking Lot, with exposed tree roots and stones. The adventurous can head off-trail to jump from stone to stone in the creek until reaching the falls. Sticking to the trail, it reaches a viewing platform overlooking Stone Creek Falls at 0.35 mile.

The falls is a popular spot to take photos, play in the creek, or simply sit and listen to the running water, birdsong, and other sounds of the surrounding forest. Hikers can turn around and return to their respective trailhead, however the forest beckons with more to explore. Continue south across the David Anderson Bridge at 0.37 mile to follow a footpath alongside the creek. The trail at 0.53 mile, marked by a sign for the ballfield and pool, leads to the western section of the park. If you want to extend your hike, turn onto this trail to wander the aforementioned cedar forest and then head to Mallet Lodge to get another bird's-eye view above the forest canopy.

Continuing southwest on the creek trail, cross Roger Sykes Bridge at 0.6 mile to reach the Falls Parking Lot; there are vault toilets at the trailhead. Turn around to follow the same trail along the creek to return to Walter Scott Jr. Lodge.

MILES AND DIRECTIONS

0.00 Begin at Lincoln Journal Tower.

0.07 Teepee.

0.11 Continue straight (north).

0.14 Keep left (southwest).

0.18 Continue straight (west).

0.21 Turn left (south) and cross the footbridge.

0.31 Continue straight (south).

0.35 Stone Creek Falls.

0.37 Cross David Andersen Bridge heading south.

0.39 Turn left to follow the footpath along the creek.

0.41 Turn left (south).

0.43 Reach a fork and keep left.

0.49 Keep left (south).

0.53 Continue straight (south) passing the sign for the ballfield and pool.

0.56 Keep right.

0.60 Roger Sykes Bridge.

0.65 Falls Parking Lot; turn around and return via the same trail.

1.25 Arrive back at the Lincoln Journal Tower.

Dogs are welcome on the trails at Platte River State Park.

H **ROWE SANCTUARY**

Just minutes from I-80, the Iain Nicolson Audubon Center at Rowe Sanctuary is one of the best places in the world to witness the sandhill crane migration. While some of its trails are closed during the annual spring spectacle, Rowe Sanctuary provides plenty of opportunities throughout the year to spot grassland birds as well as shorebirds. The center will be undergoing major renovations after the 2023 spring crane migration, with the goal of being complete before the 2024 crane migration season. The trails will also be receiving upgrades, so while some trails may be closed during renovations, keep Rowe Sanctuary on your list of places to hike once they are complete.

Start: At time of publication 2 trails begin at the visitor center: Pondering Trail heading west and the East Blind / Triplett Trail heading east.
Elevation gain: 2,101 to 2,078 feet
Distance: Over 4 miles of trails
Difficulty: Easy due to flat terrain
Hiking time: Variable depending on the trail and duration of hike
Seasons/schedule: Trails open daily from sunrise to sunset; portions of the trails are closed from Feb 15 to Apr 15 to protect migrating sandhill and whooping cranes
Fees and permits: None
Trail contact: Iain Nicolson Audubon Center at Rowe Sanctuary, 44450 Elm Island Rd., Gibbon 68840; (308) 468-5282, rowe.audubon.org
Dog-friendly: Pets not allowed
Trail surface: Mowed grass trails and crushed rock
Land status: Iain Nicolson Audubon Center at Rowe Sanctuary

Nearest town: Kearney 19 miles to the west, Grand Island 40 miles to the east
Maps: USGS Newark; paper maps available at the trailhead and visitor center (open Mon to Fri, 9 a.m. to 4 p.m.)
Other trail users: None
Special considerations: The trails are closed during the spring migration season, Feb 15 to Apr 15, to protect the cranes from human disturbance. Trails may change after renovations (scheduled to begin May 2023). Additionally, a new trail will be created through an adjacent prairie.
Amenities available: When the visitor center is open, there are restrooms and an information desk available as well as a gift shop.
Maximum grade: 1%
Cell service: Reliable throughout the entire trail system for most carriers

The trails at Rowe Sanctuary follow the Platte River and also include grasslands and riparian woodlands.

FINDING THE TRAILHEAD

From the I-80 exit 272 for Kearney, head south on NE 44 / I-80 ALT for 2.1 miles. Turn left (east) onto NE 50A. After 7 miles you will reach an intersection with Harold Warp Memorial Drive; continue straight (east) as NE 50A becomes V Road. After 2 miles, turn left (north) onto 34 Road, which becomes Elm Island Road at the intersection with Carpenter Road. Turn left at the entrance to the parking area for Rowe Sanctuary. The trailhead for the western trails is on the west side of the visitor center. **GPS:** N40° 40.170' W98° 53.200

Trail Conditions: The trails are well maintained but not waymarked; pick up a map at the visitor center. Hazards include ticks in the summer and tree snags in high winds. The trails receive light traffic.

| DARK ISLAND TRAIL

Dark Island Trail is a rail-to-trails project that connects the towns of Central City and Marquette. The 8-mile crushed rock trail crosses the Platte River via Bader Bridge, built in 1880 by the Republican Valley Railroad, with twelve viewing benches that offer year-round wildlife viewing. The trail gets its name from Lolawakohtito, a nearby island in the river that is one of the five sacred sites of the Pawnee religion. The trail signage and improvements are the work of the Platte PEER Group, Central City Trails group, Central City municipal staff, and volunteers.

Start: 28th Street trailhead in Central City
Elevation gain: 1,668 to 1,727 feet
Distance: 4.30 miles out and back; the entire trail is 8 miles from Central City to Marquette
Difficulty: Easy due to flat terrain
Hiking time: 2 hours
Seasons/schedule: Open year-round; best in spring for geese and waterfowl migration
Fees and permits: None
Trail contact: Platte PEER Group; (308) 986-2522; darkislandtrail.org/dark-island-trail/about.html
Dog-friendly: Yes, on leash
Trail surface: Crushed rock
Land status: Platte PEER Group

Nearest town: Central City
Maps: USGS Central City East and Central City West; map available at trailheads
Other trail users: Bikers
Special considerations: There are 3 trailheads near the town of Central City: 28th Street in town; north parking lot just west of NE 14 and south of town; on NE 66 south of the Platte River. All 3 have parking.
Amenities available: Parking and trash bins at the trailheads. There is a portable toilet at the north parking lot trailhead.
Maximum grade: 0%
Cell service: Full and reliable coverage along the trail

FINDING THE TRAILHEAD

From I-80, take exit 332 north on NE 14 for 19 miles. At the southern edge of Central City, turn right (east) onto 28th Street. Continue 0.3 mile to the Dark Island Trailhead. **GPS:** N41° 6.263' W97° 59.788

Trail Conditions: The trail is waymarked with half-mile markers and several interpretive signs. There is no shade for large sections of the trail. Please respect private property adjacent to the trail. Moderate traffic, mainly walkers and runners with the occasional cyclist.

Bader Bridge crosses the Platte River on the Dark Island Trail.

Prairie coneflower
(*Ratibida pinnata*).

SOUTHERN NEBRASKA

Southern Nebraska is deceiving. A cursory look would lead one to dismiss the region ecologically due to the amount of farmland. However, there are several areas of ecological importance south of the Platte River, such as the steep hills of the Loess Canyons, the Rainwater Basin, which is an important stopover for migratory birds, and the critically endangered Eastern Saline Wetlands near Lincoln. There are also several remnant tallgrass prairies and sites of historical significance, such as the first homestead claimed under the Homestead Act of 1862. The city of Lincoln itself offers a wealth of outdoor recreation opportunities, including wetlands, marshes, prairies, and wooded creeks. Get away from I-80 to explore country back roads and peaceful prairies with wildflowers from early spring to late summer.

A viewing deck overlooking Little Salt Creek at Frank Shoemaker Marsh.

32 NEW CAMP LOOP

Potter's Pasture is a network of over 100 miles of trails popular with mountain bikers and hikers. Traversing the steep loess hills and canyons 35 miles southeast of North Platte, the 1,200-acre reserve is privately owned but free and open to the public. The wide variety of trails, created and maintained by volunteers, allows hikers to create numerous day hikes and even multiday backpacking adventures. This 4.5-mile loop climbs up a ridge with sweeping views of the surrounding Loess Canyons, then descends into a valley to complete the loop.

Start: Trailhead on the west side of S Jeffrey Road, directly opposite the entrance to New Camp
Elevation gain: 2,762 to 3,041 feet
Distance: 4.48-mile loop
Difficulty: Moderate due to rugged terrain
Hiking time: 2 hours
Seasons/schedule: Trails open year-round, sunrise to sunset; best in spring and autumn for cooler temperatures
Fees and permits: None
Trail contact: Whitetail Cycle Sport, 507 North Jeffers St., North Platte 69101; (308) 530-1897; www.whitetailcyclesport.com
Dog-friendly: Yes, on leash
Trail surface: Grass and dirt
Land status: Potter's Pasture Bike and Recreation Club, Inc.
Nearest town: North Platte to the northwest, Gothenburg to the east
Maps: USGS Jeffrey Reservoir, NE 2021 and USGS Jeffrey Reservoir SW, NE 2021; trail map posted at New Camp and major junctions; trail map also available at visitnorthplatte.com/directory-posts/potters-pasture-mountain-bike-trail
Other trail users: Mountain bikers
Special considerations: The trails are popular with mountain bikers; they must yield to hikers. Cattle graze on the preserve; please close all gates behind you and maintain a safe distance from livestock. Camping is allowed at New Camp, Old Camp, and within Potter's Pasture; pack out what you pack in, only make fires in rings with grates, and put fires out completely upon leaving.
Amenities available: Toilets are available at New Camp and Old Camp.
Maximum grade: 14%
Cell service: Coverage by most carriers along the top of ridges and in open clearings; poor to no reception in valleys, canyons, and under tree cover

FINDING THE TRAILHEAD

From exit 199 on I-80, head south on NE 56D Link / S Banner Road. After 2.8 miles, turn east onto E Banner Road for 1 mile, then turn south onto S Banner Road / S Jeffrey Road for 2 miles. Turn west onto S Jeffrey Road and continue southwest for 5 miles until reaching New Camp on the east side of the road. The trailhead is directly opposite the camp entrance. **GPS:** N40° 52.417' W100° 24.011'

Trail Conditions: The trails are meticulously waymarked with color-coded tags attached to posts throughout the preserve. A trail map is available on the website (see trail contact) and trail maps are posted at major junctions that are listed on the trail map. There is no tree cover on substantial sections of the trails, and no safe and reliable water sources are available. The trails receive light to moderate traffic.

Potter's Pasture is located in the Loess Canyons south of the Platte River.

THE HIKE

Potter's Pasture is open to the public thanks to Steve Potter, an attorney from North Platte. Steve and a friend were avid mountain bikers and frequently rode the canyon country around Jeffrey Reservoir, which required the consent of landowners. They wanted to ride as often as possible without having to ask for permission each time, so Steve began to look for land to purchase. After acquiring land from a former client, Steve added a few more parcels to create the 1,200-acre Potter's Pasture.

The trail system at Potter's Pasture is one of the best in the state, thanks to the work of volunteers who created and continue to maintain the trails. The trails traverse ridge tops and valley bottoms, with a variety of different difficulty levels that challenge both mountain bikers and hikers. The trails are color-coded: green are easy, blue are moderate, and red are the most difficult trails. Tags have been nailed to posts, trees, and other objects along the trails and at junctions to help guide bikers and hikers. The helpful trail map also distinguishes ridge trails from valley trails, allowing visitors to create a diverse ride or hike that explores the unique Loess Canyons area south of the Platte River near North Platte.

The hills, canyons, and valleys of the Loess Canyons are mixed-grass prairie that have been heavily grazed over the years. Like most prairies after European settlement, they have been invaded by eastern redcedar. The ridges at Potter's Pasture are largely free of cedar trees, while the steep canyon sides and valley bottoms have dense cedar groves. The New Camp Loop hike takes hikers up Trail Ridge Trail to Team Trail Junction, then continues along another ridge following High Line Trail. The final leg of the hike follows Freeway Trail along a valley bottom.

Beginning at New Camp, pass through the gate and head northwest toward OK Corral Junction. Keep to the left and find the trail posts with tags directing you to Escalator, which climbs up a steep, rutted hillside to reach Team Trail Junction at the top of a ridge at 0.63 mile. Hike southwest along the open ridge with views south of the Loess Canyons country. The trail enters a cedar grove as it approaches Church Grove and the southern edge of Potter's Pasture. Church Grove Junction at 1.29 miles is located in an open meadow.

NEW CAMP LOOP

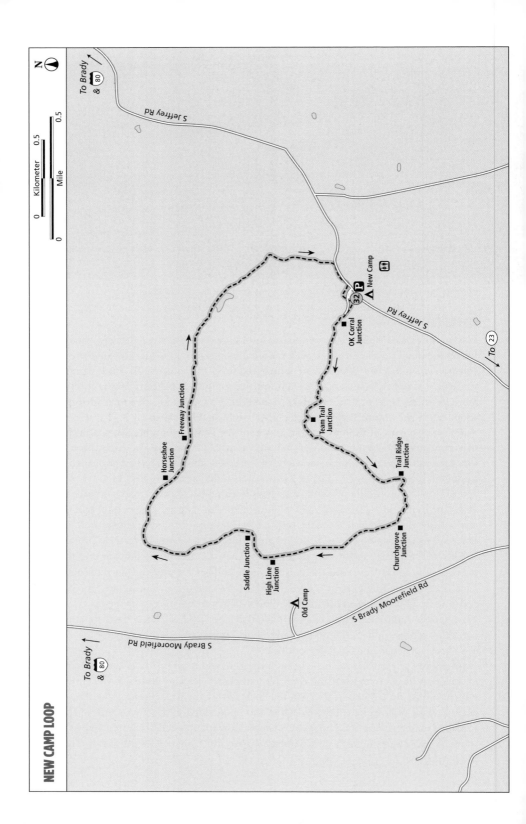

Left: Helpful trail markers are posted on trees and posts at important junctions.
Center: Old Camp, located on the west side of Potter's Pasture, also offers camping.
Right: New Camp offers primitive camping, parking, and a pit toilet.

Head north on High Line for the next 1.75 miles, passing through High Line, Saddle, and Horseshoe junctions while always staying on High Line Trail. The trail heads east and descends into a valley bottom before reaching Horseshoe Junction at 2.83 miles. Continue east at the next junction, Freeway at 3.03 miles, to follow Freeway Trail along the wide valley bottom. The pond on Freeway at 3.57 miles was dried up during the late summer. At the end of Freeway Trail, head south on The Desert at 3.91 miles; this trail begins to run parallel to Jeffrey Road at 4.18 miles before reaching OK Corral Junction and the trailhead.

MILES AND DIRECTIONS

0.00 Begin at the trailhead on the west side of S Jeffrey Road; head northwest toward OK Corral Junction.

0.11 Reach a fork; keep left (northwest) on Escalator.

0.50 Turn right (north) onto Trail Ridge.

0.63 Team Trail Junction; head southwest on Trail Ridge.

1.11 Trail Ridge Junction; continue south on Church Grove.

1.29 Church Grove Junction; continue on High Line until Freeway Junction.

1.84 High Line Junction; continue north on High Line.

2.04 Saddle Junction; continue north on High Line.

2.83 Horseshoe Junction; continue east on High Line.

3.03 Freeway Junction; continue east on Freeway.

3.91 Turn right (south) onto The Desert.

4.34 Turn left (southwest) toward OK Corral Junction.

4.36 OK Corral Junction.

4.48 Arrive back at the trailhead.

33 ROCK CREEK PRAIRIE LOOP

Created as a supply station and campground for emigrants on the Oregon and California Trails, Rock Creek Station gained infamy in 1861 when Wild Bill Hickok earned his moniker after a deadly shootout with the McCanles Gang at the East Ranch Cabin. The station was also a staging point on the Pony Express. The trail from the park office leads past reconstructed buildings from this frontier period, crosses Rock Creek over the Toll Bridge, then hikes the perimeter of a tallgrass prairie bordered by wooded creek bottoms and cropland.

Start: Park office
Elevation gain: 1,381 to 1,436 feet
Distance: 3.49-mile loop
Difficulty: Easy
Hiking time: 1.5 hours
Seasons/schedule: Trails open year-round, sunrise to sunset
Fees and permits: A park entry permit is required and may be purchased at the park, statewide Game and Parks offices and permit vendors, or online at outdoornebraska.gov.
Trail contact: Rock Creek Station State Historical Park, 57426 710th Rd., Fairbury 68352; (402) 729-5777; outdoornebraska.gov/rockcreekstation/
Dog-friendly: Yes, on leash no longer than 6 feet

Trail surface: Mostly mowed grass paths with some dirt footpaths
Land status: Rock Creek Station State Historical Park
Nearest town: Fairbury 9 miles to the northwest
Maps: USGS Endicott, NE, KS 2021; park map available at the park office and online on the park website (see trail contact)
Other trail users: Bikers and equestrians
Special considerations: Hikers and bikers must yield to equestrians; bikers must yield to hikers.
Amenities available: Toilets, water, information, and a gift shop at the park office
Maximum grade: 7%
Cell service: Reliable coverage on most carriers

FINDING THE TRAILHEAD

From Fairbury, head south out of town on NE 15. Shortly after leaving town, turn east onto NE 8 then take the next right onto PWF Road / 711 Road to head north then east past Fairbury Cemetery. After 4.5 miles, turn south onto 573rd Avenue for 1 mile. Turn east onto 710 Road for 1.8 miles to reach the entrance to Rock Creek State Historical Park. Turn south onto the park road until reaching the park office. The trailhead is on the west side of the building. **GPS:** N40° 6.784' W97° 3.620'

Trail Conditions: The trails are well maintained. The lack of trail signage does not complicate hiking, as the trail map is accurate and helpful. Ticks are common in the summer. The trails receive moderate traffic.

THE HIKE

Rock Creek Station State Historical Park was established in 1980 on 350 acres that includes tallgrass prairie and wooded draws and creeks, including the steep and rocky creek giving the park its name. The buildings around Rock Creek were reconstructed to represent the frontier era that made the station famous. West Ranch was the site of a post

Top: Wagons and stagecoaches on the Oregon Trail stopped at Rock Creek Station.
Bottom: Reconstructed buildings on the east side of Rock Creek.

office, while the Pony Express station and the site of Wild Bill Hickok's first shoot-out were across Rock Creek at East Ranch. The park office has brochures detailing a self-guided walking tour to Rock Creek and the ranches.

The trail begins on the west side of the park office. Deep ruts run parallel to the trail, carved by the thousands of stagecoaches and wagons that passed through Rock Creek Station on the Oregon and California Trails. The first building you encounter is a re-creation of the post office from 1865. The West Ranch Cabin, next to the post office, was a privately run road ranch for travelers. A nearby interpretive panel cites several traveler journals on the difficulties crossing Rock Creek because of its steep banks and rocky bottom. The toll bridge built by David McCanles solved the problem of the creek crossing; many travelers were willing to pay the toll ranging from 10 to 50 cents.

Hikers do not need to pay the toll to cross the reconstructed bridge. The East Ranch at 0.35 mile consists of several buildings, all reconstructed as the only remaining feature of the original ranch is the well. The Pony Express station was located here, as is the East Ranch Cabin, the site of the infamous gunfight that turned James Butler Hickok into Wild Bill Hickok. David McCanles and his gang were killed by Hickok and other gunmen from Rock Creek Station, but the story was later exaggerated giving Hickok

ROCK CREEK PRAIRIE LOOP

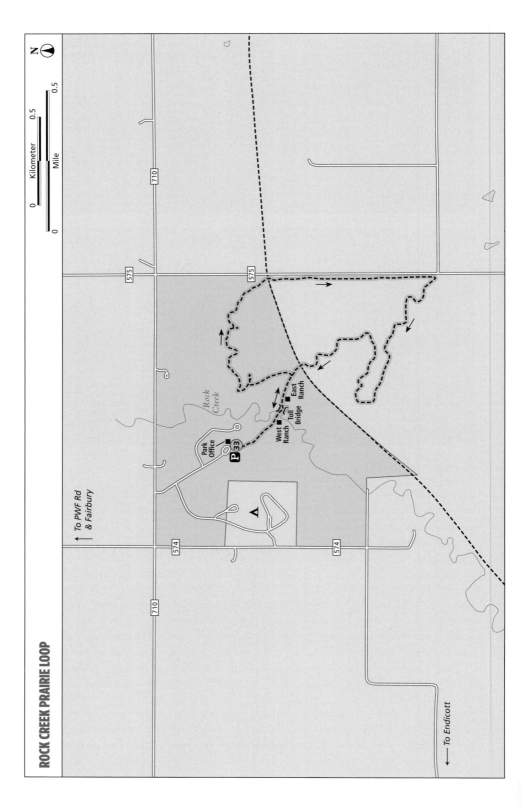

credit for killing each member of the gang himself. Despite his reputation, Hickok later apologized to David McCanles's widow and gave her all the money he had at the time.

The self-guided walking tour ends at East Ranch but the trails explore the eastern half of the park through upland prairie and wooded draws and creeks. Toward the end of East Ranch, at 0.38 mile, turn north to follow a path mowed through the prairie. Take the trail into the forest at 0.53 mile, then leave the forest at 0.73 mile to continue east along the edge of the woods and prairie. The creek crossing at 0.93 mile can be muddy; after the crossing, head southwest until the trail meets 575th Avenue and heads south running parallel to the road for more than half a mile. Upland tallgrass prairie covers much of the eastern half of Rock Creek Station State Historical Park. The trail leaves the road at 1.85 miles when it turns to head northwest. There are mowed paths that follow the edge of the wooded draw, but this hike continues northwest through the prairie. After 2.48 miles, the trail bends east then back to the northwest as it skirts two wooded ravines. Reach East Ranch at 3.16 miles, cross Rock Creek, and continue northwest uphill to reach the park office.

MILES AND DIRECTIONS

0.00 Begin west of the park office and head south.

0.06 Continue straight (south).

   Side trip: Turn left (east) to the gravesites.

0.15 1865 Post Office and West Ranch Cabin.

0.25 Cross Toll Bridge over Rock Creek heading southeast.

0.35 East Ranch.

0.38 Turn left (north) onto a mowed grass path.

0.53 Keep left (north) to enter woodland.

0.61 Turn right (east).

0.73 Continue straight (east) on the edge of the woodland and prairie.

0.93 Creek crossing.

1.25 Continue straight (south).

1.85 Turn right (northwest).

2.48 Keep right (east).

3.11 Continue straight (northwest)

3.16 East Ranch.

3.28 Toll Bridge.

3.36 1865 Post Office and West Ranch Cabin.

3.49 Arrive back at the park office.

Appropriately named Rock Creek.

34 UPLAND PRAIRIE LOOP

Homestead National Historical Park is located on the original 160-acre homestead of Daniel and Agnes Freeman, the first claim filed after passage of the Homestead Act in 1862. A 3-mile network of trails explores the T-shaped acreage that includes the second-oldest restored prairie in the United States, oak woodlands along Cub Creek, and the osage orange hedgerow planted by Freeman as a windbreak on the southern edge of the homestead.

Start: Trailhead is located between the Heritage Center and Palmer-Epard Cabin
Elevation gain: 1,252 to 1,312 feet
Distance: 1.92-mile loop
Difficulty: Easy
Hiking time: 1 hour
Seasons/schedule: Trails open year-round, sunrise to sunset
Fees and permits: None
Trail contact: Homestead National Historical Park, 8523 West NE 4, Beatrice 68310; (402) 223-3514; nps.gov/home
Dog-friendly: No pets allowed
Trail surface: Grass and dirt

Land status: Homestead National Historical Park
Nearest town: Beatrice 5 miles to the east
Maps: USGS Beatrice West, NE 2021; trail map available at the Heritage Center and nps.gov/home
Other trail users: None
Special considerations: Please enjoy the trail by staying on the path.
Amenities available: Restrooms, water, information, museum, and a gift shop inside the Heritage Center
Maximum grade: 4%
Cell service: Good coverage by most carriers throughout the trail system

FINDING THE TRAILHEAD

From Beatrice, head west on NE 4. After 4.9 miles, turn south onto SW 75 Road, then turn west at the entrance to Homestead National Historical Park. The trailhead is located between the Heritage Center and Palmer-Epard Cabin.
GPS: N40° 17.127' W96° 49.610'

Trail Conditions: The trails are marked with signs that list trail directions and distances. Watch for poison ivy, stinging nettles, and ticks. The trails receive moderate traffic.

THE HIKE

On January 1, 1863, Daniel Freeman filed a claim on 160 acres of tallgrass prairie and oak woodlands along Cub Creek 5 miles west of the town of Beatrice. Freeman's claim was the first under the Homestead Act of 1862, which spurred American expansion westward but at a tragic cost for Native Americans and wildlife and their habitat. Fortunately, organizations and institutions like the National Park Service conserve the natural and cultural history of these events and the places where they took place, like at Homestead National Historical Park.

The Heritage Center is a beautiful building with a wealth of information inside and outside. The building's architecture resembles a single-bottom plow moving through the sod, a common sight on the prairie after the Homestead Act. The display along the sidewalk outside the building's entrance illustrates the proportion of homesteaded land in

Left: The Heritage Center resembles a single-bottom plow moving through the sod.
Right: A contemplative spot on Cottonwood Loop Trail.

each state. Inside, the interpretive displays provide information on the Homestead Act's influence on American history.

Outside the center 3 miles of trails explore remnants and re-creations of Daniel Freeman's homestead and its era. The Palmer-Epard Cabin, south of the Heritage Center, was originally located 14 miles from the current national monument site. The cabin was relocated here in 1950 and is representative of the architecture of the homestead era. The trailhead for this hike is located just north of the cabin at an interpretive display about barbed wire fence.

Head north along the west side of the Heritage Center until reaching the gravesite of Daniel and Agnes Freeman at 0.1 mile. Head northwest on Grain Growers Highway, named after a proposed highway from Beatrice to Yellowstone National Park that was never finished. The tallgrass prairie south of the trail is the second-oldest prairie restoration in the United States. The National Park Service planted seed from a nearby farm after it acquired the land in 1939. Continuous restoration efforts have created a diverse prairie with 330 species of plants. A prairie plant list is available in the Heritage Center that outlines blooming times for wildflowers.

The Prairie Plaza at 0.5 has several benches to enjoy the shade of cottonwoods and view of the prairie. The monument placed by Daughters of the American Revolution is the final stop on Grain Growers Highway Trail until reaching the junction at 0.6 mile.

UPLAND PRAIRIE LOOP

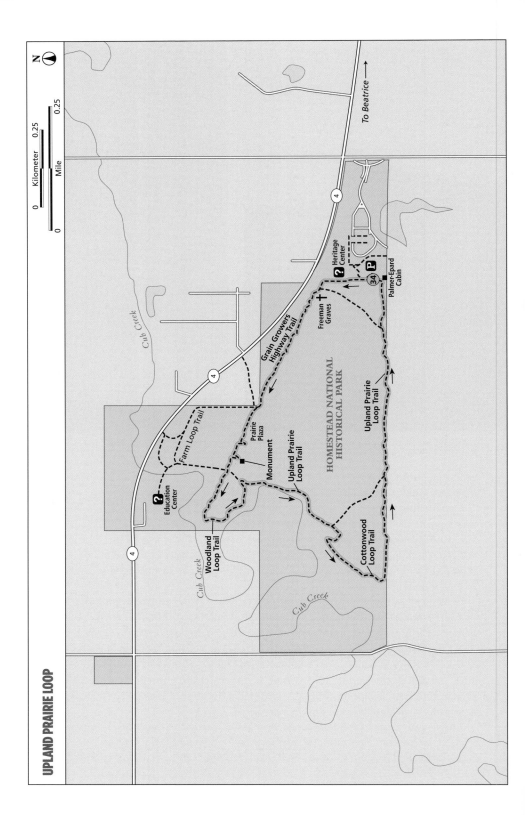

If you'd like to take a side trip, turn north at the junction to reach the Native Prairie Exhibit and cross the suspension bridge over Cub Creek. Otherwise, continue straight onto Woodland Loop Trail. The hardwood forest along the creek provided Freeman needed timber to construct buildings and equipment.

The loop through the woodland is completed at 0.85 mile, where you turn south onto Upland Prairie Trail with Cub Creek on your right to the west. Keep right at 1.08 miles onto Cottonwood Trail. Stop at the bench at 1.17 miles to meditate underneath the forest canopy, then continue southwest until reaching the southern boundary of the park. The trail heads east along an osage orange hedgerow, planted by Daniel Freeman as a windbreak, for six-tenths of a mile until reaching the end of the hike at Palmer-Epard Cabin.

MILES AND DIRECTIONS

0.00 Begin at the interpretive display about the barbed wire fence between the Heritage Center and Palmer-Epard Cabin.

0.10 Daniel and Agnes Freeman gravesite; head northwest onto Grain Growers Highway Trail.

0.40 Continue straight (northwest).

0.50 Prairie Plaza.

0.56 Daughters of the American Revolution Monument.

0.60 Continue straight (northwest) onto Woodland Loop Trail.

Option: Turn right (north) to visit the Native Plants Exhibit and the suspension bridge across Cub Creek.

0.85 Turn right (south) onto Upland Prairie Loop.

1.08 Keep right (southwest) onto Cottonwood Loop Trail.

Painted lady (*Vanessa cardui*) on Baldwin's ironweed (*Vernonia baldwinii*).

1.17 Bench.

1.50 Continue straight (east) onto Upland Prairie Loop.

1.82 Continue straight (east).

1.92 Arrive back at the Palmer-Epard Cabin.

Four miles of trails wind through one of Nebraska's largest remaining tracts of native tallgrass prairie, the most threatened ecosystem in North America. Spring Creek Prairie Audubon Center has been designated one of Nebraska's twenty-five Important Bird Areas, and with 238 documented species, it is a bird-watchers' paradise. The easy trails winding through grasslands and woodlands are perfect for a leisurely weekend hike with family exploring prairies, ponds, wetlands, and forest just 20 minutes from Lincoln.

Start: Spring Creek Prairie Audubon Center visitor center
Elevation gain: 1,328 to 1,460 feet
Distance: 3.00-mile loop
Difficulty: Easy
Hiking time: Up to 2 hours
Seasons/schedule: Trails open year-round, sunrise to sunset; best in spring for wildflowers
Fees and permits: None
Trail contact: Spring Creek Prairie Audubon Center, 11700 SW 100th St., Denton 68339; (402) 797-2301; springcreek.audubon.org
Dog-friendly: No pets allowed
Trail surface: Crushed limestone and mowed grass paths
Land status: Spring Creek Prairie Audubon Center

Nearest town: Lincoln 16 miles to the northeast, Crete 9 miles to the southwest
Maps: USGS Denton, NE 2021; trail map and interactive trail map available at springcreek.audubon.org
Other trail users: None
Special considerations: Check the center's social media in spring for prescribed burns. There is no shade for the majority of the trail, so plan and pack accordingly. Cattle may be grazing the prairie during the summer.
Amenities available: Restrooms in the visitor center, however none if the visitor center is closed. Information and gift shop in the visitor center.
Maximum grade: 10%
Cell service: Coverage not reliable

FINDING THE TRAILHEAD

From Lincoln, head west on US 6 / W O Street for 4.5 miles. Turn left (south) onto Nebraska S55A / SW 84th Street. After 5.2 miles turn right onto W Denton Road and drive west for 0.5 mile. Turn left (south) onto SW 100th Street for 3.3 miles. Turn left (east) at the entrance to Spring Creek Prairie Audubon Center. The trailhead is near the visitor center near the southeast corner of the building. **GPS:** N40° 41.617' W96° 51.185'

Trail Conditions: The mowed grass paths are not waymarked at junctions or intersections but with a map in hand it is not difficult to get lost. As with any trail through grasslands, long pants and sleeves and a thorough body check after hiking are the best protection against ticks. The trails receive moderate traffic.

THE HIKE

The Audubon Society of Nebraska purchased the O'Brien Ranch in 1998, and after adding more acreage over the following years, Spring Creek Prairie Audubon Center now totals 850 acres of tallgrass prairie, riparian woodlands, and wetlands. The rolling grassy hills, among the highest points in Lancaster County, were sculpted by a receding

Top: An animal cemetery on the prairie honors the former land owner's prized horse, Jube.
Bottom: Many of the grasses and wildflowers surrounding the visitor center are identified with plaques.

glacier during the last ice age. The quartzite boulders strewn across Spring Creek Prairie are relics of that glacier, some brought by the ice from as far away as South Dakota and Minnesota. Because of this rocky substrate, approximately 650 acres of Spring Creek Prairie were never plowed and cropped, leaving it as one of Nebraska's largest remnant tallgrass prairies. One of the few signs of human activity across this pristine prairie are wheel ruts left by freight wagons that used the Nebraska City–Fort Kearny Cutoff Trail from 1859 to 1869 to haul supplies to army forts in western Nebraska and mines in Colorado.

There are four trails through Spring Creek Prairie, and this hike uses sections of all four. Beginning on the south side of the visitor center, head south to cross a footbridge over a pond to reach the beginning of the Elizabeth Rubendall Birding Trail, a 0.7-mile trail that loops back to the footbridge. Continuing south, take the right fork of the loop as it skirts the edge of a wooded area to the west. As you walk along the trails, try to find some of the plants that were labeled in the garden outside the visitor center.

After 0.47 mile, you will reach the top of a hill with great views of the surrounding prairie and Lancaster County. The trail descends the hillside heading southeast toward a

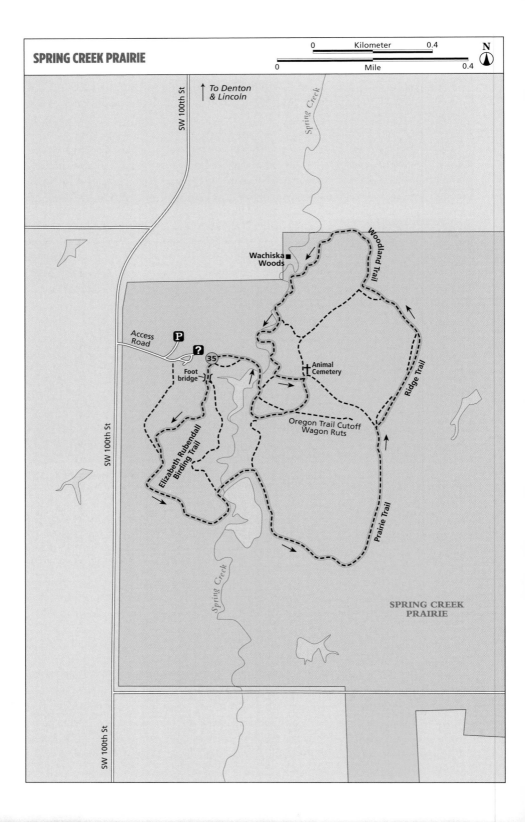

pond. Take the connector trail at 0.67 mile around the north end of the pond to reach Tallgrass Loop Trail at 0.77 mile, where you turn south. Follow Tallgrass Loop Trail until you reach Bobolink Ridge Trail at 1.44 miles, and turn right to head north for the next mile through tallgrass prairie atop the highest point of Spring Creek Prairie. There are several boulders immediately adjacent to Bobolink Ridge Trail, oddities in typically rock-free eastern Nebraska. The quartzite boulders are perfect places to sit down and listen to prairie songbirds while the breeze blows through the tallgrass prairie.

Bobolink Ridge Trail bends to the northwest as it descends toward Wachiska Woods. Turn right (north) onto Oak Savannah Loop Trail at 1.85 miles to follow the trail through bur oak, hackberry, and honey locust along the banks of Spring Creek. At the southern terminus of Oak Savannah Loop Trail, at 2.53 miles, turn left (east) onto Tallgrass Loop Trail. Shortly ahead, at 2.6 miles, the trail reaches an animal cemetery dedicated to the former ranch owner's favorite championship horse, Jube. At the cemetery, turn right (south) to continue on Tallgrass Loop Trail until the Oregon Trail cutoff wagon ruts at 2.71 miles. The ruts, still visible in the tall grasses, were created by freight wagons, settlers, and gold seekers headed west, the direction we take toward the pond. There is a sign next to the pond describing the cutoff trail and a limestone path that leads back to the visitor center.

MILES AND DIRECTIONS

0.00 Begin behind the visitor center. Cross the footbridge to the west of the pond heading south.

0.07 Elizabeth Rubendall Birding Trail begins.

0.32 Reach a junction. Keep right (south).

0.67 Turn right (northeast) onto a spur trail that connects to Tallgrass Loop Trail.

0.77 Reach a bench and turn right (southeast) onto Tallgrass Loop Trail.

1.44 Turn right (north) onto Bobolink Ridge Trail.

1.85 Turn right (north) onto Oak Savannah Loop Trail.

Monarch butterfly on a prairie blazing star.

2.16 Reach a Wachiska Woods sign and a bench.

2.32 Turn right (south) onto the trail leading into the woods.

2.45 Cross a footbridge.

2.53 At the junction, turn left (east) toward the animal cemetery.

2.60 Animal cemetery. Turn right to head south.

2.71 Oregon Trail Cutoff wagon ruts to the left. At the fork, keep left (south) toward the pond.

2.79 Reach another fork and bear right heading toward the pond and visitor center.

2.85 Arrive at a sign about the Nebraska City-Fort Kearny Trail. Follow the limestone path north around the pond toward the visitor center.

3.00 Arrive back at the visitor center.

36 MARTIN PRAIRIE AND WETLANDS LOOP

Since 1963, Pioneers Park has served the city of Lincoln as an environmental education center and wildlife sanctuary. This hike combines two loops to explore the 668 acres of tallgrass prairie, woodlands, and wetlands on the western edge of Nebraska's capital. The loop through Martin Prairie, surrounded by modern development, passes a restored homestead cabin and a frontier schoolhouse. Additionally, a small herd of bison can be viewed from the western edge of Martin Prairie and the wetland trails. The loop through the wetlands offers a plethora of educational exhibits and bird-watching, as well as a suspension bridge across Haines Branch Creek.

Start: Parking lot adjacent to the Prairie Building
Elevation gain: 1,152 to 1,280 feet
Distance: 4.34-mile loop
Difficulty: Easy
Hiking time: 2–3 hours
Seasons/schedule: Open year-round, except closed on City of Lincoln holidays; non-gated trails are open during Pioneers Park hours, while gated trails close at posted times (4:30 or 5 p.m.)
Fees and permits: None
Trail contact: Pioneers Park Nature Center, 3201 S Coddington Ave., Lincoln 65822; (402) 441-7895; lincoln.ne.gov/City/Departments/Parks-and-Recreation/Parks-Facilities/Pioneers-Park-Nature-Center

Dog-friendly: Not permitted
Trail surface: Mowed grass, dirt footpaths, asphalt, boardwalk
Land status: Pioneers Park
Nearest town: Lincoln
Maps: USGS Emerald, NE 2021; park map available online
Other trail users: None
Special considerations: Access to the wetlands trails closes at posted times. The network of trails in the wetlands and Martin Prairie allow a myriad of hiking options.
Amenities available: Toilets and water at the Prairie Building and Chet Ager Building
Maximum grade: 8%
Cell service: Coverage available throughout Pioneers Park

FINDING THE TRAILHEAD

From downtown Lincoln, head west on Rosa Parks Way. After crossing US 77, continue south on S Coddington Avenue. After 1 mile, head west on West Van Dorn Street until reaching the entrance to Pioneers Park. Turn left (south) into the park and continue for 1.5 miles until the parking lot between the golf course and the Prairie Building. **GPS:** N40° 46.455' W96° 46.543'

Trail Conditions: Trails are maintained, but there is no specific route marked on the trails. Ticks are present and to be expected during the warmer months. The trails receive heavy usage due to the park's proximity to Lincoln.

THE HIKE

In addition to the 8 miles of trails at Pioneers Park, the Prairie Corridor Trail connects the park to the multitude of other trails and nature parks in the Lincoln area, including Wilderness Park and eventually Spring Creek Prairie Audubon Center near Denton.

Muskrat Wetlands.

This hike can be split into two shorter loops, roughly 2 miles each, if time is short or children are present. Martin Prairie also has additional mowed paths to explore the most endangered ecosystem in North America: tallgrass prairie.

Before setting out into the prairie, head inside the Prairie Building (check hours) to learn about the plants and animals of the Great Plains and prairie ecosystems, as well as the history of Pioneers Park. A visit to Elk Pond, just to the west of the Prairie Building, allows a closer look at the small herd of bison that graze an enclosed section of Martin Prairie. Continuing north on Martin Prairie Trail, reach the Hudson Cabin at 0.2 mile. Built with oak logs in 1863, it was considered a large and grand house at the time. The cabin was moved from its original location on Salt Creek to another location near 9th and South Streets in Lincoln in the late 1800s. The cabin was a feature of the old State Fairgrounds in the latter half of the 1900s, then moved again to Pioneers Park in 2010.

Hudson cabin (foreground) and Heritage School (background) on Martin Prairie.

Suspension bridge of Haines Branch Creek

Martin Prairie Trail continues north, and a network of mowed paths allow the hike to be extended or opportunities to return to the parking lot. After passing a bench near a pond at 0.7 miles, head north through the prairie to consider the encroaching urban development that, along with crop fields, have reduced the remaining tallgrass prairie in North America to 1 percent of its original extent. The housing development north of West Van Dorn Street and Pioneers Golf Course are two examples of what Martin Prairie would look like now, were it not for conservation efforts to preserve wild places.

After reaching the Cunningham One-Room Schoolhouse and the parking lot at 2.4 miles, you can call it a day or continue across the park road to enter the wetlands and woodland trails (note the closing time of the gated entrances and plan accordingly). There is a children's play area, an herb garden and pollinator garden, and outdoor bird exhibits to explore on the trails. Keep right immediately after entering the gate to explore the wetlands. A boardwalk (3.08 miles) meanders through the Muskrat Wetlands. You can continue on the trail along the southern end of Heron Wetlands, however, a fun suspension bridge over Haines Branch Creek at 3.42 miles will delight children.

After crossing the suspension bridge, follow Harrington Trail as it heads east on the south side of Haines Branch Creek. Cross the Prairie Corridor Bridge at 3.85 miles and head northwest on the edge of Fleming Woods to return to the parking lot.

MILES AND DIRECTIONS

0.00 Beginning at the trail map in the parking lot, head west toward the Prairie Building on a sidewalk.

0.01 Turn right (north) onto a grass trail just before the Prairie Building.

0.10 Reach the entrance to a pond and wildlife viewing area; continue straight (north) on Martin Prairie Trail.

0.20 Hudson Cabin; continue straight (north).

0.32 Continue straight (north).

0.40 Turn left (west) and then continue straight (west) at the next junction.

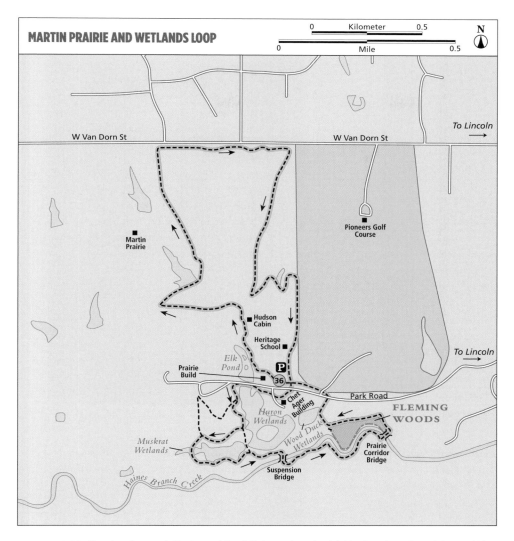

0   Kilometer   0.5

N

0   Mile   0.5

W Van Dorn St

W Van Dorn St

To Lincoln
→

Pioneers Golf
Course

Martin
Prairie

Hudson
Cabin

Heritage
School

Elk
Pond

Prairie
Build

P

36

Chet
Ager
Building

Park Road

To Lincoln

FLEMING
WOODS

Huron
Wetlands

Wood Duck
Wetlands

Muskrat
Wetlands

Prairie
Corridor
Bridge

Haines Branch Creek

Suspension
Bridge

0.60 Reach a fence at the top of the hill; turn sharply right to head northeast toward the pond.

Option: If the gate is open, you can head west to explore mowed trails through the western section of Martin Prairie.

Option: Turn left (south) to follow a mowed path that leads to the enclosed bison pen.

0.70 Reach a bench and fork at the southeast corner of the pond; keep left (north) to continue on Martin Prairie Trail. At the next junction, continue north on the same mowed path.

1.13 Northern boundary of Martin Prairie; turn right (east) to follow the path running parallel with West Van Dorn Street.

1.29 Trail passes a windmill to the south.

1.35 Trail crosses a wooded slough.

1.52   Keep right (south).

1.98   Turn left (northeast).

2.07   Turn right (southeast).

2.10   Cross a marshy area.

2.20   Trail heads south along the eastern boundary of Martin Prairie, with the Pioneers Golf Course east of the boundary fence.

2.29   Continue straight (south).

2.40   Cunningham School; continue south toward the parking lot.

2.49   Reach the parking lot; continue south and cross the road.

2.55   After entering the gate (note closing time), immediately turn right (west).

2.62   Pollinator Garden.

2.79   Pass an outdoor classroom to the west of the fence.

2.80   Outdoor bird exhibits.

2.90   At a sign about ducks and geese, turn right (west).

3.04   Turn left (south) and cross a wooden footbridge.

3.08   Boardwalk.

3.12   Bench.

3.32   Keep right (east).

3.39   Keep right.

Purple coneflower (*Echinacea purpurea*) in the Pollinator Garden.

3.42   Keep right (south) and cross the suspension bridge (note closing time).

3.47   At a bench, turn right (east) onto Harrington Trail.

3.61   Keep right (southeast).

3.85   Turn left (northeast) and cross the Prairie Corridor Bridge over Haines Branch Creek.

3.94   Turn left (west) onto the path that enters the northern edge of Fleming Woods.

4.20   The path leaves the woods and heads north toward the park road.

4.25   Cross the road and turn left to follow Prairie Corridor Trail toward the parking lot.

4.34   Arrive back at the parking lot.

37 NINE-MILE PRAIRIE

Go slow. Bring a camera and field guides, ideally on wildflowers and insects. Stop frequently, get down on your knees if need be, and accept the inevitability of ticks. All are great ways to experience Nine-Mile Prairie. This tallgrass prairie on the outskirts of Lincoln has never been plowed, and university researchers have studied it since the 1920s and continue to do so to this day. Head to the visitor registry directly south of the trailhead to study the topographical map and wildflower blooming calendar, then hike this 2.8-mile loop around the perimeter while also wandering the interior trails on this historical remnant prairie.

Start: Nine-Mile Prairie Historical Marker
Elevation gain: 1,270 to 1,373 feet
Distance: 2.80-mile loop
Difficulty: Easy
Hiking time: 1–2 hours
Seasons/schedule: Open year-round, dawn to dusk; best in spring and summer for wildflowers (check the visitor registry for wildflower blooming calendar)
Fees and permits: None
Trail contact: University of Nebraska Center for Grassland Studies; (402) 472-3471; grassland.unl.edu/nine-mile-prairie
Dog-friendly: Yes

Trail surface: Mowed grass
Land status: University of Nebraska
Nearest town: Lincoln 9 miles to the southeast
Maps: USGS Emerald, NE 2021
Other trail users: None
Special considerations: The address of the parking lot is 6201 West Fletcher Ave.; it is directly north of the historical marker and the gated entrance to the prairie.
Amenities available: None
Maximum grade: 8%
Cell service: Reliable coverage available at the parking lot and on the trails.

FINDING THE TRAILHEAD

Coming from the west on I-80, take exit 395 and head north on NE 55K Link / NW 48th Street. After nearly 4 miles, turn left (west) onto West Fletcher Avenue. Reach the parking lot after 1 mile. Coming from the east on I-80, take exit 401B and turn right (north) onto US 34. After 4 miles, turn left (southwest) onto NW 48th Street, then turn left (west) after 0.7 mile onto West Fletcher Avenue to reach the parking lot. **GPS:** N40° 52.298′ W96° 48.344′

Trail Conditions: The trails are mowed but not waymarked; they create a large network of paths through the prairie. Ticks are prevalent and certain to catch a ride regardless of the amount of repellant used. The proximity to Lincoln results in moderate trail traffic.

THE HIKE

Nine-Mile Prairie is located 5 miles west and 4 miles north of the University of Nebraska campus in downtown Lincoln, hence its name. The remnant tallgrass prairie is owned by the University of Nebraska Foundation as a research and natural area open to the public. No hunting is allowed, and only foot traffic is permitted, contributing to a peaceful setting on the northwestern outskirts of Lincoln that allows visitors to explore the 230-acre

Left: Prairie blazing star (*Liatris pycnostachya*).
Right: Rough blazing star (*Liatris aspera*).

preserve, home to 392 plant species and over 80 bird species. The prairie is ecologically important and as a result various scientific and conservation studies are conducted on the land. When you visit, please do not disturb any research equipment and do not collect plants or wildlife.

The mowed grass trails are accessed via the gate on the south side of West Fletcher Avenue. Head south toward the kiosk at 0.13 mile. Inside the kiosk there is a topographic map of Nine-Mile Prairie with the names of different areas of the preserve. There is also a helpful wildflower blooming calendar that will help your identification as you hike through the prairie. Snap a photo of both and then continue heading south through East Ridge Prairie. The trail crosses the East Ridge Ravine at 0.4 mile then heads west at 0.5 mile along a fence and underneath power lines.

As you hike west, there are several trails that lead north into Middle Ridge and West Ridge Prairies. Feel free to explore portions or all of these trails as you may encounter different plant species and other interesting things, such as protective nets surrounding vegetation that protect caterpillars as they undergo the process of becoming monarch butterflies. Please do not disturb any materials for conservation or scientific research.

Cross West Ridge Ravine at 0.7 and continue west through Gentian Prairie, which has more woody and shrubby plants than the previous areas of the prairie. The power lines head south at 0.95 mile as the trail continues to head west along the southern bound-ary of Nine-Mile Prairie. Take advantage of the picnic table at 1.17 miles to soak in the views of South Flader Prairie. Once you are back on the trail, make a decision at 1.28 miles whether to head west through West Flader Ravine and hike the westernmost sliver of land on Nine-Mile Prairie via a loop that returns to this junction. Otherwise, turn north before West Flader Ravine to hike on its eastern edge with East Flader Prairie on your right. The north end of East Flader Prairie has an extensive sumac grove, illustrative of how woody plant species invade a prairie and outcompete grasses and wildflowers.

NINE-MILE PRAIRIE

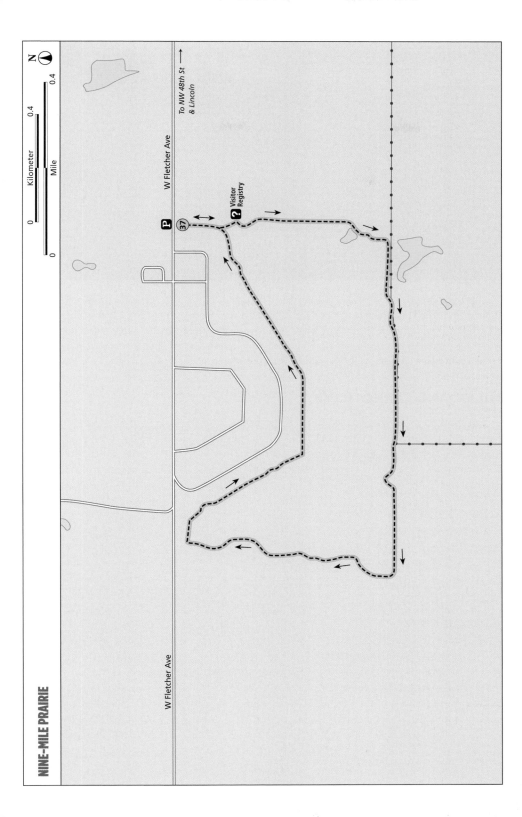

W Fletcher Ave

W Fletcher Ave

To NW 48th St
& Lincoln →

Visitor
Registry

Kilometer
0   0.4

Mile
0   0.4

N

Nine-Mile Prairie on a late summer morning.

The final stretch of the hike follows the chain-link fence that separates Nine-Mile Prairie from the Lincoln Airport storage facility to the north, returning to the trailhead after hiking the 2.8-mile perimeter loop. Again, it is recommended to explore the interior trails on the prairie, going slow and getting up close to observe the diversity of plants, insects, and other life that call Nine-Mile Prairie home.

MILES AND DIRECTIONS

0.00 Begin at the Nine-Mile Prairie Historical Marker; after closing the gate behind you, head south.

0.10 Keep left (southeast) toward the kiosk.

0.13 Visitor registry; continue south.

0.21 Continue straight (south).

0.30 Continue straight (south).

0.39 Continue straight (south).

0.43 Continue straight (south).

0.48 Turn right (west).

0.62 Continue straight (west) following the power transmission lines.

0.95 Continue straight (west) as the power lines head south.

1.17 Picnic table; continue west.

1.28 Turn right (north).

      Option: Continue straight (west) to hike a loop through the westernmost section of Nine-Mile Prairie, returning to this junction at the end of the loop.

1.51 Continue straight (north).

2.14 Turn left (east).

2.64 Keep left (east).

2.70 Turn left (north).

2.80 Arrive back at the trailhead.

38 FRANK SHOEMAKER MARSH

Frank Shoemaker Marsh is a restored wetland located in the ecologically unique and critically imperiled Eastern Saline Wetlands of the Salt Creek watershed north of Lincoln. Extensive restoration efforts by City of Lincoln Parks and Recreation have restored habitat for the endangered Salt Creek tiger beetle as well as restoring 160 acres of wetlands and upland prairie. Shorebirds, waterfowl, and grassland birds find refuge on the preserve that is just 8 miles north of downtown Lincoln. Over 3 miles of trails explore the restored wetlands and grasslands.

Start: Northwest corner of the parking area
Elevation gain: 1,139 to 1,186 feet
Distance: 3.32 miles out and back
Difficulty: Easy
Hiking time: 1–2 hours
Seasons/schedule: Trails open year-round, sunrise to sunset; best in Apr and May to view migrating birds
Fees and permits: None
Trail contact: City of Lincoln Parks and Recreation; (402) 441-7847; lincoln.ne.gov/City/Departments/Parks-and-Recreation/Parks-Facilities/Parks-A-to-Z/Frank-Shoemaker-Marsh
Dog-friendly: Yes, on leash

Trail surface: Mowed grass and crushed rock
Land status: City of Lincoln Parks and Recreation
Nearest town: Lincoln 8 miles to the south
Maps: USGS Davey, NE 2021
Other trail users: Bikers
Special considerations: Extensive restoration work has been done on this fragile ecosystem; please be respectful and do not collect plants or wildlife.
Amenities available: None
Maximum grade: 4%
Cell service: Adequate coverage by most carriers

FINDING THE TRAILHEAD

 From exit 403 on I-80, head north on N 27th Street for 0.3 mile. Turn right (east) onto Arbor Road, then immediately turn left (north) onto N 27th Street again and continue for 1.3 miles. Turn left (west) into the parking area for Frank Shoemaker Marsh. The trailhead is located in the northwest corner of the parking area. **GPS:** N40° 54.715′ W96° 40.932′

Trail Conditions: The trails are not waymarked but are well maintained and regularly mowed. Ticks are common in summer. Trails may be muddy after heavy rain. The trails receive moderate traffic.

THE HIKE

The Eastern Saline Wetlands in Lancaster and Saunders Counties form a regionally unique ecosystem that is critically endangered. Once totaling more than 20,000 acres, now there are only 4,000 acres of wetlands and marshes on the Salt Creek, Little Salt Creek, and Rock Creek floodplains north of Nebraska's capital. Groundwater brings salt buried deep under the soil to the surface, increasing the salinity of the waters, changing the characteristics of the soil, and creating habitat for a number of rare species found nowhere else in Nebraska. The state-listed endangered saltwort plant is found nowhere

A sheltered viewing deck overlooking Frank Shoemaker Marsh.

else in the state, while the only known population in the world of the federally endangered Salt Creek tiger beetle is found in the Little Salt Creek wetlands.

The city of Lincoln purchased the land along the Little Salt Creek in 2003 and named it after Frank Shoemaker, an amateur naturalist who moved to Nebraska in 1897 and meticulously studied the saline wetlands. Extensive restoration work was done on the badly degraded site to return it to as close a natural state as possible. Work was completed

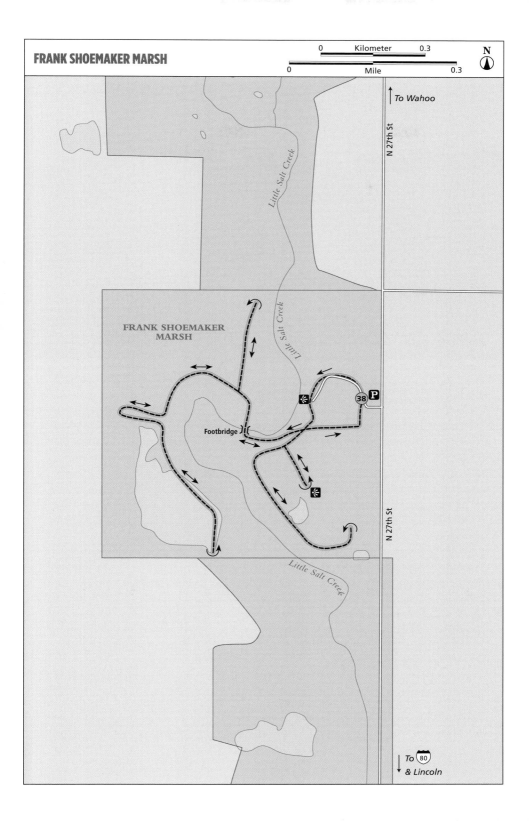

FRANK SHOEMAKER MARSH

0   Kilometer   0.3
0   Mile   0.3

N

To Wahoo

Little Salt Creek

N 27th St

FRANK SHOEMAKER
MARSH

Little Salt Creek

38 P

Footbridge

N 27th St

Little Salt Creek

To 80
& Lincoln

in 2007, and the ecosystem has responded positively. Salt-tolerant plants like saltgrass, seablite, and saltwort grow in the wetlands, while a variety of birds breed, nest, and raise their young in the marshes and upland prairie. Red-winged blackbirds are common in the wetlands while dickcissels and other grassland birds find habitat in the upland prairie.

Over 3 miles of trails explore the 160-acre preserve. The trailhead is located in the northwest corner of the small parking area. After a short walk, reach a viewing platform at 0.17 mile overlooking the Little Salt Creek. From here, hikers can choose several options. If you are rushed for time or simply want to enjoy the viewpoint, you can return to the parking area. If you want to visit another viewpoint overlooking the marsh, you can follow the trails south. If you'd like to explore all the trails, keep right at 0.26 mile to head west.

Cross the footbridge at 0.37 mile over Little Salt Creek and then continue straight at 0.45 mile. This trail explores the marsh, so if you want to identify saltwort, seablite, saltgrass, and other plant species, bring a field guide or use an application on your phone. Wetland bird species, like red-winged blackbirds, are abundant in this area of the preserve. The trail makes an arc through the marsh, eventually heading south where it reaches a dead end at a fence after 1.08 miles. Turn around and return via the same trail. Before you reach the footbridge, turn left (north) at 1.7 miles to follow a trail leading to the northern boundary of the marsh.

After crossing the footbridge over Little Salt Creek, hike east then turn south at 2.23 miles to explore two trails in the southeastern section of the preserve. Keep right at 2.25 miles to follow another dead-end trail with the creek on your right. Turn around and return to the junction at 2.96, turning right (south) to reach a covered viewpoint over-looking the marsh at 3.04 miles. The trailhead is a short hike, less than half a mile, from this viewpoint.

MILES AND DIRECTIONS

0.00 Begin at the trailhead at the northwest end of the parking lot and head north on the crushed rock path.

0.17 Viewing platform above Little Salt Creek.

0.26 Keep right (west).

0.37 Cross the footbridge over Little Salt Creek.

0.45 Continue straight (west).

1.08 Reach a dead end; turn around and head north on the same trail.

1.70 Turn left (north) onto a trail leading to the northern boundary of the preserve.

1.87 Northern boundary of the preserve; turn around and head south toward the footbridge.

2.11 Cross the footbridge over Little Salt Creek heading south.

2.23 Turn right (south).

2.25 Continue straight (west).

2.61 Reach a dead end; turn around and return via the same trail.

2.96 Turn right (south) to hike to a sheltered viewpoint.

3.04 Viewpoint; turn around and return to the previous junction.

3.12 Keep right (northwest).

3.32 Arrive back at the trailhead.

Eastern kingbirds (*Tyrannus tyrannus*).

J **WILLA CATHER MEMORIAL PRAIRIE**

"That shaggy grass country had gripped me with a passion that I have never been able to shake. It has been the happiness and curse of my life." The prairie occupies a monumental place in the work of Willa Cather, and the Willa Cather Memorial Prairie is representative of that "shaggy grass country" that awed Nebraska's most renowned writer. The 612-acre remnant prairie, never plowed, lies 6 miles south of Cather's childhood home in Red Cloud. A short trail lends itself to a slow prairie walk, best in spring through fall, in the company of grassland birds like meadowlarks and bobolinks and plants such as coneflowers, prairie clovers, and the 6-foot-tall big bluestem.

Start: Willa Cather Memorial Prairie Historical Marker
Elevation gain: 1,909 to 1,938 feet
Distance: 0.62 mile out and back
Difficulty: Easy
Hiking time: Less than 1 hour
Seasons/schedule: Open year-round, sunrise to sunset; a brochure on the prairie website lists spring, summer, and fall bird species, wildflowers, and grasses
Fees and permits: None
Trail contact: National Willa Cather Center, 413 N Webster St., Red Cloud 68970; (402) 746-2653; www.willacather.org/learn/cather-prairie
Dog-friendly: Yes, on leash
Trail surface: Grass

Land status: Willa Cather Foundation
Nearest town: Red Cloud 6 miles to the north
Maps: USGS Red Cloud, NE, KS 2021; a trail map is included in the brochure on the prairie website (see Trail Conditions below)
Other trail users: None
Special considerations: Cattle grazing is used as a land management technique; please close all gates and maintain a safe distance from livestock.
Amenities available: None
Maximum grade: 4%
Cell service: Good reception for most carriers

FINDING THE TRAILHEAD

From Red Cloud, head south on US 281. After 6 miles, turn west at the entrance to the Willa Cather Memorial Prairie Historical Marker. **GPS:** N40° 0.244' W98° 31.363'

Trail Conditions: At the time of publication, the trails listed on the brochure on the prairie website were not visible on the ground; the only trail was from the gate at the historical marker to another gate less than half a mile north. Check with the Willa Cather Foundation on trail conditions. There is not a storm shelter in case of severe weather; check the forecast before you go to the prairie. The trail receives light traffic.

The Willa Cather Memorial Prairie lies 6 miles south of Red Cloud, the author's childhood home.

K OAK CREEK TRAIL

Settled primarily by Czech immigrants in the late 1800s, the gentle, rolling hills of eastern Butler County and western Saunders County became informally known as the Bohemian Alps due to their resemblance to the immigrants' homeland. The Oak Creek Trail, which follows an abandoned Union Pacific line, is a great way to explore the prairie, oak woodlands, and farmland written about by former poet laureate and Bohemian Alps resident Ted Kooser in *Local Wonders: Seasons in the Bohemian Alps*. Trailheads in Valparaiso, Loma, and Brainard allow hikers to break the 13-mile trail into shorter day hikes.

Start: North Oak Bridge in Valparaiso, Loma (half-way point), or Brainard

Elevation gain: 1,309 to 1,670 feet (from Valparaiso to Brainard)

Distance: 13-mile point-to-point

Difficulty: Easy due to level grade following an abandoned railroad line

Hiking time: Variable depending on the section of trail hiked

Seasons/schedule: Open year-round, sunrise to sunset; best in autumn for fall colors

Fees and permits: None, however, voluntary trail pass donations are used to maintain existing trails. Passes are available at boxes along the trails or by contacting the Lower Platte South National Resources Distict (LPSNRD).

Trail contact: Lower Platte South Natural Resources District, 3125 Portia St., Lincoln 68521; (402) 476-2729; www.lpsnrd.org/oak-creek-trail

Dog-friendly: Yes, on leash

Trail surface: Crushed rock

Land status: Lower Platte South Natural Resources District

Nearest town: Valparaiso, Loma, and Brainard

Maps: USGS Loma, NE 2021; USGS Valparaiso SW, NE 2021; USGS Valparaiso, NE 2021; trail map available on LPSNRD website (see trail contact)

Other trail users: Cyclists; a separate equestrian trail shares the trail corridor

Special considerations: Voluntary trail pass donations are used to maintain existing trails. Passes are available at boxes along the trails or by contacting the LPSNRD. Check the LPSNRD website for trail closures and other information before hiking the trail. There are more than 100 geocaches along the trail; search "Oak Creek Trail Challenge" at geocaching.com to learn more.

Amenities available: Trail parking and other services are available at all 3 communities (Valparaiso, Loma, Brainard) on the trail; restrooms are available at the Valparaiso trailhead and in Loma.

Maximum grade: 4%

Cell service: Spotty in areas with most carriers

FINDING THE TRAILHEAD

The Valparaiso trailhead is on S Oak Street between W 2nd Street and W 3rd Street. The Loma trailhead is on West Road across from St. Luke's Catholic Church. The Brainard trailhead is at the intersection of S Lincoln Street and W Novak Street / 30 Road on the southeastern edge of Brainard.

GPS (Valparaiso): N41° 4.861' W96° 50.130'
GPS (Loma): N41° 7.691' W96° 56.570'
GPS (Brainard): N41° 10.624' W96° 59.908'

Bridge over Oak Creek near the trailhead in Valparaiso.

Trail Conditions: The trails were damaged by the 2019 floods and erosion issues; sections that were closed have been reopened as of October 2022 (check the LPSNRD website for current trail closures). Trail rules and regulations are posted at trailheads.

L WILDERNESS PARK

Lincoln's largest public park offers 31 miles of meandering multiuse trails along Salt Creek, allowing hikers to create their own adventure as they explore Wilderness Park's dense forest, meadows, and creek beds. Eight trailheads give access to the trail system, and updates in 2020 to the park's master plan aim to upgrade the state's wildest urban park and its trail infrastructure. Some of the trails may follow traditional trails used by the Otoe-Missouria and Pawnee, the original stewards of the lands that make up Wilderness Park.

Start: 8 trailheads in total: Day Camp, Epworth, Pioneer, 1st Street, Old Cheney, GPTN Connector, 14th Street, and Saltillo; refer to the park map for trailhead locations

Elevation gain: Variable; between 1,142 to 1,198 feet

Distance: 31 total miles of hiking trails

Difficulty: Easy to moderate, depending on distance of hike

Hiking time: Variable

Seasons/schedule: Trails open year-round, sunrise to sunset

Fees and permits: None

Trail contact: City of Lincoln Parks and Recreation; (402) 441-8258; www.itsyourwilderness.com

Dog-friendly: Yes, on leash

Trail surface: Dirt footpaths

Land status: City of Lincoln Parks and Recreation

Nearest town: Lincoln

Maps: USGS Lincoln, NE 2021 and Roca, NE 2021; trail map available online and at trailhead kiosks

Other trail users: Cyclists and equestrians (equestrians are only allowed on select trails)

Special considerations: The trails are frequently muddy; please refrain from using muddy trails to prevent trail degradation. On multiuse trails, hikers must yield to equestrians. The trail map lists a lot of helpful information, such as numbered intersections, water crossings, frequently wet areas, and historical features. The maps on the trailhead kiosks also include the mileage for each trail segment in the park.

Amenities available: Picnic facilities; seasonal restrooms are planned for some trailheads

Maximum grade: Variable

Cell service: Adequate to good reception on most carriers

FINDING THE TRAILHEAD

Refer to the park map for the location of the eight trailheads. To reach the 1st Street Trailhead, head south from Lincoln on US 77. Turn east onto W Pioneers Boulevard, then turn south onto S 1st Street. Continue south until reaching the 1st Street Trailhead.

GPS (1st Street Trailhead): N40° 45.766' W96° 43.220'

Trail Conditions: The trailheads have information kiosks with a trail map (take a photo for reference), which lists numbered intersections and the users that can use each trail. Muddy trails and occasional flooding can make the trails impassable; to prevent trail degradation, do not hike on muddy trails. The trails receive heavy traffic due to the park's location in Lincoln.

The trail system at Wilderness Park is well marked and maintained.

Whitetail deer at Ponca State Park.

MISSOURI VALLEY

The Missouri River today would largely be unrecognizable to the river that Captain Merriweather Lewis and Second Lieutenant William Clark explored in 1804. Much of the Missouri has been channelized to control flooding and aid navigation. The logjams and sandbars that complicated Lewis and Clark's journey are gone; however, flooding is still a concern, as the historical 2019 floods confirmed. Recovery is still ongoing after those devastating floods, but most of the parks and preserves along the Missouri River are open and ready to explore. Like the Loess Hills across the river in western Iowa, the bluffs lining the Nebraska side of the Missouri contain tallgrass prairies on ridgetops and hardwood forests in valley bottoms. The eastern deciduous forest reaches its westernmost range along the Missouri Valley, which means that various woodland bird species are found in the forests along the river bluffs and nowhere else in Nebraska.

Bloodroot Trail.

39 SOUTH SHORE TRAIL

In 1804, the Corps of Discovery expedition camped near present-day Lewis and Clark Lake. In 1957, construction of Gavins Point Dam created Nebraska's second-largest reservoir, forever changing the wild Missouri River that Lewis and Clark explored. South Shore Trail leads hikers along the edge of a steep cliff with views of eroded cliffs plunging into the water and boats dotting the lake. The second half of the hike passes through oak woodland where blue jays, indigo buntings, warblers, and other birds can be seen.

Start: South Shore Trailhead
Elevation gain: 1,231 to 1,355 feet
Distance: 3.5-mile loop
Difficulty: Moderate, due to some inclines and steep cliffs
Hiking time: 1.5–2 hours
Seasons/schedule: Open year-round, dawn to dusk.
Fees and permits: A park entry permit is required and may be purchased at the park, statewide Game and Parks offices and permit vendors, or online at outdoornebraska.gov.
Trail contact: Lewis and Clark State Recreation Area, 54731 897 Rd., Crofton 68730; (402) 388-4169; outdoornebraska.gov/lewisandclark/
Dog-friendly: Yes, on 6-foot leash
Trail surface: Dirt and grass
Land status: Lewis and Clark State Recreation Area

Nearest town: South Yankton 6 miles to the east
Maps: USGS Gavins Point Dam, SD, NE 2021; park map does not include South Shore Trail
Other trail users: Bikers, equestrians; cross-country skiers and snowmobiles in winter
Special considerations: Hunting is allowed during hunting season, so dress accordingly. Take precautions at the viewpoints of the lake, as the cliffs are very steep.
Amenities available: Vault toilets and water pump at the boat launch parking area near the trailhead
Maximum grade: 12%
Cell service: Reliable coverage at the trailhead; coverage may be spotty under tree canopy

FINDING THE TRAILHEAD

From Crofton, head north on NE 121. After 8.3 miles, turn left (north) into the South Shore Recreation Area. From South Yankton, head west on NE 121. After 3.5 miles, turn left (south) to stay on NE 121 and continue for 1.4 miles. Turn right (north) at the entrance to South Shore Recreation Area. The boat launch, with toilets and water pump, is at the end of the gravel road near the lake. The trailhead is south of the boat launch. **GPS:** N42° 50.650' W97° 29.336

Trail Conditions: Trails are well maintained. There are brown trail markers at trail junctions, but they do not provide navigational cues. Moderate traffic.

THE HIKE

Despite the drastic change since Lewis and Clark camped in the early nineteenth century, this impounded stretch of the Missouri River still attracts campers and boaters, albeit in search of recreation instead of the Pacific Ocean. Other recreation opportunities at Lewis and Clark State Recreation Area include fishing, hunting, and various hiking trails on both the Nebraska and South Dakota side of the lake. South Shore Trail offers

Top: Dramatic cliffs dot the south shore of Lewis and Clark Lake.
Bottom: Dame's rocket blooming along South Shore Trail.

year-round recreation, as the trail is groomed in the winter for cross-country skiing. Spring is another excellent time to explore the trail, as migratory songbirds return, such as indigo buntings and warblers, and wildflowers bloom both in the woodlands and ridgetop prairies that overlook Lewis and Clark Lake.

The trailhead is at the north end of the South Shore Area parking lot and boat launch, where there are also vault toilets. The dirt trail meanders through a mixed forest of eastern redcedar, bur oak, green ash, hackberry, and basswood for nearly one and a half miles until reaching a short spur trail at 1.3 miles, which leads to a viewpoint overlooking Lewis and Clark Lake. Gavins Point Dam is visible to the east, while a chain of light-yellow bluffs highlight the landscape to the west. These cliffs plunge directly into the lake below, and caution should be taken when approaching the edge of the bluffs.

From the viewpoint, South Shore Trail continues along the edge of the bluffs, heading southwest for more than one-half mile until reaching another viewpoint with a bench and selfie station at 1.95 miles. Look for eastern kingbirds, yellow warblers, and cliff swallows as boats silently motor atop the lake. Here the trail turns on itself to head east,

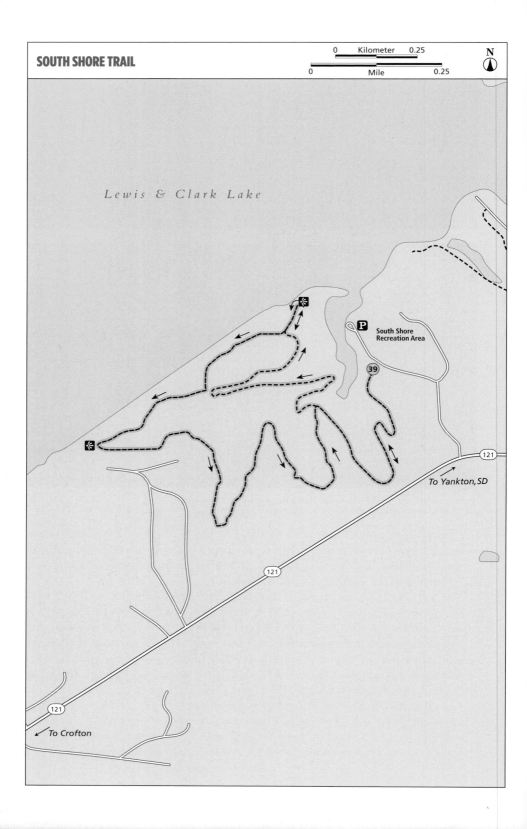

0   Kilometer   0.25

0   Mile   0.25

N

Lewis & Clark Lake

P South Shore
   Recreation Area

39

121

121

To Yankton, SD

121

To Crofton

passing a large clearing with numerous dead cedars, before entering woodlands once again at 2.0 miles. As the trail heads south, it passes several private residences. Have your binoculars on this section of the trail, as many woodland birds can be observed, including blue jays, indigo buntings, and orioles. Don't get too comfortable, however, as this final section of the loop traverses several inclines before reaching the trail at 2.95 miles back to the trailhead.

MILES AND DIRECTIONS

0.00 Begin at the trailhead at the north end of the boat launch and parking area.

0.56 At a junction, keep right (west).

0.73 Reach a hairpin turn as the trail heads west up a steep incline.

1.00 Turn right (northeast) at a crossroads.

1.30 Turn right (north) to reach a viewpoint of Lewis and Clark Lake; turn around.

1.65 At the crossroads, turn right (west) to continue along the trail following the cliff.

1.95 Viewpoint with bench and selfie station.

2.95 Keep right (southeast) at the junction to return to the trailhead.

3.50 Arrive back at the South Shore Trailhead.

Views of Lewis and Clark Lake.

40 OLD OAK TRAIL AND BLOODROOT TRAIL

Ponca State Park has 22 miles of trails that explore upland hardwood forest, tallgrass prairie remnants, and the floodplain of one of the last unchanneled stretches of the Missouri River. Old Oak Trail features the highlight of the park: the oldest tree in Nebraska, a bur oak dated to 1644. The trail is a short 1-mile loop but can be connected with Bloodroot Trail, which receives significantly less foot traffic, allowing for a peaceful forest walk. Visit throughout the year to witness blooming Dutchman's breeches in the spring, the nocturnal calls of migratory whip-poor-wills in summer, fall colors, and bald eagles in winter.

Start: Small parking area above the Old Oak Tree
Elevation gain: 1,153 to 1,348 feet
Distance: 2.90-mile loop
Difficulty: Easy
Hiking time: 1.5–2 hours
Seasons/schedule: Open year-round. For migratory songbirds, late Apr to early May; woodland and prairie wildflowers from late Apr to early June; autumn for fall colors and migratory ducks, geese, and other birds; winter for bald eagles
Fees and permits: A park entry permit is required and may be purchased at the park, statewide Game and Parks offices and permit vendors, or online at outdoornebraska.gov.
Trail contact: Ponca State Park, 88090 Spur 26 E, Ponca 68770;

(402) 755-2284; outdoornebraska .gov/ponca/
Dog-friendly: Yes, on 6-foot leash
Trail surface: Dirt footpaths
Land status: Ponca State Park
Nearest town: Ponca 2.5 miles to the south
Maps: USGS Ponca, NE, SD 2021; park map available at the park office and online at outdoornebraska.gov/ ponca/
Other trail users: Bikers
Special considerations: Take appropriate precautions during tick season.
Amenities available: Vault toilets and picnic shelters along the trail. Water pumps available in season throughout the park.
Maximum grade: 10%
Cell service: Yes, reliable in clearings but less so under tree canopy.

FINDING THE TRAILHEAD

From Ponca, head north on NE 26E Spur for approximately 2 miles. After passing the park's main gate, keep left at the fork to continue north. After 1.1 miles, turn left (south) and continue for 0.2 mile until reaching the small parking area at the top of the stairs which lead down to the Old Oak Tree. There is additional parking nearby farther west along the park road. **GPS:** N41° 49.718′ W103° 42.427

Trail Conditions: The trail is well marked and maintained. There are interpretive panels along the trail highlighting the flora and fauna of the park. Heavy foot traffic.

THE HIKE

The bluffs along the un–channelized section of the Missouri River in Dakota, Dixon, and Cedar Counties take their name from the Ponca Tribe, as does the state park 25 miles northwest of Sioux City. Ponca State Park has numerous attractions such as the

Tri-State Overlook and Towers of Time. This unchanneled stretch of the Missouri River resembles its natural state when Lewis and Clark passed what is now Ponca State Park on August 22, 1804.

The Old Oak Tree was already 160 years old when the duo led the Corps of Discovery westward. A core sample determined the bur oak was a sapling in 1644, making it the oldest tree in Nebraska and older than the United States itself. There are two main ways to reach the Old Oak Tree: a parking area south of the tree, requiring a climb up Old Oak Trail, or a smaller parking area just north of the tree where a staircase descends directly to the tree. This trail follows the north access via the staircase. As mentioned, the parking area here can fit a maximum of four cars (double-parked) but there are two additional parking pull-offs to the west on the park road. Take the staircase down to reach the Old Oak Tree, a bur oak with a thick trunk and equally thick limbs that extend over the forest floor, seemingly defying gravity. This is an example of a "wolf tree," as it wolfs up space and prevents saplings and other growth underneath its extensive canopy.

The Old Oak Tree, a sapling in 1644, is the oldest tree in Nebraska.

Old Oak Trail passes directly by the eponymous tree, meandering the hillside below underneath a canopy of bur oak, hackberry, green ash, and basswood. Head right at the tree (southwest) until reaching a fork at 0.2 mile. Keep left (southeast) to continue on Old Oak Trail; the right fork is a connector trail to Bloodroot Trail. Old Oak Trail descends to nearly the bottom of the hill and passes close to a picnic shelter and parking area at 0.4 mile. There are interpretive signs along the trail that explain the various flora and fauna at Ponca State Park.

At 0.7 mile, keep left (northwest) as Old Oak Trail begins to snake its way back up the hill toward the Old Oak Tree. Before reaching the tree again, keep right (west) at the 1-mile mark to take a connector trail to Bloodroot Trail. Cross a park road at 1.3 miles and continue west at a junction after 1.44 miles before reaching Bloodroot Trail at 1.53 miles.

Bloodroot Trail, receiving far less foot traffic than Old Oak Trail, is a peaceful loop through pristine forest. In spring and summer, the forest floor is covered in a carpet of wildflowers, beginning with Dutchman's breeches in early spring to other wildflowers such as red columbine, Virginia waterleaf, and bloodroot, which gives the trail its name.

The southern section of the loop passes through forest dominated by eastern redcedar. After completing the loop, keep right at 2.46 miles on a connector trail that crosses a park

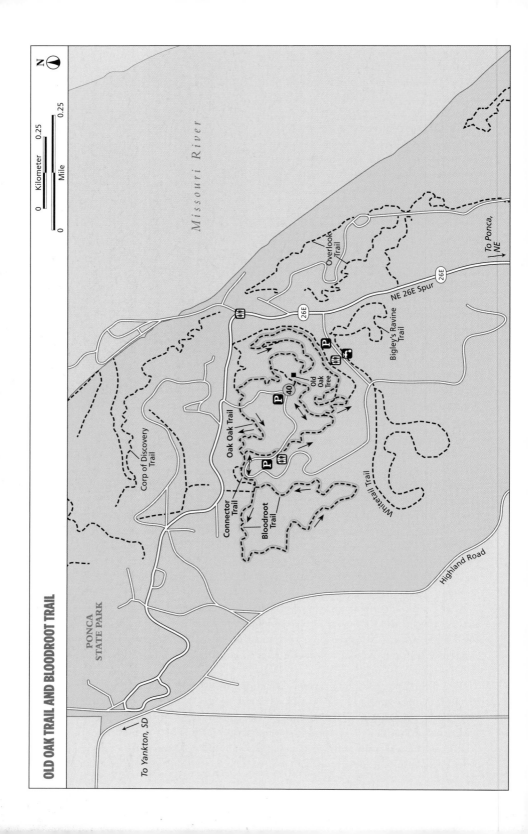

OLD OAK TRAIL AND BLOODROOT TRAIL

N

Missouri River

PONCA
STATE PARK

To Yankton, SD

Corp of Discovery
Trail

Oak Oak Trail

40

Old
Oak
Tree

Connector
Trail

Bloodroot
Trail

Whitetail Trail

Bigley's Ravine
Trail

Overlook
Trail

26E

NE 26E Spur

26E

To Ponca,
NE

Highland Road

Kilometer
0   0.25

Mile
0   0.25

road near a picnic shelter and toilets. From here it is possible to follow the park road back to the parking area at the Old Oak Tree trailhead. The connector trail, however, continues south to reach Old Oak Trail at 2.74 miles. Turn left (north) to visit the Old Oak Tree again before climbing the stairs to reach the trailhead.

MILES AND DIRECTIONS

- **0.00** Begin at the small parking area above the Old Oak Tree, marked by a sign. Head south down the stairs.
- **0.01** Old Oak Tree; turn right (southwest).
- **0.20** Keep left (southeast) at the fork to continue on Old Oak Trail.
- **0.40** Keep left (west).
- **0.70** Keep left (northwest) on Old Oak Trail.
- **1.00** Keep right (west) to follow a connector trail to Bloodroot Trail.

   Bailout: Keep left (southwest) to return to the Old Oak Tree and the trailhead.

- **1.30** Cross the park road and continue straight (southwest) following the sign for Bloodroot Trail.
- **1.44** Keep right (west) to continue on Bloodroot Trail.
- **1.53** Continue straight (west) on Bloodroot Trail.
- **2.37** Turn right (east) to follow the connector trail back to Old Oak Trail.
- **2.46** Keep right (east) to continue on the connector trail to Old Oak Trail.

Top: Eastern red columbine (*Aquilegia canadensis*).
Bottom: Red admiral (*Vanessa atalanta*).

- **2.56** Continue straight (south) crossing the park road to continue on the connector trail.
- **2.74** Turn left (north) onto Old Oak Trail.
- **2.88** Old Oak Tree and the stairs leading up to the trailhead.
- **2.90** Arrive back at the trailhead.

41 COTTONWOOD AND GRASSLAND NATURE TRAILS

DeSoto National Wildlife Refuge straddles the border of Nebraska and Iowa, but lucky for this guidebook the trails on this hike lie in the Cornhusker State. Cottonwood and Grassland Nature Trails meander through cottonwood-dogwood riparian forest and tallgrass prairie along the west bank of DeSoto Lake, a 7-mile-long oxbow lake that was notoriously hazardous when it was a bend of the Missouri River—the Bertrand steamboat that ran aground in 1865 is testament to the danger. DeSoto is a birder's delight: a peak of 50,000 ducks during the fall migration as well as wintering bald eagles, red-headed woodpeckers, warblers, gulls, shorebirds, and songbirds.

Start: Cottonwood and Grassland Nature Trails parking area
Elevation gain: 995 to 1,006 feet
Distance: 2.22-mile loop
Difficulty: Easy due to short distance and flat terrain
Hiking time: 1–2 hours
Seasons/schedule: Open daily year-round, half hour before sunrise and after sunset; best in late Nov, Dec, and early Mar for bald eagles; summer for wood ducks; mushroom foraging is allowed on open area from Apr 15 to Oct 14
Fees and permits: Federal fee area: valid entry permit (self-pay at entrance) or valid pass required
Trail contact: DeSoto National Wildlife Refuge, 1434 316th Ln., Missouri Valley, IA 51555; (712) 388-4800; fws.gov/refuge/desoto/
Dog-friendly: Yes, on leash
Trail surface: Crushed rock and asphalt

Land status: DeSoto National Wildlife Refuge
Nearest town: Missouri Valley (Iowa) to the east, Blair to the west
Maps: USGS Modale; available at the visitor center, trailhead, and fws.gov/refuge/desoto/
Other trail users: None
Special considerations: Hunting is allowed with a special permit. Meander and Green Heron Nature Trails near the visitor center are open seasonally. Some refuge roads are closed during bird migration season; check the website or call the visitor center beforehand.
Amenities available: Restrooms, water, gift shop, information desk, and interpretive exhibits at the visitor center. Vault toilets (2) and a picnic shelter at the trailhead.
Maximum grade: 2%
Cell service: Reliable coverage throughout the refuge

FINDING THE TRAILHEAD

From Omaha take I-29 north to US 30, exit 75 at Missouri Valley. Continue west on US 30 for 5 miles to the refuge entrance. Turn left (south) onto the refuge road, DeSoto Avenue. Continue for 3.7 miles, passing the visitor center. At the sign for Bertrand Discovery Site, turn left (north) and continue for 1 mile to reach the parking area of Cottonwood and Grassland Nature Trail.

From Blair, head west on US 30 and cross the Missouri River to enter Iowa. Turn right (south) onto DeSoto Avenue. Continue for 3.7 miles, passing the visitor center. At the sign for Bertrand Discovery Site, turn left (north) and continue for 1 mile to reach the parking area of Cottonwood and Grassland Nature Trail. **GPS:** N41° 31.591' W96° 1.678

Trail Conditions: The trails are well maintained but not waymarked. High winds could create tree and snag hazards in the forested sections of the hike. Moderate foot traffic.

THE HIKE

The Corps of Discovery, also known as the Lewis and Clark Expedition, set up camp on DeSoto Bend in 1804 after their first council with Indians across the river in present-day Iowa, noting the abundance of wildlife. The refuge was created in 1958 to protect and manage the floodplain forest, tallgrass prairie, and wetland habitat that is crucial for migratory birds and resident wildlife.

A portion of the refuge east of the Missouri River lies in Nebraska because, in 1960, the United States Army Corps of Engineers cut off DeSoto Bend from the river, creating an oxbow lake. DeSoto Lake is no longer part of the river but it is still the border between Nebraska and Iowa. The refuge entrance is in Iowa but shortly after passing the visitor center, the refuge road enters Nebraska. This "island" of forest, prairie, and wetlands is home to Cottonwood and Grassland Nature Trail and the Bertrand Discovery Site. There are parking areas for both but we begin this hike at the Cottonwood and Grassland Trailhead.

After the toilets and interpretive panels, the trail enters riparian forest with a cottonwood canopy and dogwood, hackberry, and ironwood understory. Mushroom foraging is permitted in the wildlife refuge, so Cottonwood Nature Trail would be an excellent place to start. The trail bends to complete the second half of the loop with DeSoto Lake on your right to the west. There are several

Top: Cottonwood Nature Trail.
Bottom: Grassland Nature Trail.

small viewpoints along the trail, including a viewing blind at 0.7 mile, so don't forget to bring your binoculars and bird-watch from the lakeshore.

Reach the end of Cottonwood Nature Trail after 0.85 mile and continue south on Grassland Nature Trail. The name is misleading at first, as it continues through the

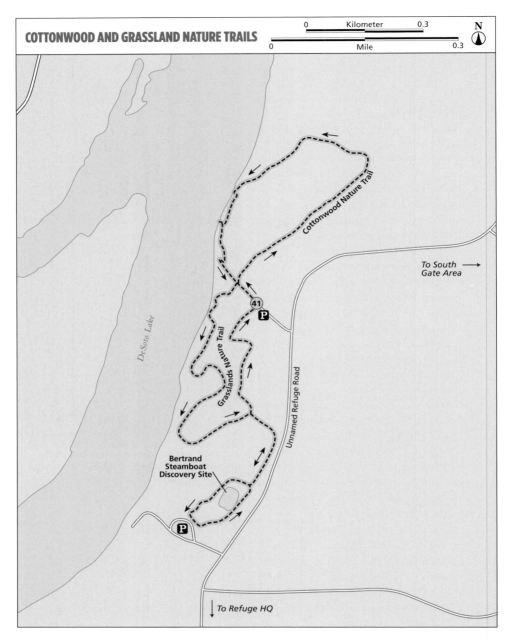

Kilometer

Mile

N

To South Gate Area

Cottonwood Nature Trail

41
P

DeSoto Lake

Grasslands Nature Trail

Unnamed Refuge Road

Bertrand Steamboat Discovery Site

P

To Refuge HQ

cottonwood riparian forest for a short distance until it reaches tallgrass prairie at 1.09 miles, with grasses and forbs reaching shoulder-height or taller in late summer.

Grassland Nature Trail connects with a spur trail at 1.38 miles to then connect to a loop trail at 1.54 miles leading to an overlook platform at Bertrand Discovery Site. The excavation pond is the result of a salvage project in 1968 to recover artifacts from the steamboat *Bertrand* that sank along DeSoto Bend in 1865. The most valuable cargo and machinery were removed after it sank, but much was left in the hull and forgotten for a century. The recovered artifacts can be viewed in the visitor center.

Continue to the parking area, where you can explore the shore of DeSoto Lake before continuing on the loop to return to Grassland Nature Trail and the parking area where the hike began.

MILES AND DIRECTIONS

0.00 Begin at the Cottonwood and Grassland Nature Trail parking area; head northwest through a gate on a loose gravel path.

0.05 Reach an intersection; turn right (north) onto Cottonwood Nature Trail.

0.28 Bench.

0.37 Trail bends west.

0.43 Bench.

0.63 Viewpoint of DeSoto Lake.

0.70 Viewing blind.

0.79 Viewpoint of DeSoto Lake.

0.85 Reach an intersection to complete the Cottonwood loop; turn right (south) onto Grassland Nature Trail.

0.89 Narrow footpath to a viewpoint of the lake.

Top: Viewing blind overlooking a frozen DeSoto Lake.
Bottom: A wet meadow adjacent to DeSoto Lake offers excellent bird-watching.

0.93 Viewpoint of DeSoto Lake.

1.09 Trail leaves riparian forest and enters tallgrass prairie.

1.38 Reach a fork; keep right (southwest) onto Spur Trail.

 Bailout: Keep left at the fork (north) to return to the parking area via Grassland Nature Trail.

1.54 Reach a fork; keep right (northwest) onto Bertrand Discovery Site loop.

1.60 Bertrand Discovery Site overlook platform.

1.68 Reach a parking area; turn left (southeast) to continue on Bertrand Discovery Site loop.

1.83 Reach a fork; keep right (northeast) onto Spur Trail.

1.98 Reach a fork; keep right (north) onto Grassland Nature Trail.

2.22 Arrive back at the Cottonwood and Grassland Nature Trail parking area.

42 NORTH ISLAND TRAIL AND ORIOLE TRAIL

The first specimen sent back to Washington by the Lewis and Clark expedition, a badger, was caught near Boyer Chute National Wildlife Refuge. The Missouri River today, however, looks drastically different than the early 1800s. Channelization made river transportation safer but devastated wildlife habitat. To mitigate the consequences, Boyer Chute National Wildlife Refuge was created in 1992 to benefit fish, migratory birds, endangered species, and local wildlife. North Island Trail takes you alongside the river to view bald eagles perched atop cottonwoods in winter or migrating waterfowl in March. Come at sunset to hear short-eared owls hooting in the floodplain forest on Oriole Trail.

Start: West Chute Unit main parking area
Elevation gain: 979 to 1,005 feet
Distance: 5.68-mile loop
Difficulty: Easy due to flat terrain
Hiking time: 2–3 hours
Seasons/schedule: Open daily year-round, half-hour before sunrise and after sunset. Excellent in winter for bald eagles atop cottonwoods along the river and Mar for waterfowl migration.
Fees and permits: None
Trail contact: Boyer Chute National Wildlife Refuge, DeSoto National Wildlife Refuge, 1434 316th Ln., Missouri Valley, IA 51555; (712) 388-4800; fws.gov/refuge/boyer_chute
Dog-friendly: Yes, on leash
Trail surface: Mowed grass

Land status: Boyer Chute National Wildlife Refuge
Nearest town: Fort Calhoun to the west, Omaha to the south
Maps: USGS Loveland; available at entrance, main parking lot, and fws.gov/refuge/boyer_chute
Other trail users: None
Special considerations: At the time of publication, CR 34 is closed east of Fort Calhoun due to flood damage; access is via a detour (see Finding the Trailhead below). Trails are closed in early Dec for a deer hunt.
Amenities available: Vault toilets at the main parking lot; picnic shelter at the beginning of Oriole Trail
Maximum grade: less than 1%
Cell service: Reliable coverage at the main parking lot and on the trails

FINDING THE TRAILHEAD

From Fort Calhoun (via detour due to road closure), head south on US 75 for 3 miles. Turn right (east) onto CR 38 for 1.2 miles. Turn left (north) onto Road 49 for 1.5 miles, then turn left (north) onto Road 51 for 1.5 miles. Turn right (east) onto Road 34 to reach the entrance to the refuge.

From the Mormon Bridge in north Omaha, take John J. Pershing Drive north for 6.6 miles. John J. Pershing Drive turns into N River Drive. Then N River Drive turns into CR 51. At a T-intersection with Road 49, turn right (north) to stay on Road 51 for 1.5 miles. Turn right (east) onto Road 34 to reach the entrance to the refuge. **GPS:** N41° 27.082′ W95° 57.054

Trail Conditions: At the time of publication, South Island Trail is impassable along the Missouri River; the three other trails (Meadowlark, Oriole, North Island) are open. The wide, mowed grass paths are maintained but not waymarked. Trails could be muddy and impassable after heavy rains or flooding. The trails receive light foot traffic.

THE HIKE

The "chute" that gives Boyer Chute National Wildlife Refuge its name was reconstructed in 1992 as a side channel of the Missouri River. The original chute was blocked in 1937 to aid river transportation, however this had devastating consequences for local wildlife. As a result, a cooperative project between the US Army Corps of Engineers and several state agencies took place to restore the chute. The refuge encompasses wetlands, floodplain forest, and tallgrass prairie that provide habitat for 240 species of birds, 80 fish, and 70 mammals. Bald eagles are a main attraction in winter, as their immense nests perched atop tall cottonwoods are easily visible from the section of the North Island Trail that follows the Missouri River.

Above: A bald eagle protecting its nest atop a cottonwood along the Missouri River.
Below: Bald eagles can be seen at Boyer Chute NWR throughout the year.

At the time of publication, the refuge is still affected by the 2019 floods that devastated eastern Nebraska and western Iowa. CR 34, which connects the refuge with the town of Fort Calhoun, is still closed and requires a detour through the northern edge of the Ponca Hills to reach the refuge via CR 51. Additionally, the section of South Island Trail along the river remains impassable at the time of this guidebook's publication. However, North Island Trail and Oriole Trail provide excellent hiking and wildlife viewing opportunities. Both trails can be accessed from the West Chute Unit main parking area.

Since the refuge lies on a floodplain, all of the trails at Boyer Chute are flat, allowing a leisurely pace that facilitates observation of wildlife and plants. After leaving the parking area, the trail crosses Boyer Chute at 0.15 mile, which has varying levels of water depending on the time of year. Immediately after crossing the bridge, on your left there

Boyer Chute is a reconstructed side channel of the Missouri River.

NORTH ISLAND TRAIL AND ORIOLE TRAIL

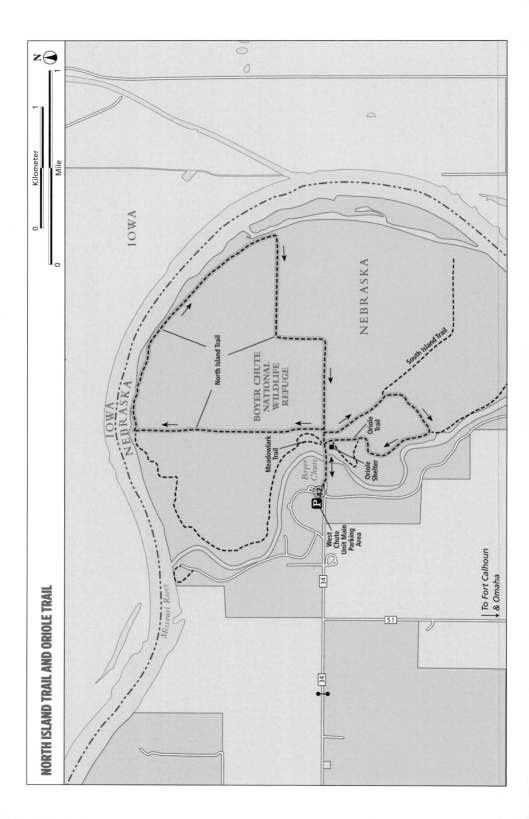

is a 0.32-mile paved loop, Meadowlark Trail, that is ADA accessible and bursts with wild-flowers during the spring and summer. Continue west on North Island Trail toward two large cottonwoods. Turn north at 0.33 mile at the trees to follow the wide, mowed grass path for 1 mile until it reaches the Missouri River after 1.31 miles.

After turning west to follow North Island Trail, keep your eyes on the top of the regal cottonwoods lining the river, as bald eagles perch on the treetops to hunt in winter and guard their immense nests in early spring. The trail follows the river along the Boyer Bend for nearly one and a half miles until reaching the junction with South Island Trail at 2.73 miles. The trail cuts the "island" of Boyer Chute in half, crossing tallgrass prairie and stands of young cottonwoods until returning to the junction of trails near the two large cottonwoods. Here you can continue west to return to the parking area or head south on South Island Trail to explore Oriole Trail, a short loop that provides direct access to the east bank of Boyer Chute. Continue through the cottonwood riparian forest, hopefully accompanied by birdsong and even owl hoots, to reach Oriole Shelter after 5.38 miles and the trail crossing Boyer Chute to return to the West Chute Unit main parking area.

MILES AND DIRECTIONS

0.00 Begin at the West Chute Unit main parking area; head east on a dirt path between the information panels and vault toilets.

0.07 Trail merges with a service road; continue west toward the bridge over Boyer Chute.

0.15 Cross the bridge over Boyer Chute and continue west.

0.26 Continue straight (west), passing Oriole Trail loop to the south.

0.30 Reach a fork; keep left (west) on North Island Trail.

0.33 Turn left (north) to continue on North Island Trail.

1.31 Reach the Missouri River; turn right (west) to continue on North Island Trail.

2.73 Reach a junction; turn right (west) to continue on North Island Trail.

3.30 Trail turns south.

3.50 Trail turns west.

4.00 Continue west, passing the turn-off for North Island Trail on the right.

4.02 Turn left (south) onto South Island Trail.

4.10 Continue straight (southeast).

4.40 Reach a fork; keep right (south) onto Oriole Trail.

4.75 Reach a fork; keep right (north) to continue on Oriole Trail.

5.38 Pass Oriole Shelter on the left and continue north.

5.42 Turn left (west) to head toward the bridge of Boyer Chute.

5.62 Veer right to follow the path back to the parking area.

5.68 Arrive back at the West Chute Unit main parking area.

43 NEALE WOODS

Managed by Fontenelle Forest, Neale Woods is a quieter and more primitive nature reserve than its bigger brother in Bellevue. Lying just 10 miles north of downtown Omaha in the Ponca Hills, Neale Woods is an excellent example of the original deciduous hardwood forest that bordered the Missouri River Valley before the arrival of European settlers. This 5.7-mile hike takes you on most of the trails through oak woodlands and restored prairies to shady valley bottoms, with wildflowers blooming in the early spring through the summer. The trails through the restored prairies are a highlight in late summer when the big bluestem towers more than 6 feet high.

Start: Junction of Gifford Trail and Neale Trail, north of the parking area
Elevation gain: 1,241 to 1,305 feet
Distance: 5.72-mile loop
Difficulty: Moderate due to distance and short but steep climbs up ridges
Hiking time: 2–3 hours
Seasons/schedule: Trails open year-round, sunrise to sunset
Fees and permits: Purchase daily admission or annual membership online at https://fontenelleforest.org/visit/, call (402) 731-3140, or pay daily fee at trailhead.
Trail contact: Fontenelle Forest, 1111 Bellevue Blvd. N, Bellevue 68005; (402) 731-3140; www.fontenelleforest.org
Dog-friendly: Pets not allowed
Trail surface: Grass and dirt

Land status: Fontenelle Forest
Nearest town: Omaha to the south, Fort Calhoun to the north
Maps: USGS Loveland, IA, NE; trail map available at the self-pay kiosk near the trailhead
Other trail users: None
Special considerations: Check the Fontenelle Forest website for trail alerts such as prescribed burns. Avoid hiking on muddy trails.
Amenities available: Composting toilet in the parking area
Maximum grade: 20%
Cell service: Good reception for most carriers at the parking area, atop ridges, and in clearings. Reception can be spotty in hollows and under tree cover.

FINDING THE TRAILHEAD

From the Mormon Bridge, head north on John J. Pershing Drive for 2 miles. Keep right (north) onto N River Drive for 0.6 mile, then turn left at the sign for Neale Woods onto White Deer Lane and continue north for 0.3 mile. Turn left (west) onto Edith Marie Avenue and drive until reaching Neale Woods and the parking area. **GPS:** N41° 23.392' W95° 57.122'

Trail Conditions: The trails are marked with signs at junctions and intersections. The trails can become icy and slippery after snow or rain, so wear appropriate footwear and avoid hiking on muddy trails. The trails receive heavy traffic.

THE HIKE

Neale Woods is named after Edith Neale, who donated the original 120 acres of land in 1971. The land was originally homesteaded by her father in the mid-1880s. Her desire for the land was that it be used for nature study. Carl Jonas, whose father was a founding member of Fontenelle Forest, donated over 100 acres of adjacent land in 1976, and Agnes

Omaha's skyline seen from Jonas Prairie on Gifford Trail.

Koley gave land to Neale Woods in 1977. These donations, in addition to others, have led to almost 600 acres of reserve in the Ponca Hills north of Omaha. The forest is an example of the Missouri River Valley's pre-European settlement of the original deciduous hardwood forest. Restoration work has returned some of the ridgetops to tallgrass prairie. This hike takes you through six prairies—Jonas, Nebraska, Hilltop, Koley, Neale, and Knull—as well as the forested valley trails of Raccoon Hollow and Settlers. Additionally, Neale Trail heads east to connect with Mink Trail, taking hikers right up to the Missouri River through a cottonwood floodplain forest.

The conservation staff at Fontenelle Forest uses various land management strategies to maintain this nature reserve just 10 miles north of downtown Omaha. Fontenelle Forest maintains six reconstructed prairies at Neale Woods and each year staff and volunteers burn the entire property, with some seasonal variations, for invasive control, habitat maintenance, and nutrient recycling. Tree thinning is also used to maintain a healthy forest. Another strategy is girdling, or ring-barking, which removes the bark around a section of the tree, killing the tree above the ring. The resulting deadwood provides wildlife habitat, replenishes nitrogen in the soil, and opens up the forest canopy offering understory plants like wildflowers more sunlight. Hike along the trails in early spring to see wildflowers such as Dutchman's breeches, bloodroot, and spring beauty. By late May, prairie phlox, white false indigo, and large-flowered beardtongue appear. Rare wildflowers at Neale Woods include showy orchis orchid and notchbract water leaf, which is only found in Nebraska at Neale Woods and nearby Hummel Park.

Beginning at the junction of Gifford Trail and Neale Trail, head south past a bench through Jonas Prairie with the Omaha skyline on the horizon. The trail heads west at the southern boundary of the nature reserve, then climbs up a hillside using several switchbacks to decrease the overall grade of the climb. Once at the top of the ridge, Gifford Trail heads north through Nebraska Prairie. The trail is cut through a beautiful prairie dominated by big bluestem, which grows over 6 feet tall late in the summer. An alternative to explore is Fox Trail that clings to the west-facing slope of the ridge.

Left: Settlers Trail traverses a ridge and valley bottom.
Right: Some trees at Neale Woods are girdled (ring-barked) to manage the forest.

At the northern end of Nebraska Prairie at 0.81 mile, continue north on Hilltop Trail. If you want to cut the hike short, continue east on Gifford Trail to return to the parking area. Hilltop Trail briefly heads north before turning west into forest. After 1 mile, head north through Hilltop Prairie, again dominated by big bluestem, before entering the forest once again at 1.13 miles. The trail continues north along the forested ridgetop. Maidenhair Trail is a difficult side trail that descends into a valley before climbing back up the ridge to rejoin Hilltop Trail.

The hike continues after descending Hilltop Trail and heading south on Raccoon Hollow Trail for the next half mile. The fourth prairie, Koley Prairie, is reached after 2 miles at the junction with Wagon Trail. Head north climbing through the prairie to reach Neale Trail on top of a treeless ridge. You can head south along Neale Trail to reach the parking area, however, turn north to explore the northern ridges and valleys on Settlers Trail and Columbine Trail.

Back on Neale Trail after 3.46 miles, head east to reach a bench with views of the Missouri River Valley and the Loess Hills of western Iowa. The steep descent to North River Drive gives access to Mink Trail, a short loop through cottonwoods to a viewpoint at 4.35 miles on the bank of the Missouri River. Return to Neale Trail by crossing the road once again. The climb is strenuous but levels off at 5.2 miles and is mostly flat for the next half mile to the trailhead and parking area.

MILES AND DIRECTIONS

0.00 Begin at the junction of Gifford Trail and Neale Trail; head west on Gifford Trail.

0.02 Turn left (south) to continue on Gifford Trail.

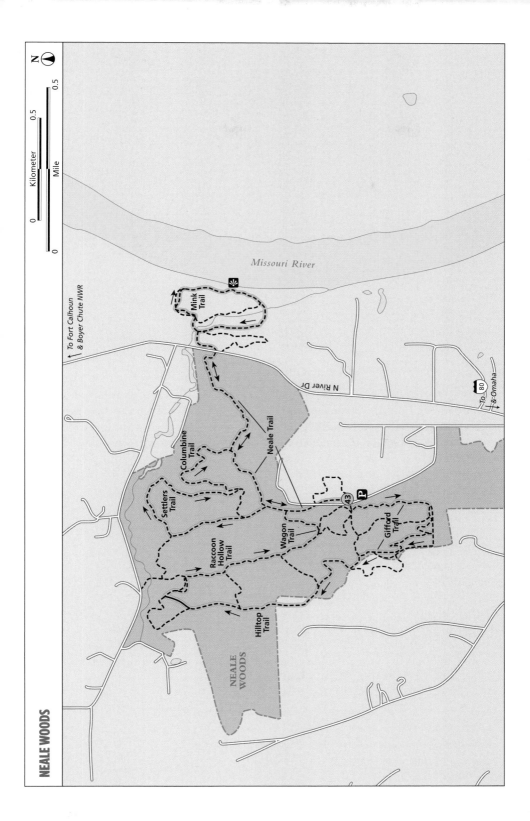

NEALE WOODS

NEALE WOODS

Missouri River

Mink Trail

To Fort Calhoun
& Boyer Chute NWR

N River Dr

To 80
8 Omaha

Columbine
Trail

Settlers
Trail

Neale Trail

Raccoon
Hollow
Trail

Wagon
Trail

Gifford
Trail

Hilltop
Trail

43

P

N

Kilometer

0   0.5

0   0.5

Mile

Raccoon Hollow Trail in winter.

0.63 Continue straight (north) on Gifford Trail.

Option: Turn left (west) onto Fox Trail.

0.75 Continue straight (north) on Gifford Trail.

0.81 Keep left (north) onto Hilltop Trail.

Option: Continue straight (east) on Gifford Trail to return to the trailhead.

1.28 Continue straight (north) on Hilltop Trail.

1.38 Keep right (northeast) on Hilltop Trail.

Option: Keep left (northwest) onto Maidenhair Trail.

1.47 Continue straight (south) on Hilltop Trail.

1.58 Turn right (south) onto Raccoon Hollow Trail.

Option: Turn left (north) onto Raccoon Hollow Trail, then turn right (east) onto Deer Trail.

2.02 Keep left (west) onto Wagon Trail.

2.16 Turn left (north) onto Neale Trail.

2.23 Keep left (north) onto Settlers Trail.

2.53 Turn right (east) to continue on Settlers Trail.

3.01 Turn left (north) onto Columbine Trail.

3.46 Turn left (east) onto Neale Trail.

3.57 Bench.

3.88 Cross N River Drive heading east.

3.91 Keep right (north) onto Mink Trail.

4.35 Viewpoint.

4.72 Keep left (west).

4.81 Cross N River Drive heading west on Neale Trail.

5.22 Continue straight (west) on Neale Trail.

5.43 Continue straight (south) on Neale Trail at the next two junctions.

5.52 Continue straight (south) on Neale Trail.

5.60 Cross Edith Marie Avenue heading southeast.

5.72 Arrive back at the trailhead.

44 UPLAND NORTH AND FLOODPLAIN

For those looking to escape the bustle of the Omaha metro, Fontenelle Forest offers a serene retreat with 17 miles of trails. A wildfire in April 2022 affected the wetlands area of the forest, closing the trails to Hidden Lake and the Great Marsh. The hike described here traverses the hardwood hollows and ridgetop oak savannas of the reserve's northern uplands as well as the northern section of the floodplain. The deciduous forest provides habitat for a plethora of birds, including pileated woodpeckers and more than thirty species of warblers! In winter, the floodplain is an excellent place to view bald eagles perched atop the towering cottonwoods along the Missouri River.

Start: Camp Logan
Elevation gain: 1,057 to 1,215 feet
Distance: 6.22-mile loop
Difficulty: Moderate due to length and steep but short inclines up ridges
Hiking time: 3 hours
Seasons/schedule: Trails open year-round, sunrise to sunset; best in fall for leaves and winter for wildlife viewing.
Fees and permits: Purchase daily admission or annual membership online at https://fontenelleforest.org/visit/, call (402) 731-3140, or pay daily fee at trailhead.
Trail contact: Fontenelle Forest, 1111 Bellevue Blvd. N, Bellevue 68005; (402) 731-3140; www.fontenelleforest.org
Dog-friendly: No pets allowed

Trail surface: Dirt footpaths
Land status: Fontenelle Forest
Nearest town: Bellevue; Omaha to the north
Maps: Omaha South, NE, IA 2021; trail map available at the nature center or fontenelleforest.org
Other trail users: None
Special considerations: Check the nature center's website for trail alerts such as prescribed burns. Be aware of tree and flood hazards while hiking in the floodplain.
Amenities available: None at Camp Logan; restrooms, water, information, and gift shop at the nature center
Maximum grade: 18%
Cell service: No reception at Camp Logan, but there is coverage on top of ridges and in clearings in the floodplain.

FINDING THE TRAILHEAD

From Omaha, head south on US 75 / Kennedy Freeway. Take the Chandler Road / Fort Crook Road exit and turn left (east) onto Chandler Road W at the traffic light. After 0.4 mile, turn slightly right (south) onto Fort Crook Road N. Turn left (east) onto Childs Road E and continue for 1.3 miles until reaching Camp Logan. There is a small parking area below Camp Logan. The trailhead is up the short stairs and on the north side of the building marked by a Bladdernut Trail sign. **GPS:** N41° 10.268′ W95° 54.346′

Trail Conditions: The trails are well marked with signs at trail junctions and intersections. Tree snags in the floodplain can be hazardous in high winds. To prevent trail degradation, do not hike on muddy trails. The trails receive heavy traffic.

The ADA-accessible Riverview Boardwalk offers year-round access to Fontenelle Forest.

THE HIKE

Fontenelle Forest has been voted one of the top three best children's attractions in Omaha by *Omaha Magazine* for four years in a row (2019–2022). The Raptor Woodland Refuge, Acorn Acres, and other programming have made the reserve an excellent place to introduce children to nature. With separate admission you can experience the forest from the treetops at TreeRush Adventures. While the distance of this hike may be too long for some children, there are several points along the hike that allow you to shorten the distance. Additionally, hikers can start from the visitor center instead of Camp Logan, where there is a 1-mile, ADA-accessible wooden boardwalk that is great for kids and strollers. However, for a quieter experience, begin your exploration of the northern uplands and floodplain from Camp Logan. Climb the stairs and pass the former education building to reach the trailhead for Bladdernut Trail, which climbs from 1,078 feet at the parking area to 1,215 feet at 0.53 mile, the highest point on the hike. As you climb, notice the piles of wood stacked against trees, part of an extensive oak woodland restoration project to create a healthier forest through thinning and prescribed fire.

Bladdernut Trail heads north along a ridge before reaching a junction with Oak Trail after 0.72 mile. Turn east onto Oak Trail briefly before turning north onto Handsome Hollow. The half-mile trail through the appropriately named hollow descends from 1,200 to 985 feet at the junction with the railroad at 1.26 miles. The trail through the shady and cool valley is often muddy, so wear appropriate footwear.

Once you cross the footbridge over the marsh and the railroad tracks, head toward the trail sign for the floodplain and turn east onto Cottonwood Trail at 1.33 miles. Cottonwood Trail heads southeast to join Missouri Trail at 1.84 miles, where you turn north to continue through the floodplain with towering cottonwoods. Missouri Trail reaches the Missouri River at 2.45 miles and heads west on the south bank of the river for nearly half a mile. In winter, it is not uncommon to see bald eagles perched atop the tall cottonwoods as they hunt for fish in the icy waters of the Missouri River.

White snakeroot (*Ageratina altissima*) blooming in mid-September on Bladdernut Trail.

At 2.96 miles, safely cross the railroad tracks to reenter the northern uplands. Head southwest into Mill Hollow on Hawthorn Trail to reach a footbridge at 3.02 miles. If you wish to return to Camp Logan, do not cross the footbridge but keep left to follow Oak Trail back to Camp Logan. If you wish to explore more of the northern uplands, cross the footbridge and then turn south onto Hawthorn Trail. It's a steep climb up the ridge to the junction at 3.51 miles, where you keep left to descend into Child's Hollow. Follow Child's Hollow downstream to reach Chickadee Trail at 4.2 and climb steeply once again up the ridge. The roller coaster is not over, however, as you will descend steeply into Mill Hollow to return to the footbridge at 5.0 miles and climb one final time up Oak Trail to reach the ridge that leads back to Camp Logan.

The wildfire that burned over 300 acres of wetlands at Fontenelle Forest in April 2022 could have been much worse. However, the knowledge and experience gained by the conservation staff using prescribed fire helped control the wildfire and limit its damage. At the time of publication, Hidden Lake Trail and Redbud Trail remained closed as recovery efforts continued. Once the two trails are reopened to the public, hikers can explore the southern uplands and wetlands starting from Camp Wakonda using History Trail, Hidden Lake Trail, Marsh Trail, and Mormon Hollow Trail.

MILES AND DIRECTIONS

0.00 Begin at Camp Logan parking area. After climbing the stairs, turn left to head to the north of the building to reach the Bladdernut Trailhead.

0.72 Turn right (east) onto Oak Trail.

0.77 Turn left (north) onto Handsome Hollow.

1.26 At the end of Handsome Hollow, cross the footbridge over the marsh, then cross the railroad tracks heading northeast.

1.33 Turn right (east) onto Cottonwood Trail.

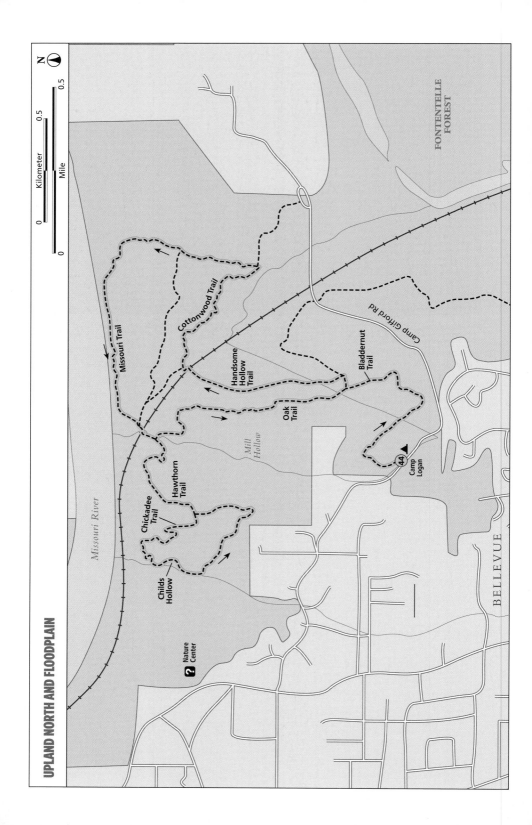

UPLAND NORTH AND FLOODPLAIN

Left: Northern red oak (*Quercus rubra*) lives up to its name in the fall.
Right: Mushrooms are common in the shady hollows of Fontenelle Forest.

1.84 Turn left (north) onto Missouri Trail.

2.10 Continue straight (northeast) on Missouri Trail.

2.45 Reach the Missouri River.

2.96 Arrive at an interpretive panel about the floodplain. Cross the railroad tracks to begin Hawthorn Trail heading southwest.

3.02 Turn right (north) and cross the footbridge over Mill Hollow. After crossing the bridge, turn left (south) onto Hawthorn Trail.

   Bailout: Keep left instead of crossing the bridge to follow Oak Trail back to Camp Logan.

3.51 Turn left (south) to continue on Hawthorn Trail.

3.96 Turn right (north) onto Childs Hollow Trail.

   Option: Turn left (south) to continue on Hawthorn Trail to explore the trails around the nature center.

4.20 Bear right (east) onto Chickadee Trail.

4.52 Keep left (northeast) to continue on Hawthorn Trail.

5.00 At the footbridge, turn right (east) and cross the bridge. Then, turn right onto Oak Trail.

5.60 Keep right (south) at the fork.

5.90 Continue straight on Bladdernut Trail.

6.22 Arrive back at Camp Logan parking area.

45 INDIAN CAVE VIA EAST RIDGE TRAIL

East Ridge Trail climbs steeply up the edge of a narrow ridge with views of the Missouri River Valley to the east and mature eastern deciduous forest to the west. The roller-coaster hills of Indian Cave State Park will make your lungs burn, but the effort is worth the views of the forest river bluffs. Birds found only along the Missouri River in Nebraska, such as whip-poor-wills and pileated woodpeckers, can be seen in the oak hickory forest. Descend steeply from the ridge to see petroglyphs at Indian Cave from the newly renovated viewing platform.

Start: Trailheads 9 and 10, next to the Indian Cave Bend Shallow Water Habitat Area
Elevation gain: 892 to 1,290 feet
Distance: 4.25-mile loop
Difficulty: Difficult due to steep climbs
Hiking time: 2 hours
Seasons/schedule: Trails open year-round, sunrise to sunset; best in Oct for fall colors, cooler temperatures, and the park's annual Haunted Hollow events
Fees and permits: A park entry permit is required and may be purchased at the park, statewide Game and Parks offices and permit vendors, or online at outdoornebraska.gov.
Trail contact: Indian Cave State Park, 65296 720 Rd., Shubert 68437; (402) 883-2575; outdoornebraska .gov/indiancave
Dog-friendly: Yes, on leash

Trail surface: Dirt and grass
Land status: Indian Cave State Park
Nearest town: Falls City 15 miles to the south, Auburn 22 miles to the northwest
Maps: USGS Langdon, MO, NE 2021 and USGS Barada, NE, MO 2021; trail map available online or at the park headquarters
Other trail users: Bikers and equestrians
Special considerations: Avoid hiking on muddy trails. Hikers and bikers must yield to equestrians; bikers must yield to hikers.
Amenities available: Vault toilets at the trailhead; water is available seasonally through the state park
Maximum grade: 24%
Cell service: Weak coverage at the trailhead and under tree cover; reception is available but spotty along open ridges along the park road

FINDING THE TRAILHEAD

From Auburn, head east on US 136 for 8 miles. Before reaching the town of Brownville, turn south onto NE 67 and continue for 9 miles passing through the town of Nemaha. Turn east onto NE 64 Spur and continue until reaching the park entrance. Continue on the main park road, Indian Cave Recreation Road, for 3.7 miles following signs for Indian Cave until you reach a parking area near the Indian Cave Bend Shallow Water Habitat Area. Trailheads 9 and 10 are located on the south side of the park road. **GPS:** N40° 15.071' W95° 32.236'

Trail Conditions: The trail system is one of the best in the state, with helpful trail signage that includes trail names and directional information. Ticks are abundant in summer. The trails receive heavy traffic.

Indian Cave contains Native American petroglyphs from an unknown date and origin.

THE HIKE

The sandstone cave that gives Indian Cave State Park its name has been a refuge for humans for over 1,000 years. Little is known about the history of the cave or the people who carved drawings in the sandstone, which include a bird, a man riding a horse, and several bison. One theory suggests the multiple bison figures are evidence the cave was the Bison Lodge, a sacred Pawnee religious site. What is known is that as far back as 1,500 years ago, nomadic tribes used the cave as temporary shelter, and it has been more or less continuously used by humans since. Picnickers and other visitors have added graffiti to the cave, sadly defacing a fascinating piece of native cultural history.

Indian Cave State Park is located in the southeastern corner of Nebraska, which receives more annual rainfall than anywhere in the state. The climate supports a high diversity of plant and animal species. The forested river bluffs of southeastern Nebraska, like at Indian Cave State Park, are the only places in the state capable of supporting southern flying squirrels. The chance you will encounter one on this hike, however, is virtually zero unless you hike in near total darkness when the little squirrels are active. It is common to see gray squirrels and hear their predator, barred owls, hooting in the forest of oak, hickory, and basswood. There are remnants of tallgrass prairies on top of the steep bluffs along the Missouri River—the East Ridge Trail, accessed via Trailhead 9 and 10, climbs one of these bluffs to reach a prairie.

The climb begins immediately after taking Trail 10; you will climb 365 feet in less than 1 mile with a precipitous drop on your left. Some of the bur oaks along the trail have

INDIAN CAVE VIA EAST RIDGE TRAIL

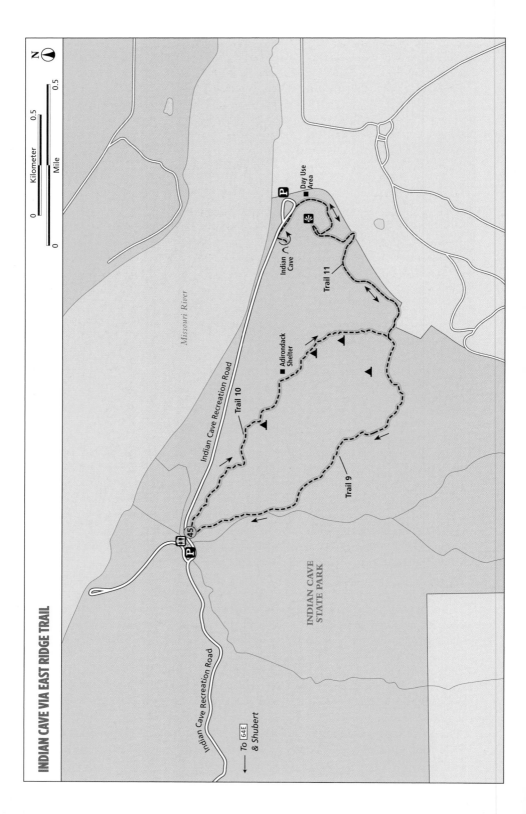

Missouri River

Indian Cave Recreation Road

To 64E
& Shubert

Indian Cave Recreation Road

45

P

Trail 10

Adirondack Shelter

Indian Cave

Day Use Area

P

Trail 11

Trail 9

INDIAN CAVE STATE PARK

N

Kilometer
0   0.5

Mile
0   0.5

been tagged as part of a scientific study. The campsite at 0.5 mile has incredible views of the sun setting behind the forested horizon. An Adirondack shelter at 0.7 mile and another campsite at 0.83 mile are additional options for backpackers.

Reach a junction after 1.1 miles where you take Trail 11 down a steep path to reach Indian Cave. The Missouri River is visible at the viewpoint at 1.7 miles. The final descent from the junction at 1.76 miles follows a narrow and cool ravine over rocky terrain to the day-use area along the river at 1.95 miles. Continue northwest on the park road until you reach the new ADA-accessible boardwalk that leads to the viewing platform of Indian Cave. A landslide in March 2019 damaged the old boardwalk. Head across the park road to a small area along the river at 2.25 miles, then follow Trail 11 to return to the junction on top of East Ridge at 3.16 miles. Continue northwest on Trail 9 as it descends along a valley to return to the trailhead.

East Ridge Trail is just one of several recommended hikes at Indian Cave State Park. Rock Bluff Run Trail (Trails 8 and 8A) traverses another steep ridge with the Missouri River below. History Trail (Trails 2, 3, and 3A) includes a beautiful viewpoint and also passes by a cemetery from the abandoned village of St. Deroin. Hardwood Trail (Trails 5 and 5A) explores the wooded ridges and valleys west of Indian Cave and East Ridge Trail.

MILES AND DIRECTIONS

0.00 Begin at Trailhead 9 and head south, then keep left onto Trail 10 to begin climbing East Ridge Trail.

0.33 Keep left (south).

0.50 Hike-in campsite.

0.70 Adirondack shelter.

0.83 Continue south along East Ridge Trail; spur trail to hike-in campsite to the right.

1.10 Reach a junction; turn left (east) onto Trail 11.

1.66 Reach a junction; head straight (north) to a viewpoint of the Missouri River Valley.

1.70 Viewpoint; return to previous junction.

1.76 Turn left (east) to follow Trail 11 to Indian Cave.

1.95 Reach Trailhead 11 and day-use area; continue (northwest) toward the park road.

2.12 Boardwalk to Indian Cave.

2.25 Missouri River; return to Trailhead 11 in the day-use area at the end of the park road loop.

2.35 Trailhead 11; continue southeast.

2.60 Turn left (south) to follow the sign toward Trailheads 9 and 10.

3.16 Turn left (south) onto Trail 9.

3.30 Continue straight (southwest) passing a hike-in campsite on the right.

3.38 Turn right (northwest) to stay on Trail 9.

Option: Continue straight (west) to explore Trail 5 / Hardwood Trail (see park map).

3.87 Continue straight (northwest) on Trail 9, passing Trail 5 on the left.

4.25 Arrive back at Trailhead 9.

HONORABLE MENTIONS

M **DEER CREEK TRAIL**

Located at the confluence of the Niobrara and Missouri Rivers, Niobrara State Park is a popular summer destination. The buffalo cookouts on Sundays throughout the summer, complete with cowboy poets and storytellers, and the scenic 3 Mile Loop drive around the park make it a great weekend getaway. Among the 14 miles of trails in the park, Deer Creek Trail follows the creek through cedar forest before climbing through upland prairie with views of the Missouri River backwaters.

Start: Trailhead behind campsites 10 and 11
Elevation gain: 1,261 to 1,463 feet
Distance: 2.09-mile loop
Difficulty: Moderate due to lack of trail signage and maintenance and hill climb on second half of loop
Hiking time: 1–1.5 hours
Seasons/schedule: Open year-round, dawn to dusk
Fees and permits: Valid park permit; available for purchase at the Schramm Education Center, kiosks near the park entrance, and online at outdoornebraska.gov
Trail contact: Niobrara State Park, 89261 522 Ave., Niobrara 68760; (402) 857-3373; outdoornebraska.gov/niobrara/
Dog-friendly: Yes, on leash

Trail surface: Mowed grass and dirt footpaths
Land status: Niobrara State Park
Nearest town: Niobrara 2.5 miles to the east
Maps: USGS Niobrara, NE, SD 2021; available at the park office and online at outdoornebraska.gov/niobrara/
Other trail users: Mountain bikers
Special considerations: The eastern section of Deer Creek Trail has several footpaths and little signage that can make navigation difficult.
Amenities available: Vault toilets, water, and picnic areas throughout the state park
Maximum grade: 11%
Cell service: Coverage is available throughout the state park. Reception may be limited under tree cover.

FINDING THE TRAILHEAD

From the town of Niobrara, head west on NE 12. After crossing the Niobrara River, turn right (north) onto the park entrance road. Keep left (north) after the park entrance kiosk, then continue on the park road past the visitor center. Keep left at the next fork to follow the 3 Mile Loop park road. After 1.3 miles, turn right (south) then take the next right (west) to continue on the 3 Mile Loop. Reach campsites 10 and 11 after nearly 1 mile. The trailhead is located behind the campsites. **GPS:** N42° 45.931′ W98° 4.058′

Trail Conditions: There is a Deer Creek Trail sign at the trailhead, however the trail itself has very little trail signage. The park map shows most of the trails, but there are some trails on the ground that do not appear on the map, which can make navigation difficult. The trails receive moderate traffic.

The trailhead is located behind campsites 10 and 11.

N **STEAMBOAT TRACE TRAIL**

Beginning in Nebraska City and running parallel to the Missouri River for 22 miles until Brownville, the Steamboat Trace Trail is a scenic hike and bike trail following an abandoned railroad line. Two of the best sections for day hikes are the 3-mile (one-way) stretch from the Peru trailhead south to the Missouri River and a 2-mile (one-way) stretch north from the Brownville Bridge along the Missouri River. Sandstone bluffs, open farmland, wildlife along the Missouri River, and impressive fall colors make this easy-to-access trail ideal for families and hikers of all levels.

Start: Trailheads located in Brownville, Peru, and south of Nebraska City (near the OPPD coal plant)
Elevation gain: 892 to 960 feet
Distance: 22-mile point-to-point
Difficulty: Easy
Hiking time: Variable
Seasons/schedule: Trail open year-round except during rifle deer hunting seasons (see special considerations); best in autumn for fall colors
Fees and permits: None
Trail contact: Nemaha Natural Resources District, 62161 US 136, Tecumseh 68450; (402) 335-3325; www.nemahanrd.org/recreation/steamboat-trace
Dog-friendly: Yes, on leash
Trail surface: Crushed limestone

Land status: Nemaha Natural Resources District
Nearest town: Brownville, Peru, and Nebraska City
Maps: USGS Hamburg, IA, MO, NE; USGS Julian, NE, MO, IA 2021; USGS Nebraska City, NE, IA 2021; USGS Peru, NE, MO 2021; trail map available on Nemaha NRD website (see trail contact)
Other trail users: Cyclists
Special considerations: The trail is closed during rifle deer hunting seasons (10 days in Nov, 2 weeks in Jan).
Amenities available: Restroom available seasonally at the trailhead in Peru
Maximum grade: 4% (overall grade of the trail)
Cell service: Reception can be spotty along the trail

FINDING THE TRAILHEAD

For the Nebraska City trailhead, head south on US 75 for 2.5 miles, then turn left onto K Road for 4 miles. K Road turns into S 70th Road and then L Road before reaching the trailhead west of the OPPD power plant. For the Peru trailhead, head north on 5th Street for 1 mile from the town of Peru until reaching the trailhead. The Brownville trailhead is located just south of the US 136 Brownville Bridge over the Missouri River.

GPS (Brownville trailhead): N40° 23.846' W95° 39.203'
GPS (Peru trailhead): N40° 29.218' W95° 43.877'
GPS (Nebraska City trailhead): N40° 37.205' W95° 47.893'

Trail Conditions: The trail follows an abandoned railroad corridor and is mostly flat. Flooding in 2019 severely damaged sections of the trail but as of October 2022 the entirety of the trail has been reopened. The trail receives moderate traffic.

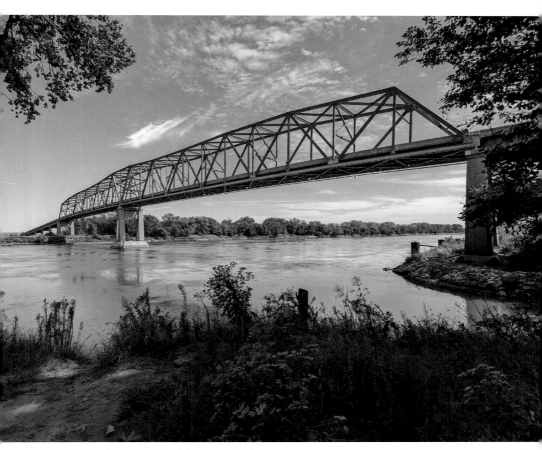
Brownville Bridge spanning the Missouri River.

HIKE INDEX

Bead Mountain, 46
Black Hills Overlook Trail, 72
Blue Jay Trail, 100

CCC Fire Tower Trail, 104
Chimney Rock Trail, 38
Coffee Mill Butte, 90
Cottonwood and Grassland Nature
    Trails, 224
Cowboy Trail, 143
Crane Trust Prairie Trail, 154

Dark Island Trail, 174
Deer Creek Trail, 248
Derr House Prairie, 150

East End Access Trail, 118

Fort Falls Trail, 126
Fossil Hills Trail and Bone Cabin, 25
Frank Shoemaker Marsh, 203

Gjerloff Prairie, 158
Government Canyon, 122

Hackberry Trail and Red Cedar
    Trail, 162

Indian Cave via East Ridge Trail, 244
Island Lake Loop, 116

Long Pine Creek and Dale Mundorf
    Memorial Nature Trail, 139
Lovers Leap and Red Cloud Buttes, 63

Martin Prairie and Wetlands Loop, 194
Mexican Canyon, 59

Neale Woods, 234
New Camp Loop, 178
Nine-Mile Prairie, 199
Niobrara Valley Preserve, 135
North Island Trail and Oriole Trail, 228
North Platte River Trail, 146

Oak Creek Trail, 210
Old Oak Trail and Bloodroot Trail, 220
Olson Nature Preserve, 112
Oregon Trail to Medicine Wheel, 42

Pine Ridge Trail, 88

Roberts Loop, 68
Rock Creek Prairie Loop, 182
Rowe Sanctuary, 172

Saddle Rock Trail, 29
Sandhills Nature Trail, 96
Scott Lookout National Recreation
    Trail, 108
Smith Falls Trail and Jim MacAllister
    Nature Trail, 130
South Shore Trail, 216
Spotted Tail Loop, 80
Spring Creek Prairie, 190
Steamboat Butte Trail, 76
Steamboat Trace Trail, 250
Stone Creek Falls, 166
Strong Canyon, 92

The Cliffs, 84
Toadstool Trail, Bison Trail, and Great
    Plains Trail, 20
Trooper Trail and Boots and Saddle
    Trail, 50

Oglala National Grasslands.

Turkey Run Trail to Monument View, 33

Turtle Rock Trail, 55

Upland North and Floodplain, 239

Upland Prairie Loop, 186

Wilderness Park, 212

Willa Cather Memorial Prairie, 208

THE TEN ESSENTIALS OF HIKING

 **American Hiking Society**

American Hiking Society recommends you pack the "Ten Essentials" every time you head out for a hike. Whether you plan to be gone for a couple of hours or several months, make sure to pack these items. Become familiar with these items and know how to use them. Learn more at **AmericanHiking.org/hiking-resources.**

 1. Appropriate Footwear

 6. Safety Items (light, fire, and a whistle)

 2. Navigation

 7. First Aid Kit

 3. Water (and a way to purify it)

 8. Knife or Multi-Tool

 4. Food

 9. Sun Protection

 5. Rain Gear & Dry-Fast Layers

 10. Shelter